# HOW TO MAKE THE WORLD A BETTER PLACE

# HOW TO MAKE THE WORLD A BETTER PLACE

## A Guide to Doing Good

**JEFFREY HOLLENDER**

**This book is printed on recycled paper.**

*William Morrow and Company, Inc.*
*New York*

**Library of Congress Cataloging-in-Publication Data**

Hollender, Jeffrey A.
    How to make the world a better place : a guide to doing good / Jeffrey A. Hollender.
      p.  cm.
    ISBN 0-688-09577-1
    0-688-08479-6 (pbk)
    1. Social problems—Handbooks, manuals, etc.  2. Quality of life—
Handbooks, manuals, etc.  3. Human ecology—Moral and ethical
aspects—Handbooks, manuals, etc.  4. Consumer education—Handbooks,
manuals, etc.  5. Social action—Handbooks, manuals, etc.
    I. Title.
    HN18.H67  1990
    361.2—dc20                        89-13132
                                                           CIP

Printed in the United States of America

First  Edition

  2  3  4  5  6  7  8  9  10

BOOK DESIGN BY ARLENE GOLDBERG

*This book is dedicated to my wife, Sheila, for creating the space and providing me with the encouragement I needed. It is written especially for my children, Meika and Alexander, for whom it matters most.*

# Acknowledgments

To David Levine and the Learning Alliance, my guide into many new worlds; to Maggie Scott, who typed this complete manuscript and corrected all of my unbearably bad spelling and grammar; to my agent, Richard Pine, my editor, Doug Stumpf, and his assistant, Jared Stamm; to the New York City and Bridgehampton public libraries at which the book was written; to Mark Barcohana, for research assistance; to Rosen, Rudd, Kera, Graubard & Hollender who provided me with an office and a telephone; to Joan and Alan Gussow, Josh Mailman, Larry Martin, and my father, Alfred Hollender, who graciously agreed to review the manuscript; and to the hundreds of organizations who so freely and helpfully supplied me with information.

# Foreword

# How to Put This Book into Action

The 120 actions that make up the book you're holding in your hands can be read in any order you choose. You can start at the beginning and work your way through each of the six chapters or you can skip around, picking those actions that appeal to you most.

Each action is introduced by background and explanatory material followed by a "What You Can Do" section that contains one or a series of specific actions. Don't get bogged down by all the introductory facts—if they seem overwhelming you can always skip ahead to the action. However, if you like facts, figures, and some fairly amazing information, you'll find more than enough to meet your appetite in each introduction.

Clearly, this book does not address all of the problems that the world currently faces. Issues such as health, education, homelessness, and the AIDS epidemic are conspicuous by their absence. I plan to cover them and other subjects in a second book.

# Contents

# Prologue

# A Sand Castle Builder's Refresher Manual

A homeless man sleeps in a giant cardboard box by the hot air vent of a new apartment building; starving children with swollen bellies, ragged clothes, and distant, empty eyes have no energy to cry; rain forests burn, rivers are poisoned, and acid rain scars the earth; a war, which might use only two percent of our nuclear arsenal, threatens to alter life on our planet forever. Where do we begin to make the world a better place?

Descriptions of the world's problems blare from TV sets, fill endless pages of newsprint, are the focus of international symposiums and are studied, monitored, and evaluated by governments, universities, multinational corporations, and independent agencies. This book is not yet another description of our problems. It is, in the most basic, simple, and straightforward manner possible, about solutions to those problems and what you can do today to help bring them about.

But how do we solve problems that appear too large to approach and too complex to understand? What stands between our sincere and noble desire to help and the concrete, effective actions necessary to effect change? Why are we so lost in sadness, not believing that we can make a difference, distrustful that our efforts will ever bear meaningful results?

We tremble and turn our eyes away as famine wipes out millions in distant places, as wars engulf nations and children are forever separated from their parents. We are no better equipped

to face the violence and poverty that shatter our own neighborhoods. No fences are high enough to guard those we love from
the pain and suffering the world seems so full of.

As a child playing by the seashore, I was amazed at the
strength of my sand castles to stand up to the ocean's mighty
swells. Deeper and deeper I would dig, rushing to pack sand,
hurrying to build moats as I raced against the incoming tide.
Through my sand castles I felt the simple beauty of my ability
to reach out into the world and have it respond to my touch.
We've lost that sense of power. We've allowed the tide to overcome us. Today we've left sand castle building to professional
architects, engineers' drawings, and construction crews. But the
sand castles they build wipe out parks and forests, spew deadly
fumes into the air, and leave us in windowless rooms under the
hum of artificial light.

We've lost our touch—we need to rediscover how to build
our own sand castles, reexperience our own ability to reach out
into the world and effect change. We can still beat the tide. This
book in a way is a "Sand Castle Builder's Refresher Manual."
The tools we'll use are different—you won't need to rush out and
purchase buckets, pails, and plastic shovels. Instead, you'll learn
about the hidden power that lurks in your shopping list, a new
way to use credit cards, the unrivaled power of the U.S. Mail
and, of course, how to make some unusual connections with the
telephone. You'll learn how your rights as a citizen, shareholder,
customer, or employee will bring presidents, politicians, and corporate executives to almost any bargaining table. This book will
help you build hundreds of little sand castles, each one setting
off many waves of change.

These simple actions, grounded in solid information, can
make the world a better place. When postcards mailed from rock
concerts were received by heads of state, political prisoners were
set free. When enough people stopped eating Nestle's Crunch,
Third World mothers were no longer induced to give up breast
milk for infant formula that would ultimately kill their children.
The toothpaste you use can support a company that selects women
and minorities for positions of responsibility, or one that manufactures nuclear weapons and supports apartheid in South Africa. A dollar spent with a cooperative venture spreads the ethics
of fair, responsible, and honest business in a marketplace full
of inferior products manufactured by uncaring corporations. Each
white grape you eat perpetuates dangerous working conditions
that bring serious injury to over 300,000 farm workers every

year. Handcrafted goods purchased from Third World craftsmen help eliminate hunger and encourage self-sufficiency.

Only a few minutes are needed for many of the actions that will result in positive social change. This book will equip you with the basic facts, introduce you to specific issues, provide clear and concise instructions and lots of inspiration. You'll learn to make the world a better place as you wheel your cart down the aisle of a supermarket, travel on business or pleasure, select an insurance policy, open a bank account, prepare dinner, relax around the house, and even as you soap up in the shower.

We'll cover issues ranging from hunger and homelessness to apartheid in South Africa, ozone depletion, water pollution, corporate responsibility, citizen diplomacy, plus how to protect children from the pervasive violence of this world. You'll learn how to help build low-income housing, use recycled products, contribute to a food bank, invest money in a socially responsible manner, free prisoners of conscience, pass legislation through the U.S. Congress, and encourage world peace.

Everything you need to step into action is included, from phone numbers and addresses to names, titles, background statistics, and quotable information. Each action is designed to generate the greatest impact in the least amount of time. Results are guaranteed without marching on Washington, quitting your job, or giving away your life savings.

If I've left out any good ideas that you know of, important organizations, or useful resources (and I'm sure I have), please let me know. They will be added to new editions of the book.

The shape of the future is in our hands. It is our responsibility, for it can be no one else's. The world won't be destroyed tomorrow, but it can be made better today. Step by step, one by one, find the actions that suit you best, try them out, tell your friends, and things will change. They always have in the past, and no matter what anyone says, you and I do have the power to begin to make the world a better place.

# Avoid the Pitfalls That Line the Road to Effective Activism*

## Clark W. Bullard

To be a successful activist, you must learn to avoid or outwit mind traps. Mind traps are those little sinkholes that your mind falls into when it tries to contemplate cultural or environmental problems and is boggled at their magnitude. They are reinforced by the media and our leaders because they preserve more options for those currently in power. They are also sprung by friends who have an interest in getting you to accept one of their own mind traps.

Here are some of the mind traps I've identified and my response:

**MIND TRAP NUMBER ONE:** *Someone knows what to do and is in control.*

Sorry, but "they" do not know what to do. They are not in control and they are not doing it.

**MIND TRAP NUMBER TWO:** *Even if I do my share nobody else will, so why bother.*

I can't prove that you are wrong, but it's a self-fulfilling prophecy. We all must take responsibility for the world we share. The lure to do otherwise is strong. For example: One person or one factory can benefit by polluting the air, but the costs of cleaning it up are spread over all. It's like going to a restaurant with twenty people and deciding to put the whole bill on one

* Excerpted with permission from *Audubon Activist*, January-February 1988, p. 11.

check and split it equally. That makes it hard to avoid the temptation to order steak and lobster.

**MIND TRAP NUMBER THREE:** *I can't take the first step unless I know the whole route.*
The only way to learn a new path is to take a few steps, make mistakes (like writing a really embarrassing letter to the editor), experiment and learn, and adopt an explorer or research mentality. Recognize that your friends are making mistakes and that they need encouragement from you—especially after writing an embarrassing letter to the editor.

**MIND TRAP NUMBER FOUR:** *These are all long-term problems.* Let's just ignore them and work on the short-term ones.
A year from now they are still going to be long-term problems, and they are often easier and cheaper to deal with early on.

**MIND TRAP NUMBER FIVE:** *Disaster is coming anyway no matter what I do, so why bother.*
Disaster only occurs if everybody does nothing. We live in a diverse and pluralistic society, so when a disaster is coming a few people start making changes. Be one of those people. Don't get hung up trying to prevent disasters; just work on ways to make things better.

**MIND TRAP NUMBER SIX:** *Don't worry, technology and the market system will take care of everything. When oil gets scarce, some new technology or new resource will be discovered and developed.*
That's like saying the hammer will build the house. Remember that the market system and technologies are just tools of our society. Technologies simply reflect our values and concerns, our resources and constraints. We are responsible for controlling our technologies.

**MIND TRAP NUMBER SEVEN:** *I can't do it all, therefore I won't do anything.*
What you *can* do is make up your mind to give a certain amount of time, money, and influence. Something small enough that you can sustain the commitment. Then, as you get more efficient and productive, increase the level.
The problems that confront us are big and they are messy.

But we live in the United States, a self-governing democracy. We have the freedom and the luxury to take action on the issues that concern us. We also have an overriding responsibility to make time for activism and to exercise our democratic privileges.

By avoiding the mind traps that keep others idle, we can take action and make a difference.

## Part 1

# PROTECTING THE ENVIRONMENT

*What you can do today to prevent everything from acid rain to the "greenhouse effect" while you shop, bathe, travel to work—even while you read this book!*

# 1

# Introduction

## *What on Earth Are We Doing?**

Like the evil genies that flew from Pandora's box, technological advances have provided the means of upsetting nature's equilibrium, that intricate set of biological, physical, and chemical interactions that make up the web of life. Starting at the dawn of the Industrial Revolution, smokestacks have disgorged noxious gases into the atmosphere, factories have dumped toxic wastes into rivers and streams, automobiles have guzzled irreplaceable fossil fuels and fouled the air with their acid rain causing fumes. In the name of progress, forests have been denuded, lakes poisoned with pesticides, underground aquifers pumped dry. For decades, scientists have warned of the possible consequences of all this profligacy. No one paid much attention.

This year the earth spoke, like God warning Noah of the deluge. Its message was loud and clear, and suddenly people began to listen, to ponder what portents the message held. In the summer of 1988, a three-month drought baked the soil from California to Georgia, reducing the country's grain harvest by

* Excerpted with permission from the introduction to "Planet of the Year," Thomas A. Sancton, *Time* magazine, January 2, 1989, pp. 26–30.

31% and killing thousands of head of livestock. A stubborn seven-week heat wave drove temperatures above 100°F across much of the country, raising fears that the dreaded "greenhouse effect"—global warming as a result of the buildup of carbon dioxide and other gases in the atmosphere—might already be under way. Parched by the lack of rain, the Western forests of the U.S., including Yellowstone National Park, went up in flames, also igniting a bitter conservationist controversy. And on many of the country's beaches, garbage, raw sewage, and medical wastes washed up to spoil the fun of bathers and confront them personally with the growing pollution of the oceans.

Similar pollution closed beaches on the Mediterranean, the North Sea, and the English Channel. Killer hurricanes ripped through the Caribbean, and floods devastated Bangladesh, reminders of nature's raw power. In Soviet Armenia a monstrous earthquake killed some 55,000 people. That too was a natural disaster, but its high casualty count, owing largely to the construction of cheap high-rise apartment blocks over a well-known fault area, illustrated the carelessness that has become humanity's habit in dealing with nature.

There were other forebodings of environmental disaster. In the U.S. it was revealed that federal weapons-making plants had recklessly and secretly littered large areas with radioactive waste. The further depletion of the atmosphere's ozone layer, which helps block cancer-causing ultraviolet rays, testified to the continued overuse of atmosphere-destroying chlorofluorocarbons emanating from such sources as spray cans and air-conditioners. Perhaps most ominous of all, the destruction of the tropical forests, home to at least half the earth's plant and animal species, continued at a rate equal to one football field a second.

What would happen if nothing were done about the earth's imperiled state? According to computer projections, the accumulation of $CO_2$ in the atmosphere could drive up the planet's average temperature 3° to 9°F by the middle of the next century. That could cause the oceans to rise by several feet, flooding coastal areas and ruining large tracts of farmland through salinization. Changing weather patterns could make huge areas infertile or uninhabitable, touching off refugee movements unprecedented in history.

Toxic waste and radioactive contamination could lead to shortages of safe drinking water, the sine qua non of human existence. And in a world that could house between 8 billion and 13 billion people by the mid–21st century, there is a strong likelihood of mass starvation on a scale previously unknown to our civilization.

Taking effective action to halt the massive injury to the earth's environment will require a mobilization of political will, international cooperation, and sacrifice unknown except in wartime. Yet humanity is in a war right now, and it is not too Draconian to call it a war for survival. It is a war in which all nations must be allies. Both the causes and effects of the problems that threaten the earth are global, and they must be attacked globally. "All nations are tied together as to their common fate," observes Peter Raven, director of the Missouri Botanical Garden. "We are all facing a common problem, which is, How are we going to keep this single resource we have, namely the world, viable?"

As we head into the last decade of the 20th century, we find ourselves at a crucial turning point: The actions of those now living will determine the future, and possibly the very survival, of the species. "We do not have generations, we only have years, in which to attempt to turn things around," warns Lester Brown, president of the Washington-based Worldwatch Institute. Every individual on the planet must be made aware of its vulnerability and of the urgent need to preserve it. No attempt to protect the environment will be successful in the long run unless ordinary people—the California executive, the Mexican peasant, the Soviet factory worker, the Chinese farmer—are willing to adjust their life-styles and values. Our wasteful, careless ways must become a thing of the past. We must recycle more, procreate less, turn off lights, use mass transit, do a thousand things differently in our everyday lives. We owe this not only to ourselves and our children but also to the unborn generations who will one day inherit the earth.

---

## Cleaning Up Our Act*

Every pound of coal, gallon of gasoline, or gram of uranium that our society consumes represents some degree of insult to the environment. The fossil fuels we burn send soot into the air along with noxious chemicals that help contribute to smog and acid rain. In the United States each year we burn over two billion

* Excerpted with permission from *Energy Unbound*, by L. Hunter Lovins and Amory B. Lovins. (San Francisco: Sierra Club Books, 1986), pp. 198–201.

tons of fossil fuel—more than the combined weight of all the food and timber, iron and steel, copper and aluminum, cement and concrete that we grow, mine, and use. Nearly all that fuel ends up in the air. A house heated with electricity from a coal-fired plant is responsible for the release into the air every year of a couple of hundred pounds of nitrogen oxides and as much as 400 to 500 pounds of sulfur oxides, creating over 1,500 pounds' worth of acid rain.

In the atmosphere, all of these gases mix with clouds, rain, and snow, and come down as a witches' brew of acids that has already decimated aquatic life throughout the Northeast and is spreading to the Great Lakes, the Rockies, and the Pacific Coast. Such acids are already well on the way to wiping out the forests of Germany and Czechoslovakia. And anyone who has been to a city dominated by cars—such as Los Angeles, Denver, or Phoenix—knows what an eye-watering, throat-scratching brown pall fills the air.

When industries mine coal and uranium they leave behind mountains of tailings that actually leach poisons into the local streams. To mine the uranium needed to provide only one house with nuclear electricity, eight tons of dirt must be moved, leaving a residue of one third of a ton of uranium mill tailings.

Coal is often strip-mined, with enormous machines tearing the tops off entire mountain ranges for miles, or eating away whole ranching valleys. Even if some effort is then made to replant the vegetation, mountains and underground aquifers do not easily recover from being skinned and turned upside down.

Oil is an ecological culprit also. Offshore oil drilling and crude oil shipping are responsible for dumping six million tons of petroleum into the oceans every year. Jacques Cousteau reports that now it's hard to find any part of the world's oceans that doesn't have oil tracings floating on the surface.

Perhaps worst of all, the burning of fossil fuels has raised the amount of carbon dioxide in the atmosphere. This accumulation is the major contributor to the phenomenon known as the "greenhouse effect." This warming trend could turn temperate climates into deserts and would melt large parts of the polar ice caps, raising the level of the oceans and flooding the coasts of every country in the world.

Is there anything we can do to stop all this from happening? Of course there is. We've known for years what to do. But business, government, and we as consumers have been unwilling to take the necessary action. Some say, "That's the price we must pay to have the life-style we want." Others claim, "The evidence isn't yet conclusive." Of course, if we wait for all the evidence to be in, New York will be under ten feet of water, and stockbrokers will set off for Wall Street in scuba gear—or, the lucky ones, in private submarines.

The real point that ought to be driven home to everyone is that we've been ignoring the best way of solving these problems. The first thing we need to do is to start using energy more efficiently. If we insulate our houses, we'll need to burn less fuel to keep warm, we won't release as much pollution into the atmosphere, and we won't have to tear up as much land to get the fuel we need. The same is true of all kinds of efficiency improvements—more efficient light bulbs, better-made appliances and motors, better water conservation, cars that get more miles per gallon, and of course improved public transportation. We need to create less waste and recycle more of what we consume. We need to stop poisoning the planet with chemicals to which insects can develop immunities quicker than humans.

Every aspect of our lives has some environmental impact. We must acknowledge the responsibility we were all given as citizens of the planet and act on the hundreds of opportunities to save our planet that present themselves every day. The actions that follow will help you get started and explain why you can really make a difference.

The following sections on the environment will provide you with specific actions you can take to protect and heal our ailing planet.

# 2

# Home and Appliance: Energy Efficiency and Conservation

Today modern lighting technology could save the U.S. $30 billion a year; Renault has a car that gets 124 miles to the gallon; and homes can be built with super-insulation so they need no heating in temperatures down to 40 below zero.

## The Problems Are Clear— but So Are the Solutions!

—Our lights, refrigerators, and televisions are powered by electricity from coal-burning generators that spew out the gases responsible for acid rain and the greenhouse effect.

—Most American households waste half the energy they consume, with the average home guzzling 1,253 gallons of oil a year at a cost of $1,123.*

—If every household in the United States lowered its average heating temperature six degrees for *only twenty-four hours* this could save more than 570,000 barrels of oil.[†]

—If everyone raised air-conditioning temperatures six degrees, we could save the equivalent of 190,000 barrels of oil every day.[‡]

*U.S. Department of Energy, Washington, D.C.
[†] Ibid.
[‡] Ibid.

—Better yet, if everyone improved their home insulation using the most efficient materials, the same amount of energy would be saved, and they wouldn't even need to touch the thermostat. During the summer, trees properly planted around your home can cut your energy bills and use of electricity by 10 to 50 percent.*

If we spent the equivalent of what it costs to keep the Rapid Deployment Force active in the Middle East for one year (to protect oil tankers passing through the Persian Gulf) on weatherizing American buildings, we'd save enough oil to be able to eliminate oil imports forever![†]

—The average cost of generating nuclear power per kilowatt-hour is 10 to 13 cents. (This is the equivalent of buying oil at $240 a gallon, one of the many reasons we've so far abandoned $15 billion worth of nuclear plants before construction was complete).[‡] This compares to the average cost to generate one kilowatt-hour of nonnuclear electricity of 6 cents.*

—To generate a savings of one kilowatt-hour through energy conservation would cost only 1 to 4 cents.[†]

So why does the U.S. Treasury continue to spend $15 to $20 billion a year on subsidizing the nuclear power industry and only $200 million on energy conservation and development?

Energy efficiency even creates jobs! One million dollars spent on energy efficiency will directly create fifty jobs. The same million dollars spent on the petroleum industry will only create ten jobs. That means money invested in saving energy creates 400 percent more employment than the same numbers of dollars spent on creating new energy.[‡]

Unfortunately, much energy efficiency has helped those that need the help least. Private homes have been constructed to be more and more efficient—but rental units that disproportionately house minorities, the poor, and the elderly remain the most

---

*The American Forestry Association, Washington, D.C.
[†]*Energy Unbound*, by L. Hunter Lovins and Amory B. Lovins (San Francisco: Sierra Club Books, 1986), p. 17.
[‡]*Greenpeace* magazine, Vol. 13, No. 2, p. 17.
*Greenpeace* magazine, Vol. 13, No. 2, p. 17.
[†] Ibid.
[‡]*Energy Unbound*, p. 52.

wasteful of energy. Rental housing poses a serious problem. Since tenants usually pay oil, gas, and electric bills, landlords have little incentive to spend extra dollars to reduce their tenants' costs. Tenants, who don't own their own property, are equally reluctant to make the investment, even though the payback period is often less than a year. This is one area where legislators must step in with national, state, or even local efficiency standards for all rental housing.

> The extraordinary levels of efficiency possible today can be seen in Scandinavia, Canada and the northern Great Plains of the United States, where new homes have been built to get through the winter on $200 worth of heat. Montana-based builder Brian Curran goes so far as to guarantee his homes will have heating bills of under $100—otherwise, he pays the difference.
>
> These "superinsulated" homes, first developed in Sweden, combine high-quality, air-tight construction with ample insulation, double- or triple-glazed windows and efficient appliances. Walls and ceilings are insulated to twice the standard level, and the entire structure is enclosed in a vapor and windproof barrier. So thermally sound are these houses that most of the heating actually comes from occupants, lights and appliances. Indeed, until recently it was difficult to find furnaces small enough to meet their minuscule heating demands.*

But let's not get carried away—we're not all ready to build or buy new homes. Let's simply start with a careful look at our appliances and some other inexpensive but effective ways to conserve energy.

---

**Action 1**        *Energy-Efficient Lighting*

Compact fluorescent lighting could save enough energy to eliminate the need for all the nuclear power plants currently operating in the United States.

A compact fluorescent bulb provides huge environmental benefits. Over its lifetime, using the new light bulb will slow global warming and reduce acid rain by cutting down on emis-

*World Watch* magazine, May-June 1988, Worldwatch Institute, pp. 27–28.

sions from a typical U.S. coal plant of one ton of $CO_2$ and about twenty pounds of $SO_2$. Or if instead it is used to save nuclear electricity, it will help avoid the production of half a curie of strontium-90 and cesium-137 (two high-level waste components) and about 25 milligrams of plutonium—nearly equivalent in explosive power to 850 pounds of TNT, or equal in radiotoxicity, if uniformly distributed into the lungs, to about two thousand cancer-causing doses.*

Compact fluorescents will also save you money! A standard 60-watt light bulb burning twenty-four hours a day consumes 526 kilowatt-hours of electricity every year. At a national average cost of 8 cents per kilowatt-hour, that's $42.08 per year. But a 16-watt compact fluorescent bulb, which produces the same amount of light and fits into any household lamp, consumes only 140 kilowatt-hours of electricity at a yearly cost of $11.20. Into this formula we must add the significantly higher cost of compact fluorescent bulbs, which can run $15 to $18 each compared to the $1 you would pay for a regular bulb. But don't worry—you'll still come out ahead.

The Panasonic Light Capsule lasts an average of nine thousand hours, the equivalent of nine standard incandescent bulbs. Over its lifetime the Panasonic capsule, at $18 plus the cost of electricity at $11.50, totals $29.50. Nine standard bulbs would cost $9 plus the cost of electricity at $43.50, or a total of $52.50. Each compact fluorescent will save you an average of $23 over its life span. If there are fifteen bulbs in your house that's a savings of $345. Don't get hung up on the cost of the fluorescent bulb—though it seems expensive, it's a bargain in the long run.

Our nation has 2.5 billion light-bulb sockets. Of these, more than one billion could easily use high-efficiency bulbs, though only forty million are now in use. The potential savings of $30 billion a year if the United States converted to the most efficient lighting technology boggles the imagination.†

In the home, most of the incandescent bulbs in use are manufactured by General Electric, one of the nation's top ten defense contractors, currently the target of a boycott by INFACT (see Action 117). Switching to fluorescent bulbs will save money,

---

*Rocky Mountain Institute Newsletter*, November 1988.
†The World Bank spent $100,000 to upgrade the energy efficiency of the lighting in its headquarters building. In 1984 alone it saved $500,000 in electricity costs. Over ten years, assuming no increase in the cost of electricity, the World Bank will save over $5 million (Source: *Greenpeace* magazine, Vol. 13, No. 2, March/April 1988, p. 17).

reduce the demand for electricity, and thus the output of pollution, and can support the GE boycott all at the same time.

### WHAT YOU CAN DO:

Order compact fluorescent bulbs from Seventh Generation —Products for a Healthy Planet (800) 456-1177, twenty-four hours a day, or write to them and request a copy of their mailorder catalog at:

> 10 Farrell Street
> South Burlington, VT 05403

Commercial or industrial users contact:

> Rising Sun Enterprises, Inc.
> P.O. Box 586
> Old Snowmass, CO 81654
> (303) 927-8051

---

**Action
2**          *The Refrigerator*

How can you help eliminate the need for at least twelve nuclear power plants while you freeze ice and keep your juice chilled.

Your refrigerator motor is probably underneath your refrigerator so that heat from the motor rises up into the food compartment, and the fridge ends up using an average of 50 percent of its cooling capacity to eliminate the heat of its own motor!

Manufacturers have also been working for years on another neat trick—making the inside of the refrigerator bigger without enlarging the outside. What they're doing of course is making the walls thinner and thinner and thus eliminating more and more insulation.

When you open the door to the fridge, cold air comes out, and the walls inside frost up. To remove the frost, manufacturers came up with the brilliant idea of installing a little electric heater inside the refrigerator. If you tried really hard you'd probably never be able to come up with a less efficient way to use electricity. That's why, unless you use an electric water heater or electric space heating, your refrigerator is probably the costliest electric appliance in your home.

—Nationally, refrigerators use the equivalent of about half the output of all nuclear power plants.*

—If all households had the most efficient refrigerators available, the electricity savings would eliminate the need for about twelve large nuclear plants.†

—Most refrigerators operate with freon gas, which when released damages the earth's ozone layer.

—Generally, models that have the refrigerator and the freezer side by side use *35 percent more* energy than models with the freezer on top. Models with manual defrost use *50 percent less* electricity than those with automatic defrost.

## WHAT YOU CAN DO:

**1.** When you purchase a new refrigerator make sure that you first consult the American Council for an Energy-Efficient Economy booklet titled *The Most Energy-Efficient Appliances*. See page 000 for ordering information.

**2.** If you're serious about saving the environment by drastically cutting your energy consumption, consider a Sun Frost refrigerator, which uses 80 percent less electricity than the average model. Consider the facts: Most consumers spend $1,000 on a refrigerator, an additional $120 to $180 annually for electricity, or a total of $4,000 over the machine's twenty-year lifetime. The Sun Frost, at a cost of $1,550, will save more than 75 percent of your energy expenses, or $3,000 worth of electricity over the appliance's lifetime. For more information about the Sun Frost refrigerator contact: Real Good News at (800) 762-7325. They also sell the Sibir Propane Refrigerator, which uses *no* electricity and only 1.5 gallons of propane per week; the cost: $1,025.

---

* Excerpted from *Energy Unbound*, pp. 24–26.
† Ibid.

| Action | ***Hot Water*** |
|--------|-----------------|
| **3**  |                 |

How to heat more water with less energy for fewer dollars.

### WHAT YOU CAN DO:

**1.** Consider replacing your electric hot water heater if you've got one; gas and oil heaters are generally at least 40 percent more efficient. In addition, almost all hot water tanks waste an average of 20 to 30 percent of the electricity they consume—keeping water hot when it's not needed. This can be minimized by wrapping insulation around the tank and around all hot water pipes. Better yet, "demand-type" water heaters come on only when you turn on the tap—there's no tank and the water is heated only as it is used, with a high-powered gas burner or electric heating element that the water passes through.

**2.** No matter what type of water heater you currently own, set the thermostat to "low." For each reduction of 10 degrees on the dial you'll save roughly 3 to 5 percent on your heating bill. A setting of 110 degrees will provide you with water that is more than adequately hot. Also remember to turn off your heater if you leave home for the weekend or take a vacation.

**3.** See page 52 for information on flow-reduction shower heads and taps that will lower overall use of hot water.

**4.** See page 44 for information on solar hot water heating.

**5.** See page 48 for how to order *The Most Energy-Efficient Appliances* and *Saving Energy and Money with Home Appliances*.

| Action | ***Other Home Appliances**** |
|--------|------------------------------|
| **4**  |                              |

Residential appliances and heating and cooling equipment consume about one third of the total electricity produced in the United States.

*All of the material in this section is excerpted with permission from *Saving Energy and Money with Home Appliances*, published by the American Council for an Energy-Efficient Economy, Washington, D.C.

To begin with, let's do away with a few myths:

—*Turning off lights and the TV whenever possible is the best way to save energy in the home.* Lighting and television sets account for a relatively small portion of home electricity use. A lot more energy can be saved by buying efficient refrigerators, water heaters, and air conditioners.

—*High-powered small appliances are energy guzzlers that should be avoided to conserve energy.* While devices such as a coffee maker, hair dryer, and toaster do draw a large amount of power (typically 1,000 watts or more), they are kept on only a short time and don't contribute significantly to your electric bill. Other appliances in this category include vacuum cleaners, radios, stereos, blenders, mixers, and assorted kitchen gadgets.

—*Standing in front of an open refrigerator wastes energy.* In reality, the cold air rushes out of the refrigerator as soon as the door is opened, so keeping the door open for thirty seconds is not much worse than opening it for fifteen seconds. Of course, it's not a good idea to leave the door open for long periods of time.

When it comes to saving energy these are the appliances to focus on. Aside from your central heating system, the following are likely to be the biggest energy users in your home:

1. Water heaters
2. Refrigerator/freezers
3. Freezers
4. Air conditioners
5. Ranges
6. Clothes washers
7. Clothes dryers
8. Dishwashers
9. Portable space heaters
10. Lights

Although many appliance models may look the same, they can be very different when it comes to energy cost. That's why it pays to look closely at energy efficiency.

The following table shows how much it costs to run various appliances each year. The table compares average appliances used in American homes and apartments today and very energy-efficient appliances on the market as of 1988. Costs are shown both for locations with average energy prices and for the Northeast, an area that has high energy prices. Actual energy use varies greatly from one model to the next. As you can see from the table, considerable savings are possible with top-rated appliances.

## TYPICAL APPLIANCE OPERATING COSTS, Yearly Cost ($)*

| APPLIANCE | AVERAGE EXISTING APPLIANCE | | VERY ENERGY-EFFICIENT NEW APPLIANCE | |
|---|---|---|---|---|
| | U.S. | NORTHEAST | U.S. | NORTHEAST |
| Water heater (electric) | $300 | $400 | $150 | $200 |
| Water heater (gas) | 160 | 200 | 130 | 160 |
| Refrigerator (manual defrost) | 45 | 60 | 30 | 40 |
| Refrigerator/freezer (frost free) | 120 | 160 | 70 | 90 |
| Freezer (manual defrost) | 75 | 100 | 40 | 55 |
| Freezer (frost free) | 135 | 180 | 75 | 100 |
| Air conditioner (central) | 300 | 200 | 150 | 100 |
| Air conditioner (1 room) | 60 | 40 | 40 | 25 |
| Range (electric) | 60 | 80 | 50 | 70 |
| Range (gas) | 45 | 60 | 35 | 45 |
| Clothes washer (includes water heating) | 90 | 120 | 45 | 60 |
| Clothes dryer (electric) | 70 | 90 | 55 | 75 |
| Clothes dryer (gas) | 30 | 40 | 25 | 30 |
| Dishwasher (includes water heating) | 70 | 90 | 45 | 60 |
| Television (color) | 25 | 35 | 10 | 15 |
| Lights (household total) | 75 | 100 | 25–50 | 33–67 |

*Energy costs for the typical U.S. household are based on an electricity price of 7.5 cents per kWh and a gas price of 60 cents per therm. Energy costs for the typical household in the northeastern United States are based on 10 cents per kWh and 75 cents per therm. Air-conditioning figures include an allowance for the Northeast's cool climate.

## WHAT YOU CAN DO:

Order two booklets from the American Council for an Energy-Efficient Economy to guide all your appliance purchases to those that are the most energy efficient: *The Most Energy-Efficient Appliances* covers all the highest-rated models available in the United States, and costs $2. *Saving Energy and Money with Home Appliances*, also $2, is a companion guide to the purchase and use of energy-efficient appliances. Both are available from ACEE, Suite 535, 1001 Connecticut Avenue, N.W., Washington, DC 20036.

| Action | *Weatherproofing and* |
|---|---|
| 5 | *Insulation* |

For what it costs each year [as of 1987] to maintain the military's Rapid Deployment Force, that supposedly guarantees the safe flow of oil out of the Persian Gulf (most of which goes to Japan), we could weatherize American buildings and save enough oil *to eliminate imports forever!**

A typical house has enough cracks, leaks, and holes to be equivalent to a three-foot by three-foot hole in the wall of the living room. Not much help when you're trying to keep cool in the summer or warm in the winter. A basic weatherproofing program, consisting of weather-stripping windows and doors, tuning up the furnace, and adding some insulation to the attic, can make a big dent in your utility bills and is a major step toward reducing our overall energy needs, which at current levels are destroying the planet.

Windows are a particularly key area of energy loss—as much energy leaks through American windows every year as flows through the Alaskan pipeline! A 50-cent investment in weatherstripping and calking can save you $5 a winter. Storm windows can double a window's insulating value. If you have south-facing windows, opening the blinds means your house will soak up the solar heating equivalent of seven gallons of oil each winter. Unfortunately, unless you close the blinds at night, you'll lose just about all the heat you've gained.[†]

A "retrofitting" renovation of your whole house, while expensive, can make an even larger difference. In forty thousand retrofits monitored by U.S. Utilities, overall energy consumption fell by 25 percent, and homeowners got a 23 percent annual return on their investment.[‡]

If you start from scratch, superinsulated houses that add only several thousand dollars in construction costs, or $35 a month, to your mortgage bill can save an average of $79 a month in utility costs. That's a savings of $528 every year, and can be even more as the cost of energy rises.

*Amory B. Lovins, Rocky Mountain Institute.

[†] *World Watch* magazine, May-June 1988, p. 30.

[‡] Lester Brown, *State of the World, 1988* (Washington, D.C.: Worldwatch Institute), p. 45.

## *WHAT YOU CAN DO:*

**1.** Contact your local utility company or look in the Yellow Pages to see who offers a free energy audit of your home.

**2.** Your local hardware store probably stocks everything you need to cover windows and doors with shrink-to-fit plastic sealers, as well as liquid calk, outlet covers, draft stoppers for the bottoms of doors, and pipe insulation for hot water pipes. More than enough to get you started.

**3.** To order a complete line of weatherproofing products by mail, call Resource Conservation at 800-243-2862; request free samples as well as a copy of their catalog.

**4.** Order *The Superinsulated Home Book* by J. T. Nisson and Gautam Dutt, ($22.15). It will show you how to heat and cool your house for $200 to $300 a year. John Wiley & Sons, One Wiley Drive, Somerset, NJ 08873; (201) 469-9400.

---

**Action
6**                 *Solar Energy*

The sun can provide many of our energy needs without the devastating side effects caused by fossil fuels such as acid rain and global warming—it's renewable and environmentally sound.

Converting any part of your energy consumption from electric, gas, or oil to solar power is admittedly much more expensive, involved, and time consuming than writing letters, calking windows, or resetting thermostats. However, no discussion of energy conservation would be complete without the introduction of at least one "renewable" energy source. Oil, gas, and coal are of course "nonrenewable" sources, since as soon as you extract them from the earth they're gone. But the sun is not diminished in its strength or value by our increasingly diverse uses of it.

Solar heating has been around for years. In 1897, 30 percent of the houses in Pasadena, California, used excellent solar water heaters. Today, solar technology is so advanced that even in climates having almost constant cloud cover you can still utilize solar heating to turn cool water into steam. Commercially available solar collectors can heat water to as high as 2,600 degrees

Fahrenheit. But America is running well behind in its use of solar technology; 12 percent of Japan's, 65 percent of Israel's, and 90 percent of Cyprus's homes use water that is solar heated. Many of these systems are so simple that they cost only $500 per family to install.

Today, in addition to heating water and your entire home by the sun, you can purchase solar rechargeable batteries, solar-powered Walkmen, flashlights, fans, and even a solar barbecue. In the Mojave Desert, a private plant owned by Solar Energy Generating Systems supplies enough power for 10,000 homes. Five of these plants are already in operation in the Mojave and fourteen more are scheduled for completion by 1992.

Perhaps most important, solar power doesn't pollute our air. It does not contribute to the destruction of the environment through acid rain, to the depletion of our protective ozone layer, or to the greenhouse effect, all of which are caused by burning gas, coal, or oil.


## WHAT YOU CAN DO:

**1.** First, call or write Rodale Press for a copy of their book catalog, which contains a large number of excellent do-it-yourself guides. In addition, contact the Rocky Mountain Institute for their publications list. Addresses and phone numbers of both appear on page 46.

**2.** Consider purchasing a solar-powered calculator and watch. Seventh Generation (see page 46) also sells the Solar Cap, which (believe it or not) will blow a cool breeze onto your forehead in the summer months for only $29.95, a solar flashlight for $35, and solar-powered battery recharger that cost $15 to $26; (800) 456-1177. Catalog available free.

**3.** Also contact the American Solar Energy Society, Inc., at 2400 Central Avenue B1, Boulder, CO 80301; (303) 443-3130. The Solar Energy Society is a national membership organization open to those interested in the development and promotion of solar energy. It offers a free catalog of publications listing a variety of books on solar energy—from a guide to residential solar water heaters to technical discussions on solar equipment. It also publishes the bimonthly magazine *Solar Today,* which covers advances in solar technology.

Action         *Energy Conservation*
  7            *Resource Guides and*
               *Materials*

**1.** *ENERGY UNBOUND*, by L. Hunter Lovins and Amory
B. Lovins with Seth Zuckerman, is a complete and unrivaled
energy primer in the form of a witty modern-day parable about
Eunice Bunnyhut, a Midwestern housewife who becomes sec-
retary of energy. The book explains the relationship between the
national debt, acid rain, Third World poverty, farm failures, rainforest destruction, and our individual energy-use patterns. It
tells you what you can do at home, at work, and in your community to use energy efficiently. The book covers the politics and
economics of energy consumption with hard-hitting facts and
crystal-clear examples. It is published by Random House, New
York, NY, 1986; 377 pages, hardcover, $17.45, and is available
from the Rocky Mountain Institute (see below).

Much of the information in this section of the book is based
upon the Lovinses' work, and I am deeply indebted to them for
their pioneering efforts.

**2.** ROCKY MOUNTAIN INSTITUTE, founded by Hunter
and Amory Lovins, focuses on research and practical applica-
tions of renewable energy, energy efficiency, and conservation.
It publishes a quarterly newsletter, a *Where-to-Get-It List of
Technologies* for an ultra-efficient home ($5), and more than one
hundred other publications.

Of special note is the recently published *Resources-Efficient
Housing Guide* ($15). This incredible catalog covers everything
from an extensive list of relevant periodicals and books to information on design, construction, and retrofitting; landscaping;
appliances; financing energy-efficient resources; household environmental quality, and much, much more. Write Rocky Mountain Institute, 1739 Snowmass Creek Road, Old Snowmass, CO
81654-9199; (303) 927-3128 or (303) 927-3851.

**3.** SEVENTH GENERATION (a company I helped start; I
am currently the chairman) has an incredible array of environmentally sensitive and energy-conserving products for almost
every imaginable use. From books and magazines to recycled
paper products, compact fluorescent bulbs, photodegradable garbage bags, even solar experiments, games, and watches. It is

truly the ultimate guide and resource for people who want to live environmentally sensitive life-styles. Write Seventh Generation, 10 Farrell Street, South Burlington, VT 05403; (800) 456-1177.

**4.** JADE MOUNTAIN also offers a catalog of renewable energy products on a somewhat grander scale—from boats and cars to wind generators, hydroelectric systems, solar cooling devices, and solar electric panels. Call for a free catalog or order the *Alternative Energy Sourcebook*, 293 pages, more than 1,200 items, for only $4. Write Jade Mountain, P.O. Box 4616, Boulder, CO 80306; (303) 449-6601.

**5.** CAREIRS, under contract with the U.S. Department of Energy, offers a toll-free energy hotline that can provide a wide range of solar and consumer conservation information. Call (800) 523-2929 (U.S., including the Virgin Islands and Puerto Rico); plus (800) 462-4983 (Pennsylvania); (800) 233-3071 (Alaska and Hawaii); or write CAREIRS, P.O. Box 8900, Silver Spring, MD 20907.

**6.** NATAS, the National Center for Appropriate Technology, also has a toll-free hotline that can provide callers with more technical information on renewable energy sources and appropriate technologies. Under contract with the U.S. Department of Energy. Call (800) 428-2525, (800) 428-1718 (Montana), or write NATAS, P.O. Box 2525, Butte, MT 59702.

**7.** *HOME ENERGY: THE MAGAZINE OF RESIDENTIAL ENERGY CONSERVATION* will keep you in touch with the latest developments in the field of residential energy conservation. It contains articles about energy-efficient products, research reports, and tips on how to identify energy waste in your home. Home Energy is a nonprofit organization working to provide a continuing education on energy conservation for homeowners. Write Home Energy, 2124 Kittredge, Suite 95, Berkeley, CA 94704; (415) 524-5405; bimonthly, $35.

**8.** ALLIANCE TO SAVE ENERGY offers a free publications list on energy conservation. Call (202) 857-0666, or write Alliance to Save Energy, 1925 K Street, N.W., Suite 206, Washington, DC 20006.

**9.** APPLIANCE EFFICIENCY. Two booklets from the American Council for an Energy-Efficient Economy can help you make wise decisions when buying or upgrading home appliances.

*The Most Energy-Efficient Appliances* is the best source of current data on the comparative efficiencies of major appliances sold as of 1988. *Saving Energy and Money with Home Appliances* describes appliances that really guzzle energy in contrast to those that save energy. Shopping tips, detailed information on ten types of major appliances, and good energy buys are included. Write ACEE, 1001 Connecticut Avenue, N.W., Suite 535, Washington, DC 20036. $2 each (postpaid).

**10.** *ALTERNATIVE SOURCES OF ENERGY.* A monthly magazine covering cogeneration, hydropower, wind power, alternative fuels, waste energies, and solar power. Includes reports on important trends, new product developments, and legislative changes affecting the alternative power production industry. Subscription costs $58 a year. Write ASE, 107 South Central Avenue, Milaca, MN 56353; (612) 983-6892.

**11.** *ENVIRONMENTAL ACTION RESOURCE SERVICE (EARS).* Free mail-order catalog lists reprints, pamphlets, and paperback books in the field of appropriate technology, including items on solar rays, wind, water, biomass, energy policy, design, and technology. Write P.O. Box 8, Laveta, CO 81055.

**12.** *PRACTICAL HOMEOWNER.* Focuses on energy efficiency and conservation. A one-year subscription (eight issues) costs $12.97. Write Rodale Press, 33 East Minor Street, Emmaus, PA 18098; (215) 967-5171.

**13.** *REAL GOODS.* This five-dollar 170-page catalog/source book offers an array of energy-saving and alternative energy devices, from low-voltage refrigerators and lighting systems to solar-powered water heaters, battery chargers, and calculators. Also includes how-to books on home installation of solar heating and cooling and on hydropower and wind power systems; it offers appliances, equipment, and instructions for energy self-sufficiency. Write Real Goods Trading Company, 3041 Guidiville Road, Ukiah, CA 95482; (707) 468-9214.

**14.** *101 PRACTICAL ENERGY TIPS FOR HOME & WORK.* This ninety-six page booklet is perfect for anyone who'd like more practical actions and a wealth of additional resources. Highly recommended. $3.95 from The Windstar Foundation, Earth-Pulse Project, 2317 Snowmass Creek Road, Snowmass, CO 81654; (800) 669-4777.

# 3

# Water Conservation

Life on earth began in the water. Today much of it is unsafe to drink let alone fit to create new life. Bathers have to dodge sewage, hypodermic needles, tampons, and poisoned fish. Fishermen haul in sea life complete with cancerous tumors and deadly lesions.

## Water Is the Medium of Life*

Eighty percent of the weight of a typical living cell is water; ninety-nine out of every one hundred molecules in your body are water molecules. Trace for a moment the path of one of these water molecules. Yesterday, a bit of water may have entered your body as you bit into a tomato; before that, it was part of an oak leaf decomposing in the soil of your vegetable garden. To become that oak leaf, the water molecule surged up the oak tree from its roots, where it was first deposited by a raccoon that had drunk from a nearby pond.

Through water we are connected to the oak, the raccoon, the marsh grass, to clouds and rivers, to soil and oceans. Through water, we are intimately connected to each other and to our entire planet.

There is almost nothing that we do that does not affect or

*Excerpted with permission from Kim Allsop, *New Alchemy*, Fall 1984.

rely on water, either directly or indirectly. Every time you press the brake pedal on your car a small amount of asbestos brake lining falls to the street and is later washed by rain into a nearby stream. The product you buy in New Hampshire today was perhaps created in a sulfur-dioxide–spewing factory in Ohio last week; the acid fumes released from this factory may come down as rain in your favorite fishing spot tomorrow. And the half-used box of pesticides you toss into the trash today may leach from the town landfill into your drinking water next year.

Although each of us, on the average, uses about 150 gallons a day directly for cooking, washing, flushing, and watering, our indirect use of water amounts to an astounding 1,840 gallons per day. Of this, about 1,660 gallons are used to grow the crops and livestock we eat, and 180 gallons are used by industry to create products. Approximately 120 gallons are used in the production of just one egg, three gallons to process one can of corn, ten gallons to make a paperback book, and six to flush a toilet.

Each time we flush the toilet, those six gallons affect one or more aquatic ecosystems. If your water comes from a surface reservoir, it was diverted from its downstream course by damming a river, which concentrated pollutants and decreased the oxygen levels necessary for life. Similarly, if those six gallons were removed from underground aquifers their use could ultimately lower the water level in area ponds and lakes.

What happens to the six-gallon flush after it leaves the toilet bowl? If the septic system is malfunctioning, or if there are too many such systems in an area of poor soils, the wastes could seep into ground water and affect the water you and your neighbors use to wash with and drink. If you live in a sewered area, the waste-laden six gallons travel to a waste-water treatment plant, where it may flow untreated into a bay, river, or ocean.

Between 1972 and 1981, under the auspices of the Federal Water Pollution Control Act, we spent over $32 billion in an attempt to make all the nation's waterways suitable for fishing and swimming by 1983. Thirty-seven states did not reach that goal, and the General Accounting Office reported that it doubted whether we can afford to complete the job.

It is not surprising that this monumental clean-up effort has been at best a partial success. For while laws, good planning, and funding all help, they will never be enough until we, as a people, learn an ethic of responsible use.

As usual, ecology and economics speak with one voice. When

we conserve water in the home we save money and aquatic eco-systems. When we maintain our septic systems we help avoid the need for building expensive new sewage treatment plants that almost always degrade water quality. When we use conservation technologies to water lawns, gardens, and fields we cut our water bills and reduce the likelihood of damming yet another river. When we take action in our communities to influence water-supply and water-quality planning we inform our government officials about how much we care about saving money and our ecosystems.

Today there are numerous ways to cut daily water consumption by more than 50 percent without any modification to our comfort or change in our life-styles. What follows is a description of the simplest, most effective ways to start reducing water usage.

---

**Action
8**

## *Flushing*

At 5 to 7 gallons a flush, with an average of 23 gallons per person a day and 8,395 gallons a year, flushing uses more water than anything else in your household.

## *WHAT YOU CAN DO:*

**1.** Start by flushing the toilet less often—if you cut flushing in half you'll save up to 16.5 gallons a day.

**2.** Toilet dams cut the flow of water per flush by 50 percent [$6.50 each from Seventh Generation (800) 456-1177]. They can be installed in less than thirty seconds without tools, and can cut your water bill by as much as 30 percent, while they save in the average household over 13,000 gallons of water every year.

**3.** State-of-the-art, low-flow toilets, which use only 1 to 1½ gallons per flush, saving over 7,665 gallons a year per person [$198 plus shipping costs from Real Goods Trading Company, 3041 Guidiville Road, Ukiah, CA 95482, or call (707) 468-9214 or (800) 762-7325]. The toilet is made by Aqualine in South Carolina. Also check with local dealers for the equally efficient American Eljer model.

**Action**        *Showering and Bathing*
  **9**

At twelve gallons a minute, a two-minute shower uses twenty-four gallons of water and a ten-minute shower over one hundred, with the average bath consuming forty gallons of water.

## WHAT YOU CAN DO:

The first thing you can do is keep your shower short and avoid taking baths unless the water level in the tub is kept as low as possible.

Low-flow shower heads can cut water use as much as 75 percent by reducing the water flow from twelve gallons a minute to three. Because of their unique design these shower heads still deliver water with invigorating force. If you have four people taking showers every day, low-flow shower heads will also save about 105 gallons of hot water a day, significantly reducing your hot water heating costs. You can calculate your savings as follows: If you have two showers, your total investment for shower heads would be $28. Assuming you heat your water with natural gas costing 80 cents per therm and that the temperature of the shower water is 110 degrees Fahrenheit, the 105 gallons you don't use every day, which would take more than two thirds of a therm to heat, will save you at least 55 cents a day. Over a year you'd save $200, leaving you with $172 after you've paid for the shower heads. If you heat with electricity the savings would be much greater, up to or over $300.* These energy savings of course translate into less acid rain and fewer "greenhouse" gases.

The Europa Showerhead is available from Seventh Generation for $13.95 and fits easily in any shower without requiring special tools for installation.

Flow-reduction shower heads are also available from Resources Conservation (800) 243-2862, and Vanderburgh Enterprises (203) 853-4429.

---

*L. Hunter Lovins and Amory B. Lovins, *Energy Unbound* (San Francisco: Sierra Club Books 1986).

## Action       *Brushing, Shaving, and*
### 10           *Doing the Dishes*

With the tap running, brushing your teeth can use up to 2 gallons of water, a shave 5–10 gallons and washing dishes by hand up to 20 gallons.*

### WHAT YOU CAN DO:

Don't let the tap run while you brush, shave, or scrub. This alone can cut water consumption by 75 percent. Single-lever ON/OFF switches make shutting off the water easier, without wasting water while you adjust to the right temperature.

Faucet aerators, with ON/OFF switches, create further savings by reducing the flow from the tap by 60 percent and saving over 6,000 gallons of water every year. Available from Seventh Generation for $8.95 each.

## Action       *Clothes Washers*
### 11

Most washing machines waste over 5,304 gallons of water every year.

### WHAT YOU CAN DO:

Front-loading washing machines, used widely in European countries, consume one third less water (and two thirds less soap) than conventional top loaders. A typical family of four does twenty-six loads of clothes a month, and if you're saving seventeen gallons of water per load (5,304 gallons a year), fourteen of them hot or warm water gallons, you will save lots of energy as well as water if you have a front loader. Gibson, White-Westinghouse, and Montgomery Ward all manufacture front-loading washing machines.

* L. Hunter Lovins and Amory B. Lovins, *Energy Unbound* (San Francisco: Sierra Club Books 1986).

Action                   *When You Want a*
  12                        *Cool Drink*

## WHAT YOU CAN DO:

Don't let the tap run till the water becomes cool. This can easily waste a gallon of water. Keep a bottle of water in the refrigerator for drinking purposes.

---

Action          *Keeping Your Grass Green*
  13

## WHAT YOU CAN DO:

If you must water the lawn, do it in the early evening to prevent the sun from evaporating much of the sprinkler's efforts and cause you to waste hundreds of gallons of water over the course of the year.

# 4

# The Global
# Environmental Crisis

---

**Action**            *The "Greenhouse Effect"\**
**14**

Climatic changes from the earth's warming are expected to melt glaciers and ice caps, causing sea levels to rise five to seven feet by (the year) 2100, flooding cities from New Orleans, to Cairo and Shanghai, to Rio. In other parts of the globe, rainfall could decline by as much as 90 percent, causing mass starvation on an unprecedented scale. Hundreds of plant and animal species unable to adapt to these changes are likely to become extinct. And this is only the beginning!

Factories, utilities, and cars produce a number of "greenhouse gases," so named because of the effect they have on the planetary heat balance. Like the panes of a greenhouse, these gases are largely transparent to the sun's incoming rays, but prevent more and more of the sun's energy from escaping back into space. As a result, temperatures in the lower atmosphere have slowly begun to rise.

Carbon dioxide is the single most damaging greenhouse gas. It is created when coal, oil, natural gas, or other fossil fuels are burned. Coal is the greatest producer of carbon dioxide, followed by oil and then natural gas, which only creates half as much carbon dioxide as coal performing a similar function.

\* Excerpted with permission from the *Audubon Activist*, September-October 1988.

Industrial and agricultural activities also produce a host of "trace gases," such as methane, nitrous oxide, and chlorofluorocarbons (CFCs, the same gases that affect the ozone layer) that, taken as a group, may rival or even surpass the warming effects of carbon dioxide. To make matters worse, we are reducing the earth's ability to reabsorb carbon dioxide by deforesting millions of acres of trees around the globe. These forests are actually able to consume carbon dioxide through photosynthesis, thus helping to reverse this dangerous pattern—if only we didn't chop them down and burn them up at such an alarming rate.

By most estimates, the atmospheric concentration of carbon dioxide is expected to double by the year 2030. This will cause a rise in the global average temperature of 1.5 to 4.5 degrees centigrade. However, these temperature changes are not expected to occur uniformly: They will be considerably greater at higher latitudes—rising to 9 degrees centigrade in the Arctic—and much less severe in the tropics. These temperature changes are projected to occur at rates fully one hundred times faster than any climatic change the earth has ever experienced.

As a result of the greenhouse effect, water supplies will shrink in the American West, where serious shortages already exist. Rising sea levels will inundate many coastal areas, causing tremendous economic losses and destroying valuable wetlands.

Unable to migrate fast enough to keep pace with changing climates, many plants and animals will be doomed to extinction. North American forests may be reduced to a small remnant in northeast Canada, the Arctic tundra may cease to exist in its current form, and wetlands may be flooded by rising seas or sucked dry by high temperatures. National parks and refuges may no longer be capable of supporting the very life forms they were designed to protect.

A general increase in energy efficiency is the fastest and cheapest solution to this problem. Energy efficiency reduces fuel consumption and thus reduces the output of greenhouse gases into the atmosphere. America already lags far behind other nations in energy efficiency. Japan and West Germany are in general twice as energy efficient as we are.

## WHAT YOU CAN DO:

**1.** All of the suggested energy conservation actions covered previously will help reduce the emission of greenhouse gases into the environment:

—energy-efficient home appliances (Actions 1 to 5)
—weatherizing and insulating your home (Action 6)
—reducing your use of hot water (Actions 9 and 10)
—switching to renewable energy sources such as solar power (Action 7)

In addition, the next action on acid rain, which focuses on transportation, explains the importance of reducing fuel emissions from your automobile.

**2.** Recycling waste and purchasing products made from recycled materials also are positive actions, since they save energy and thus emit fewer greenhouse gases into the environment. (See Actions 29 to 36.)

**3.** We must also fight the destruction of rain forests (Action 18) and contribute wherever we can to making the earth a greener place. Plants and trees are able to consume a huge amount of the carbon dioxide we produce that would otherwise contribute to the greenhouse effect. Tropical forests contain 340 billion tons of carbon, equaling half the carbon in the atmosphere. This is released when we burn tropical forests to clear them for cropland, and of course we no longer have those trees to consume through photosynthesis the carbon dioxide we create.

**4.** Forest fires, urban sprawl, new highways, and parking lots all contribute adversely to the environment. Planting trees, whether outside city apartment buildings or to replace some of the cropland on farms, helps. Trees planted in the city yield extra environmental benefits, since they often shade multiple dwellings, significantly reducing energy requirements for cooling.

**5.** For more detailed information on what you can do, order a copy of *Cooling the Greenhouse: Vital First Steps to Combat Global Warming*, $5 from the Natural Resources Defense Council, 1350 New York Avenue, Suite 300, Washington, DC 20005; (202) 783-7800.

**6.** If you want to become even more active, you can join:

—Climate Change Activists, sponsored by the Audubon Society. Contact Robert T. Lester at Audubon Activist, 950 Third Avenue, New York, NY 10022.
—The American Forestry Association's Global ReLeaf program, P.O. Box 2000, Washington, DC 20013. A $15 membership fee entitles you to a free copy of their *Action Guide*

and the *Global ReLeaf Report*, a newsletter focusing on reforestation, the greenhouse effect, and what you can do.
—Greenhouse Crisis Foundation, c/o Jeremy Rifkin, 1130
17th Street, N.W., Suite 630, Washington, DC 20036; (202)
466-2823. An informal network of progressive activists
(church, environmental, agriculture, Third World, and others) in thirty-five countries. They also have an excellent
publication, *101 Things You Can Do to Help the Environment,* available for $5.

---

| Action 15 | *Controlling Acid Rain* |
|---|---|

The fish are dead in 140 lakes in Ontario, Canada; 1800 of
Sweden's fresh water lakes are near totally lifeless, 55% of the
Netherlands' forests are dying and experts say the damage has
just begun to become visible.

Acid rain is the result of our massive burning of natural,
nonrenewable fossil fuels. Three activities are primarily responsible for this: driving automobiles, creating electricity, and industrial manufacturing. These factors closely relate to many of
the destructive activities discussed in the previous section on
the greenhouse effect.

Our energy systems now put more than 5.5 billion tons of
carbon into the atmosphere each year—more than one ton for
each person on the planet. Americans contribute a disproportionately large amount, equivalent to *five tons per person.* Additionally, these activities produce one hundred million tons of
sulfur and lesser quantities of nitrogen oxides and hydrocarbons,
all dangerous pollutants that first affect the air and then return
to the earth in the form of acid rain. Though we have tried to
control this pollution, we are losing the battle and everyone must
join in to slow the destruction of our forests, lakes, and rivers.*

## WHAT YOU CAN DO:

Actions that will result in lowering the emission of these
deadly chemicals into the air, and in turn reduce acid rain, are:

* Lester Brown, *State of the World, 1988*, Worldwatch Institute, Washington, D.C.

1. Minimize the use of your automobile by walking, bicycling (see Action 17 for more information), joining a car pool, or taking public transportation. Transportation is now the largest and most rapidly growing drain on the world's oil reserves. The United States uses fully 63 percent of its oil in transportation, more than the country produces.*

2. If you must drive, use a fuel-efficient car. Unfortunately, when the price of oil dropped, America's leading automakers abandoned much of their research into fuel efficiency. Japan has continued to maintain the lead. Already there are several Japanese models on the road, achieving over fifty miles per gallon. Prototypes are in development for models that will go up to one hundred miles per gallon. The key factor to remember is if you switch from a car that gets twenty-five miles to the gallon to one that gets fifty, you'll cut in half the dangerous emissions you cause every time you drive.

### FUEL EFFICIENCY OF SELECTED FOUR-PASSENGER AUTOMOBILES, 1987

| MODEL | FUEL | FUEL EFFICIENCY* (MILES PER GALLON) |
|---|---|---|
| In Production | | |
| Peugeot 205 | gasoline | 42 |
| Ford Escort | diesel | 53 |
| Honda City | gasoline | 53† |
| Suzuki Sprint | gasoline | 57 |
| Prototypes | | |
| Volvo LCP 2000 | diesel | 71 |
| Peugeot ECO | gasoline | 73 |
| Volkswagen E80 | diesel | 85 |
| Toyota AXV | diesel | 98 |

*Composite urban-highway figure
†City driving; composite would be higher. *Source:* Deborah Blevis, *The New Oil Crisis and Fuel Economy Technologies: Preparing the Light Transportation Industry for the 1990's* (New York: Quorum Press).

3. Use energy-efficient appliances (see Actions 2 to 7) and insulate and weatherize your home to reduce energy consumption. Solar energy is nonpolluting and makes no contribution to acid rain.

4. Purchase products made from recycled materials, since they take less energy to make.

*Lester Brown, *State of the World, 1988*, Worldwatch Institute, Washington, D.C.

**5.** Remember to use the compact fluorescent energy efficient light bulbs discussed in Action 1. Over each bulb's lifetime, the burning of 400 pounds of coal will be avoided. This will prevent twelve pounds of sulfur dioxide from entering the atmosphere.*

To play an even more active role join the Citizens Acid Rain Monitoring Network, where volunteers organized by the Audubon Society collect, test, and report on the acidity of rainfall in all fifty states. Contact Dorene Bolze at Audubon's New York office for more information: 950 Third Avenue, New York, NY 10022.

---

| Action 16 | *Protecting the Earth's Ozone Layer* |
|---|---|

By 1987 the ozone hole over Antarctica was twice the size of the continental United States. Half a billion additional cases of skin cancer are predicted by 2037, and sea food is expected to almost totally disappear from the world's oceans.[†]

"Chlorofluorocarbons, or freon (CFCs), circulate in the innards of refrigerators and air conditioners, and have done so since the 1930s. They are also used as a source of pressure in aerosol spray cans; as a solvent; to clean computer parts; and to make foam cartons and other insulating materials."[‡]

"The CFCs, once considered non-toxic 'perfect chemicals,' are now believed to be destroying ozone molecules in the upper atmosphere at an eventual doomsday rate. The ozone layer shields the planet from most of the sun's ultraviolet radiation, making life on earth possible.

"Indeed, despite the U.S., Canada and Scandinavian countries voluntarily ending their use of CFCs in aerosol sprays by the late 1970s, the CFC industry simply developed other products that sent just as much of the chemicals into the atmosphere as before. In 1976, some 470,000 tons were used in aerosols, 350,000 tons in non-aerosols. By 1985, the aerosol consumption

---

* *Newsletter*, Rocky Mountain Institute, February 1989.
[†] *World Watch* magazine, May-June 1988, Worldwatch Institute, Washington, D.C.
[‡] *The Economist*, September 19, 1987.

had been halved, but non-aerosol use had escalated to 540,000 tons."*

"Once released, CFCs take about 10 years to rise 18 to 25 miles above the earth into the stratosphere. Even under the new 1986 Montreal accord, stratospheric chlorine levels are expected to double before leveling off by the middle of the next century. At that point, global ozone loss could reach 7 percent, increasing the amount of harmful ultraviolet radiation that reaches the ground by about 15 percent.

"Exposure to radiation levels of this intensity suppresses the human immune system, permitting the growth of infectious diseases. The EPA estimates that a 15 percent increase in harmful ultraviolet rays would cause 1.5 million additional skin cancer cases worldwide each year.

"Researchers are just beginning to understand the impact of ozone loss on plants and wildlife. Alan Teramura, a botanist at the University of Maryland, found that each 1 percent increase in the intensity of ultraviolet exposure depresses soybean yields by an equal percentage. Two out of three plant species are sensitive to increased ultraviolet radiation, according to Teramura. In the oceans, crab, fish, seal and whale populations may decline as the killing rays destroy phytoplankton, the microscopic plant cells that sustain the aquatic food web."†

## WHAT YOU CAN DO:

1. We must become careful and conscientious consumers, avoiding all products manufactured with Styrofoam. Do not purchase Styrofoam cups, plates, egg cartons, ice chests, or flotation devices. If your friends, school, or office still purchase Styrofoam cups, convince them of the importance of switching to paper—or, better yet, use real coffee mugs.

2. If you eat fast food, stay away from all companies that haven't already switched to paper packaging.

3. Don't use or purchase products that are excessively packaged with those little Styrofoam "eggs" or blocks.

4. Tell the butcher in your supermarket you don't want your meat or chicken on a Styrofoam tray; ask him to wrap your purchase in paper.

* *Guardian*, October 7, 1987.
† *World Watch* magazine, May-June 1988.

**5.** Refrigerators are available that don't use CFCs (see Action 2), and a company called Cyrodynamics, (1101 Bristol Road, Mountainside, NJ 07092) has developed air conditioners and refrigerators that are both CFC free.

**6.** Other products and materials that are often made with CFCs include car seats, foam mattresses, carpet padding, and chairs or couches that are made with foam padding. Ask before you buy!

**7.** Make sure that when your air conditioning or refrigerator is serviced that the service man does not allow the freon inside to escape. Special equipment is now available to capture and recycle this dangerous form of CFC.

**8.** For more detailed information and additional actions, purchase a copy of *Protecting the Ozone Layer: What You Can Do*, published by the Environmental Defense Fund, and available for $2. Write them at 257 Park Avenue South, New York, NY 10010; (212) 505-2100.

**9.** Friends of the Earth publishes a new quarterly newsletter, *Atmosphere*, which focuses on current domestic and international ozone protection news. Annual subscriptions are $10 for FOE members and $15 for nonmembers. Write FOE, 530 7th Street S.E., Washington, DC 20003; (202) 543-4312.

---

**Action 17**          *The Incredible Bicycle\**

Automobiles and trucks are responsible for 30% of the nation's carbon dioxide emissions, a major cause of acid rain and the greenhouse effect. Two-thirds of the land in the city of Los Angeles is devoted to highways, roads and parking lots. Our nation's thirst for gasoline has left traces of oil from spills and accidents that can be found in every body of salt water on the face of the planet.

Traffic noise in Beijing means the whirring of bicycle wheels and tinkling of bells. The streets of New Delhi come alive with thousands of bicycle commuters each day. Office workers in New

\*Excerpted from Marcia D. Lowe; "Pedaling into the Future" *World Watch* magazine, July-August 1988.

York City depend on bicycle messengers to cruise past bumper-to-bumper traffic and deliver parcels on time.

Outside the city, bicycles also play a vital role. Kenyan dairy farmers with milk deliveries cycle through remote regions, and Nicaraguan health workers on bikes now reach four times as many rural patients as they did on foot.

Whether a cycle rickshaw in Jakarta or a ten-speed bike in Boston, pedal power plays a key role in transportation. The bicycle is fast becoming the only way to move quickly through congested urban traffic and the only affordable personal transport in the developing world—where an automobile may cost more than a worker earns in a decade.

The United States government, however, has yet to take the bicycle seriously as a means of transportation. It collects no statistics and refers all requests for information to its "Division of Toys and Games." Our society, for the most part, has chosen to pay a high price for mobility, and overreliance on the automobile is backfiring as too many cars clutter city streets and highways, and bring rush-hour traffic to a standstill. The side effects of massive oil use show up not only in economy-draining import bills but in deadly air pollution in cities, acid rain in dying lakes and forests, and hastened global warming.

## Planning Makes a Difference

Like the United States, most other industrial countries have all but abandoned the bicycle for the automobile. Suburbanization has caused jobs, homes, and services to sprawl over such long distances that automobiles are less a convenience than a necessity. Only a handful of North American cities have extensive bike paths, and most major cities have become bicycle-proof, their roadways and parking facilities designed with only motor vehicles in mind.

There are, however, outstanding models of nationwide bicycle planning in the Netherlands, West Germany, and Japan. Local governments in these countries—spurred by traffic jams and air pollution—are demonstrating how public policy can be used to make cycling a safe and convenient alternative to the car.

The Netherlands has over nine thousand miles of bicycle paths, more than any other country. In some Dutch cities, half of all trips are made by bike. The West German city of Erlangen has completed a network of paths covering one hundred miles, about half the length of the city's streets. Bicycle use has more than doubled as a result.

So many Japanese commuters bicycle to train stations where they then ride public transportation to work that the stations need parking towers. The city of Kasukabe now has a twelve-story structure that uses cranes to park more than 1,500 bicycles.

---

## Automobiles Have Become
## the Bane of Urban Life

Industrial cities typically relinquish at least one third of their land—two thirds in Los Angeles—to roads and parking lots. In the United States, this totals 38.4 million acres—more than the entire state of Georgia.

Traffic congestion is eroding the quality of life in urban areas, and the amount of time wasted in traffic continues to expand in the world's cities. London rush-hour traffic crawls at an average of eight miles an hour. In Los Angeles, motorists waste 100,000 hours a day in traffic jams. Traffic engineers estimate that by the turn of the century Californians will lose almost two million hours daily.

Emissions from gasoline and diesel fuel use are linked to as many as 30,000 deaths annually in the United States alone, and some 100,000 people in North America, Western Europe, Japan, and Australia died in traffic accidents in 1985. Developing countries—with fewer automobiles but more pedestrian traffic and no provisions for separating the two—have fatality rates as much as twenty times higher than industrial countries.

### WHAT YOU CAN DO:

While government must take the responsibility for making roads safe for bicycles, building bike paths, constructing parking areas, and conducting safety campaigns—we can all get involved. Retrieve your bike from the cellar or attic, dust it off, oil it up, and pedal every place you can. Pedal for your health, for clean air, for the end of acid rain, and for the hope that our planet will escape the devasting climatic changes that the greenhouse effect could bring our way.

The following groups are leaders in advocating programs

that encourage the use of bicycles and are working to pass legislation that provides for cyclists' rights:

—League of American Wheelman. This one-hundred-year-old group has been active for more than a century, starting with its campaign for bicycle paths in New York City's Central Park. 6707 Whitestone Road, Suite 209, Baltimore, MD 21207; (301) 944-3399.

—Bicycle Federation of America, 1818 R Street, NW, Washington, DC 20009; (202) 332-6986.

—Bicycle Network, P.O. Box 8194, Philadelphia, PA 19101.

---

**Action 18**    *Saving the Rain Forests*

A 100 year old rain forest tree has lifted in its lifetime 2,500 tons of water from its roots to its crown and provided 20 years' worth of oxygen for a human being. Yet in the course of every hour of every day, we destroy an average of seventy-five acres of rain forest and every day of every year we permanently wipe out over one hundred different species of plants and animals.[*]

In the past thirty years, more than 40 percent of the earth's rain forests have been destroyed. Environmentalists fear that in another thirty years, there may not be any tropical forests left. What about life on earth after the rain forests are gone? Paul Ehrlich warns: "We are destroying a part of the planet's heritage that is crucial to our health, to our climate, to the very maintenance of our biosphere. Second only to nuclear war, there are few problems more critical to humanity at the moment." But the destruction continues; fifty to one hundred acres of rain forest are demolished each minute, an area larger than the size of a football field is destroyed every second of every day. A million species of plants and animals will be extinct by the turn of the century, an average of one hundred a day.

The decline in tropical forests is due, in part, to consumer demand in industrialized countries. For example, the United States obtains much of its timber from tropical forests. Each

[*]*Catalyst,* Summer 1988, Vol. V. No. 2.

year, logging removes about twenty thousand square miles of these forests—an area nearly the size of West Virginia. Meanwhile, reforestation is proceeding very slowly in the tropics. In many places, ten trees are cut for each one planted; in Africa, twenty-nine trees are cut for each one planted. The developed world's consumption of tropical hardwoods has risen fifteen times since 1950; consumption in tropical countries has increased only three times. As loggers selectively fell commercially valuable tree species—which sometimes account for less than 5 percent of the trees in any given hectare (2.47 acres) they often destroy 30 to 60 percent of the unwanted trees at the same time!

The clearing of tropical forests for cattle pasture is another reason for the decline of such areas. For example, the growing imports of beef by the United States from southern Mexico and Central America during the past twenty-five years have been a major factor in the loss of about half of the tropical forests in those areas—all for the sake of keeping the price of a hamburger in the United States about a nickel less than it would be otherwise.

Population growth, inequitable land distribution, and the expansion of export agriculture have greatly reduced the area of cropland available for subsistence farming, forcing many peasants to clear virgin rain forests. These displaced cultivators often follow traditions of continuous cropping that are ill suited to fragile forest soils. Eventually the soils become so depleted that peasant colonists must clear more forest to survive, a cycle that continues over and over.

Yet another factor is the relentless search for fuel wood. Nearly 1.5 billion people—one third of the world's population—are cutting firewood, often their only source of heat and energy, faster than the wood can be regrown.

Tropical rain forests play a critical role in our everyday lives and are essential to continued human survival on the planet—often in ways we are unaware of or take for granted.

1. We use *tropical rain forest* products when we read a book, drive a car, drink coffee, apply deodorant, eat chocolate, or take a pill. The list of industrial, medicinal, and agricultural uses is long and impressive.

2. More than one quarter of the pharmaceuticals prescribed in the United States are derived from *tropical rain forest* plants.

The rosy periwinkle of Madagascar contains alkaloids that have revolutionized the treatment of leukemia and Hodgkin's disease. Seventy percent of plants identified as having anti-cancer properties live in *tropical rain forests*.

3. Tropical deforestation will severely affect the global climate. Rain forests, as all forests do, consume carbon dioxide through photosynthesis; this counteracts much of the $CO_2$ that is pumped into the environment and is the prime cause of the greenhouse effect. Without these forests to slow global warming, Siberia may soon become the world's breadbasket and New York City a place that only scuba divers visit.

Because rain forests also store carbon, when these rain forests are burned in the clearing process, large amounts of carbon are released into the atmosphere. This, too, accelerates the greenhouse effect.

4. Tropical deforestation affects short-term global weather conditions as well. The absence of huge areas of treecover causes more sunlight to be reflected off the earth's surface, disrupting wind currents and rainfall patterns. Additionally, as the rain forests' sponge effect (their ability to absorb and recirculate rainfall) is lost, floods and droughts become exaggerated, leading to massive soil erosion on the one hand and desertification on the other.

## WHAT YOU CAN DO:

1. United States-based timber corporations active in tropical deforestation are Weyerhauser, Georgia Pacific, Scott Paper, Westvaco, and International Paper. In 1984 American consumers spent $2.23 billion for tropical hardwood products. Furniture imports accounted for slightly more than $1 billion worth of U.S. trade. Another $1 billion was spent to import semimanufactured products such as panels, plywood, veneer, and joiners (for use in the construction of floors, windows, shelves, counters, etc.).

The Friends of the Earth of England publishes the best guide to the responsible purchase of wood products. It will enable you to avoid buying rain forest woods. The guide is *very* oriented to the British market, but it is also the best source of information. Order *The Good Wood Guide* from FOE-UK, 26–28 Underwood Street, London, NI-7JU; (01) 490-1555.

**2.** For a comprehensive review of the economic and corporate factors contributing to rain forest destruction, as well as what can be done to turn the situation around on both the grass-roots and global levels, order a copy of *Listening to the Forest: An Action Guide*, by Susan Meeker-Lowry and Erik van Lennep, available (Fall 1990) from Catalyst, 64 Main Street, 2nd Floor, Montpelier, VT 05602; (802) 223-7943.

**3.** Ask before you buy: Don't purchase tropical wildlife like parrots and macaws, or tropical plants such as orchids and bromeliads, unless you can be sure they have been raised or grown in the United States rather than taken from the wild.

**4.** Encourage local merchants who sell furniture and beef products to find out where their products come from. If they come from natural tropical forests, don't buy them.

**5.** Communicate your views on saving tropical forests to the agencies and development banks that provide loans to tropical countries. Write to: President, The World Bank, 1818 H Street, N.W., Washington, DC 20433; Administrator, U.S. Agency for International Development, 320 21st Street, N.W., Washington, DC 20532; and President, Inter-American Development Bank, 1808 17th Street, N.W., Washington, DC 20577.

**6.** Look for other people and organizations in your community that may already be involved in saving tropical forests, and join in their work (the conservation groups listed below can help you).

**7. ADDITIONAL SOURCES\* OF RAIN FOREST IN-FORMATION AND ACTIONS INCLUDE:**

**New York Rainforest Alliance,** 295 Madison Avenue, Suite 1804, New York, NY 10017, which publishes *The Canopy,* a quarterly, and *Hot Topics from the Tropics,* a bimonthly newsletter for all members contributing $20 or more. Both are excellent publications, covering international developments, research reports, book reviews, and a calendar of events. For those interested in supporting beneficial rain forest legislation, the "Capital Briefs" column in *The Canopy* will be of special interest.

**Rainforest Action Network,** which publishes the *World Rainforest Report* and *RANAlert,* published monthly, for all

---

\*Compiled by *Catalyst,* a newsletter on socially responsible investing.

members contributing $15 or more. Address: 300 Broadway, Suite 29, San Francisco, CA 94113.

**Rainforest Information Centre,** P.O. Box 368, Lismore 2480 N.S.W., Australia.

**Cultural Survival,** which publishes *Cultural Survival Quarterly*, $20 a year. Address: 11 Divinity Avenue, Cambridge, MA 02138.

**Survival International,** 2121 Decatur Place, N.W., Washington, DC 20008.

**Earth Island Institute,** 300 Broadway, Suite 28, San Francisco, CA 94133. Publishes *Earth Island Journal* (see Action 19 for more information).

**Earthscan,** 1717 Massachusetts Avenue, N.W., Washington, DC 20036.

**Earthwatch,** 319 Arlington Street, Watertown, MA 02172.

**Environmental Policy Institute,** 218 D Street, S.E., Washington, DC 20003.

**Friends of the Earth,** 210 D Street S.E., Washington, DC 20003. Publishes *Not Man Apart* (see Action 19 for more information).

**American Forestry Association, Global ReLeaf,** P.O. Box 2000, Washington, DC 20013 (see Action 14 for more information).

**Natural Resources Defense Council,** 1350 New York Avenue, N.W., Washington, DC 20005.

**Oxfam America,** 115 Broadway, Boston, MA 02116.

**Sahabat Alam Malaysia,** 37 Lorong Beach 10250, Penang, Malaysia, is active in native issues and deforestation. Offers many excellent publications and resources.

**World Resources Institute,** 1735 New York Avenue, N.W., Washington, DC 20006.

# 5

# Environmental Action

---

---

**Action
19**

## *Environmental Action*
## Letters and Organizations

Whether you want to save dolphins, whales, and sea turtles; the air you breathe and the water you drink; fight new highways; save national parks; outlaw unnecessary packaging; or control acid rain—there is probably a bill in Congress that needs your support.

**WHAT YOU CAN DO:**

Writing letters, claims the *Audubon Activist,* "is the single most important thing you can do to influence environmental issues." The magazine offers these letter-writing tips, adapted from *The Right to Write* by Congressman Morris K. Udall:

## ADDRESS IT PROPERLY

| | |
|---|---|
| Honorable ——————— | Honorable ——————— |
| U.S. House of | U.S. Senate |
| Representatives | Washington, DC 20510 |
| Washington, DC 20515 | |

## IDENTIFY THE BILL OR ISSUE

## THE LETTER SHOULD BE TIMELY

## CONCENTRATE ON YOUR OWN DELEGATION

Letters written to congressmen or congresswomen in other districts are simply referred to your own representative.

## BE REASONABLY BRIEF

Many congresspeople receive more than 150 letters a day. It is not necessary that letters be typed, have perfect grammar, or be beautifully phrased, only that they be intelligible.

## ASK FOR A RESPONSE

Don't hesitate to ask questions (but don't be demanding or threatening).

## WRITE YOUR OWN VIEWS, NOT SOMEONE ELSE'S

## GIVE YOUR REASONS FOR TAKING A STAND

Your congressperson may not know how the bill may affect an important segment of his/her constituency.

## SHOW UNDERSTANDING

Try to show an awareness of how the proposed legislation would affect not just the environment, but also your community and other people's health and jobs.

## BE CONSTRUCTIVE

If you believe a bill takes the wrong approach, offer an alternative. If you have expert knowledge, share it with your elected representatives.

## USE PERSONAL OR BUSINESS LETTERHEAD WHENEVER POSSIBLE

Be sure to include a complete return address.

**There are many sources to keep yourself informed on the status of current legislation. Some of the best are:**

**1.** The **Audubon Activist** is full of suggestions on how to get involved, and is in every way an outstanding publication. As a bonus it's exceptionally well written and designed. Letters are suggested by its "Conservation Issue Update" column as well as by special "Action Alert" mailings that members and subscribers receive periodically on certain critical wildlife and wilderness issues. Six issues, $9 from the National Audubon Society, 950 Third Avenue, New York, NY 10022.

**2. Earth First! Journal.** No organization or journal presents more opportunities for action or involvement than Earth First! You may not agree with their tactics, take issue with their politics and even question their effectiveness, but they believe in individual action and provide more practical suggestions on what you can do to protect and preserve our natural environment than any other source. Each issue of their forty-page journal, published eight times a year (coinciding with the old European nature holidays), is filled with twenty to thirty "What You Can Do" briefs—one at the end of almost every article. Unlike most publications that carefully describe a problem but leave you feeling lost and quite hopeless abbout what you can do, *Earth First! Journal* is committed to making you part of the solution of every problem it is concerned with.

Earth First! has more than one hundred international, national, regional, and local chapters and groups you can join. It has special task forces that deal with specific issues, ranging from rain forests to grizzly-bear protection; a touring road show complete with musicians, speakers, and poets; a foundation that supports research and educational projects; and it has organized direct actions and demonstrations to protest dams, logging, uranium mining, and gas and oil drilling. Earth First! activists have occupied offices of antiwilderness legislators in Montana, sat in front of logging trucks in Washington, hiked into nuclear test sites, and blockaded (while dressed in bear costumes) new developments in Yellowstone National Park. And if you like to write letters, they'll tell you to write to protest illegal whaling operations, encourage the reintroduction of wolves into the wilderness, support a ban on frog exports, or help win the release from jail of Malaysian environmental activists.

For more information, to receive a free copy of the *Earth First! Journal,* or to subscribe ($15 a year), call (602) 622-1371 or write Earth First! P.O. Box 5871, Tucson, AZ 85703.

**3. Earth Island Journal** is published quarterly by the Earth Island Institute, 300 Broadway, Suite 28, San Francisco, CA 94133—$25 for annual membership. The *Journal* is an unusually activist publication with "What You Can Do" notes at the end of most articles. Earth Island Institute is involved in sponsoring, supporting, or coordinating nineteen different projects, ranging from the Japan Environmental Exchange to the Rainforest Health Alliance. Several topics are usually covered in great detail in each issue of the journal; there is a strong focus on international environmental issues and many brief news items. An excellent publication—highly recommended.

**4. Environmental Action** is a bimonthly publication dedicated to providing readers with the resources, background, and latest information they need to be effective activists. From coverage of local issues to national politics, industry trends, and scientific developments, *Environmental Action* is a wonderful resource packed with names, numbers, facts, and ideas. Six issues, for $20; 1525 New Hampshire Avenue, N.W., Washington, DC 20036.

**5. Garbage, The Practical Journal for the Environment** is a new bimonthly magazine that covers issues including good versus bad plastics; recycling in Europe; alternatives to harmful products; designing your kitchen for recycling and gardening without pesticides. $21 annually from Garbage, 435 9th Street, Brooklyn, NY 11215, or call (800) 274-9909.

**6. Greenpeace** is a quarterly publication for Greenpeace members who contribute a minimum of $15. Its "Action Access" column focuses on legislative as well as corporate issues (for example, Adidas's use of kangaroo leather for its sneakers) and international matters (rain forests in Brazil). Greenpeace USA, 1611 Connecticut Avenue, N.W., Washington, DC 20009.

**7. Newsline,** published bimonthly by the Natural Resources Defense Council for its members. It costs $10 to join and the magazine includes a "Current Legislation" column. NRDC, 122 East 42nd Street, New York, NY 10168.

**8. Not Man Apart,** the newsmagazine of Friends of the Earth, is published bimonthly and is free to members who contribute $25 or more. The publication covers the full range of environmental issues with "What You Can Do" suggestions at the end of most articles. The reporting is very strong and supported by the research and legislative work carried out by Friends of the Earth. Of special interest are their international perspective, detailed and up-to-date explanation of the issues, and coverage of special topics such as "Labor and the Environment." Friends of the Earth, 218 D Street, S.E., Washington, DC 20003; (202) 544-2600.

**9. Sierra Club Activist Network** is one of the most sophisticated and effective networks around. Divided into twenty-five specific interest areas, from air quality to mining law, it can notify you whenever environmental legislation is in need of help. Action Alerts will fill you in on the background and details of the issue and let you know who to call or write. To join, write: Campaign Desk, Sierra Club, 730 Polk Street, San Francisco, CA 94109, or call (415) 776-2211.

---

| Action 20 | *Environmental Action* Telephone Hotlines* |
|---|---|

These hotlines will provide you with up-to-date information in an 'environment' of complex and ever-changing laws. They'll also help you respond to an environmental emergency.

### NATIONAL RESPONSE CENTER HOTLINE

You can call this hotline to report accidental releases of any potentially dangerous substances, including oil and chemical spills. Open twenty-four hours, all year round; (800) 424-8802.

### CHEMICAL EMERGENCY PREPAREDNESS PROGRAM (CEPP) HOTLINE

This hotline can provide information on how well a community is prepared for chemical accidents. Call Monday through Friday, 8:30 A.M. to 4:30 P.M. EST; (800) 535-0202.

### NATIONAL PESTICIDES TELECOMMUNICATIONS NETWORK (NPTN)

Here activists can get unbiased information on the handling, effects, and disposal of any pesticides. Physicians can use this hotline to get help with toxicology and in managing poisoning

---

*This information was assembled and first published in the *Audubon Activist* and is reprinted here by permission.

by pesticides. Open twenty-four hours, all year round; (800) 858-7378.

## ASBESTOS HOTLINE

If you suspect or know that your home or workplace contains asbestos, call this number to find out what to do about it. Call Monday through Friday, 8:15 A.M. to 5:00 P.M. EST; (800) 334-8571, ext. 6741.

## CLEAN AIR HOTLINE

Call Environmental Action's hotline for legislative updates and information about how and where to write letters of support; (202) 745-4879.

## PUBLIC INFORMATION CENTER

This is the place to call for general information about the Environmental Protection Agency and its programs and activities. The center offers a variety of nontechnical publications. Call (202) 382-2080. Or write PIC (PM-211B), USEPA, 401 M Street, S.W., Washington, DC 20460.

---

| Action 21 | *Environmental Action* **Books and Resources**\* |
|---|---|

While there are hundreds of books that deal with environmental action, these are noteworthy and not mentioned elsewhere in the book.

**1.** *A Citizen's Guide to Plastics in the Ocean: More than a Litter Problem*, by Kathryn J. O'Hara, Suzanne Iudicello, and Rose Bierce, Center for Marine Conservation (formerly Center for Environmental Education), 1425 DeSales Street, N.W., Washington, DC 20036, free ($2 postage). This handy booklet is geared toward citizen activists who want to help rid their beaches of plastic litter. Profiles of successful activists are presented as proof that individuals can effect change. The authors explain what kinds of plastics are present in our waters, where they originate, the laws concerning ocean dumping, and most important, what citizens can do to reduce or halt the plastics problem

\* Excerpted from *Audubon Activist*.

in their area. Twelve appendices provide additional information, including addresses of private, state, federal, and international organizations, as well as summaries of the laws and treaties covering the use of marine waters.

**2.** *Island Press Annual Environmental Sourcebook,* Island Press, P.O. Box 7, Covelo, CA 95428, or call 1-800-628-2828, ext. 416. There are 130 books—some new and some conservation classics to choose from in this free environmental catalog from Island Press. The contents are arranged according to specialty, including wildlife management, land conservation, air pollution, and solid-waste management. It's the most complete collection of environmental books you're likely to find anywhere.

**3.** *Making Polluters Pay: A Citizens' Guide to Legal Action and Organizing,* by Andrew Owens Moore, Environmental Action Foundation, 1525 New Hampshire Avenue, N.W., Washington, DC 20036, $15 individuals ($1.50 postage). Citizen-action suits against polluters can often be complicated and arduous even for the most experienced activists. Here is an easy-to-read and detailed workbook that will get you jumping through legal loopholes.

**4.** *The Toxic Cloud: The Poisoning of America's Air,* by Michael H. Brown, Harper and Row, Perennial Library, $9.95 paper. Available in bookstores. This book is a must-read for individuals concerned about the quality of the air they breathe, as well as a primer for activists who want to see a stronger clean air act.

**5.** *The Earth Report: An Essential Guide to Global Ecological Issues,* edited by Edward Goldsmith and Nicholas Hildyard, Price/ Stern/Sloan, Inc., 360 North La Cienega Boulevard, Los Angeles, CA 90048, $12.95 paper, $19.95 cloth. In the first part of this report, noted environmental writers and scientists provide essays on such varied topics as world food supplies, the quality of the air, acid rain, and the health of our drinking water. The second section is an encyclopedia of short articles ranging from asbestos to junk food to zero population growth. The book is an excellent reference for both professional conservationists and concerned citizens.

**6.** *Blueprint for a Green Planet,* by John Seymour and Herbert Girardet, Prentice-Hall, $17.95 paper. Available in bookstores. First published in England, this is without a doubt one of the best practical handbooks to deal specifically with how you can reduce harmful activities that damage the planet. Topics covered include waste, water, drugs, gardening, energy conservation, automobiles, and household toxins.

**7.** *A Field Guide to Over 100 Leading American Environmental Groups.* This guide offers brief summaries of the activities and publications of more than one hundred groups. $2 paper, available from Seventh Generation, 10 Farrell Street, South Burlington, VT 05403; (800) 456-1177.

---

| Action 22 | *Environmental Action* **Jobs, Adventures, and Volunteer Opportunities** |
|---|---|

## WHAT YOU CAN DO:

*Jobs* There's one place to turn if you are looking for a job related in any way to the environment and that's *Environmental Opportunities,* published monthly by Sanford Berry, P.O. Box 969, Stowe, VT 05672; (802) 253-9336. Single copies are $4, with an annual subscription costing $39. The price may seem a bit steep, but it's worth every penny. With twelve pages packed with over one hundred specific job listings (including background requirements, salary, and job responsibilities), you'll find it an invaluable resource.

Listings are divided by subject areas, which range from business development and administrative positions to jobs for biologists, ecologists, teachers, graphic artists, agricultural engineers, data technicians, community organizers, graduate and postgraduate students, and many, many more!!

*Adventurers and Volunteer Opportunities* Buzzworm, a new journal, offers an extensive listing of both environmentally oriented adventure travel and volunteer options. The adventure travel options range from ocean kayaking with whales and sea lions in Mexico to treks through the Peruvian Amazon jungle and nature explorations in the Himalayas. (Also see Action 97, Socially Responsible Travel.)

Volunteer options include: for bird lovers a chance to care for crane chicks; a beach patrol to help protect sea turtle hatcheries; maintenance work on Vermont's Long Trail; planting wild flowers; wetlands preservation; and even a poison patrol.

Subscribe to *Buzzworm*: $12 for four quarterly issues. Write to P.O. Box 6140, Boulder, CO 80306-9851; pickup a copy at your newsstand, or call (303) 442-1969 for more information.

---

**Action
23**
### *Environmentally Sound Voting*
### The League of Conservation Voters

The League of Conservation Voters (LCV) is a political action committee that works at grass-roots and national levels to find, support, and elect candidates to federal office who will vote and sponsor legislation to protect the environment.

The LCV's public education activities include publication of the *National Environmental Scorecard,* the standard by which candidates for federal office may be judged on their commitment to environmental protection. The League's board compiles a list of the floor votes, co-sponsorships, and letter signatures that are most important to the environmental movement. It rates members of Congress for their records on these issues. The *National Environmental Scorecard* is distributed to members of Congress, the media, and the public at large. Other public education activities of the league have focused on grading the presidential candidate's records on environmental protection.

### WHAT YOU CAN DO:

Obtain a copy of the *National Environmental Scorecard* by writing the League of Conservation Voters at 2000 L Street, N.W., Suite 804, Washington, DC 20036; (202) 785-VOTE. And, it goes almost without saying, VOTE in the next local, state, or federal election.

# 6

# Waste and Recycling

## Controlling Waste

Every year we throw away:—eighteen billion disposable diapers, made from twenty-one million trees;—twenty-five billion Styrofoam cups, that threaten to destroy the ozone layer;—over two billion disposable razors;—two hundred million automobile tires;—enough wood and paper to heat five million homes for two hundred years;—and some seven and a half million TV sets, which if placed in a line would reach from New York to Denver!*

**Action
24**   *Throwing Away Our Future;
Starting with the Basics*

"We live in a throwaway society made up of all types of disposable products—from diapers and razor blades to throwaway cameras and even disposable phones."

*Rhode Island Solid Waste Management Corporation, *Annual Report,* 1986.

"Americans throw out ten times their weight in trash every year, or about one-half ton for every person. We throw away enough aluminum to rebuild the entire American airfleet 71 times, enough steel to reconstruct Manhattan, and enough wood and paper to heat five million homes for 200 years. Containers and packaging waste account for almost half of this, with 50% of the nation's paper, 8% of its steel, 75% of its glass, 40% of its aluminum, and 30% of its plastic used solely to package and decorate consumer products.

"The United States packaging industry spends $28 billion a year to bring everything from television sets to toasters into our homes. Consumers spend another $3 billion a year to collect and dispose of these items, and one out of every eleven dollars spent by consumers in grocery stores is used to pay for packaging costs. Remarkably, Americans spent more for food packaging last year than the nation's farmers received in net income."*

"No other country in the world can match the United States's output of garbage on a per-capita basis. Americans generate four to six pounds of garbage per day, about double that produced by the typical Japanese, Swiss, West German or Swedish citizen and almost three times that of the typical resident of Oslo, Norway. The total amount of trash generated in the United States each day—about 400,000 tons—boggles the mind. It's enough to fill about 40,000 garbage trucks or to load up an armada of 125 ocean going garbage barges."†

"Where does this country's trash go? Well, as a recent advertisement placed by the Steamfitting Industry Promotion Fund put it, 'There are four ways to dispose of garbage: Burn it. Bury it. Recycle it. Or send it on a Caribbean cruise.' "‡

Opportunities to reduce waste present themselves on a minute-by-minute basis, from the moment you rise (and don't use the new pump toothpaste dispenser because of its excessive packaging or shave with a disposable razor) to the moment you go to sleep (putting aside a library book rather than one you bought, and making sure you've hung up your clothes on a metal or wood hanger rather than one made of plastic).

---

*Rhode Island Solid Waste Management Corp., *Annual Report,* 1986.
†*Science for the People,* November/December 1987.
‡Ibid.

## *WHAT YOU CAN DO:*

Reducing waste demands an awareness of:

—what can be recycled

—what's biodegradable

—how to avoid products that you use once and throw away

—what products utilize the least amount of packaging

The action chart on page 82 will serve as an introductory guide, in addition to the following *ten general rules* for leading a less wasteful life-style:

1. Always purchase goods packaged in glass, metal, or paper— avoid plastic and Styrofoam, they're not recyclable.

2. Always purchase in bulk or family size; besides saving money you'll reduce the overall amount of packaging you're consuming.

3. Always purchase fresh produce from greenmarkets rather than produce that has already been packaged for supermarket distribution.

4. Read labels; occasionally you'll discover a company like Arm & Hammer that uses recycled paper for its laundry detergent box.

5. Always look for the recycling symbol whenever you shop.

 100% recycled

6. Buy durable, long-lasting products. The extra price you pay is usually a bargain when it comes to both quality and reduced waste. *Consumer Reports* magazine—(monthly, $18; call 800-234-1645 or write P.O. Box 2886, Boulder, CO 80322)—is a good source of information for any major purchase.

7. Borrow before you buy. Don't purchase something you're only likely to use on a rare occasion. Borrow it from a friend, whether a ladder, slide projector, power tool, or toilet plunger. Many power tools and do-it-yourself items are also available for rent. Check the Yellow Pages for everything from baby furniture to party supplies, electric sanders, and audiovisual equipment.

8. Maintain and repair the products and equipment you own. Don't put off that service call or the purchase of a replacement part. Even shoes last longer if you take care of them.

9. Donate what you no longer need. There's a Goodwill or Salvation Army store in almost every community. Your local church or synagogue will put almost anything you don't want to good use.

10. Last, avoid impulse buying. Don't leave home without a list of what you need, and try to stick to it. If you are unsure whether you need something or not, you probably don't. Shopping is not a cure for loneliness and depression. It leaves you feeling worse when the bills come. Both you and the environment end up poorer!

---

## Action 25

### SPECIFIC DO'S AND DON'TS FOR THE WASTE-CONSCIOUS CONSUMER

| WHAT AND WHERE | DON'T BUY | DO BUY |
|---|---|---|
| *In the Bathroom* | | |
| | plastic disposable razors | nondisposable or electric razors |
| | pump toothpaste dispensers | old-fashioned tubes |
| | foam shaving cream in cans | brush-on soap or shaving cream |
| | liquid soap in plastic pump bottle | soap bars |
| | toilet paper wrapped in plastic | toilet paper wrapped in paper |
| | Q-Tips in plastic box | Q-Tips in paperboard box |
| | tampons with plastic tip applicators | tampons with paperboard applicators |
| | deodorant aerosol spray | deodorant stick or roll-on |
| *Office Supplies* | | |
| | disposable cartridge typewriter ribbons | cloth reusable ribbons |
| | plastic disposable pens | fountain pens or mechanical pencils |

|                         DON'T<br>BUY | DO<br>BUY |
|---|---|
| disposable Scotch tape dispensers | permanent metal tape dispensers |
| one-sided Xeroxing | two-sided Xeroxing |
| Xeroxed memos | electronic mail |
| Styrofoam coffee cups | paper cups or ceramic mugs |

*In the Kitchen*

| | |
|---|---|
| plastic wrap | wax paper |
| liquid detergent in plastic bottles | liquid in glass or granular in paper box |
| paper towels | cloth towels |
| paper cups and plates | real cups and plates |
| plastic knives, forks, and spoons | real knives, forks, and spoons |
| plastic food storage bags | cellulose food storage bags |

*Food*

| | |
|---|---|
| eggs in Styrofoam cartons | paperboard egg cartons |
| plastic soda bottles | glass or aluminum bottles |
| meat or poultry wrapped in plastic on a Styrofoam tray | meat or poultry wrapped fresh in paper |
| butter or margarine in plastic tubs | butter or margarine wrapped in paper |
| six-packs of beer or soda with plastic rings | beer or soda in a cardboard box |
| frozen food in plastic pouch | frozen food in a cardboard box |
| pasta in plastic bags | pasta in cardboard boxes |
| catsup, vegetable oil, mayonnaise or peanut butter in plastic bottles or jars | glass bottles and jars with metal tops |

*General Household Products*

| | |
|---|---|
| plastic shopping bags | reusable string bags |
| plastic or cut Christmas trees | living plants or trees |
| plastic flowers | real potted flowers and bulbs |
| disposable lighters | matches or refillable lighters |
| plastic garbage bags | "new" biodegradable or photodegradable garbage bags |
| regular batteries | rechargeable batteries |

Now we'll move on to a more in-depth look at some of the greatest contributors to the waste problem and the toll they take on our environment.

**Action**          *Disposable Diapers\**
**26**

How can we ever live without them? The facts are sobering.
The waste is incredible, and the pollution they cause may be
enough for you to give cloth diapers a try.

Approximately 3 percent of municipal solid waste in the
United States is made up of disposable diapers. Every year we
spend about $3 billion a year purchasing over eighteen billion
of these little wonders, whose life span is only a few hours. In
just eighteen months, we in the United States use enough diapers to create a stack that would reach the moon. To make them
they use up about 75,000 metric tons of plastic and 1,265,000
tons of tree pulp, the equivalent of more than 21 million trees
per year. Their manufacturing process uses 21 trillion BTUs of
energy and results in 6.3 million pounds of air pollutants, 2,700
pounds of water pollutants, and 13.2 million pounds of solid
waste. The plastic part of the diaper even takes up to five hundred
years to decompose in a landfill.

Taxpayers spend nearly $100 million a year on disposal costs
alone, or four to twenty cents per diaper, and this expense does
not include the ultimate cost to clean up the environment. (These
costs should at a minimum be paid directly by the manufacturers
and passed on to the purchaser.)

To add insult to injury, most diapers are still filled with
fecal matter as they enter household garbage cans and end up
in municipal landfills. They then slowly leak into the earth and
pollute underground water supplies instead of being properly
disposed of through sewage systems.

The average American family spends approximately $800
on disposable diapers during their baby's first year. At seven to
eleven cents each, this means roughly 7,200 to 11,400 diapers
per year, or the equivalent of 40 pounds of plastic, 800 pounds
of paper pulp (or 6.8 trees), and 7 million BTUs of energy.

---

\* Research compiled in part by Carl Lehrburger, recycling specialist in Massachusetts,
Larry Martin, Institute for Local Self Reliance, and Trish Ferrand, Ferrand Associates,
Washington, DC.

## WHAT YOU CAN DO:

There are basically two alternatives. The first is to use a diaper service, which will cost $400 to $600 per year—a savings of $200 to $400 over what you pay for disposable diapers. The second is, launder your own diapers. Including the costs of purchasing cloth diapers at $10 to $15 a dozen, laundry detergent, electricity, and water for your washing machine (if you have one), laundering your own diapers will save an additional 20 to 30 percent.

Look in the Yellow Pages for the diaper service nearest you, or contact the National Association of Diaper Services, (800) 462-6237; or write them at 2017 Walnut Street, Philadelphia, PA 19103.

*Biodegradable Disposable Diapers:* While clearly a second and, we hope, avoidable choice, biodegradable diapers are the next best thing to cloth diapers. Major innovations have created a disposable product that uses half the number of trees as do regular disposable diapers, due to a special type of pulp that also does not produce dioxin in the bleaching process. The plastic wrap on the biodegradable diaper is manufactured with a cornstarch base that degrades in two to five years rather than the two hundred to five hundred years that regular plastic takes to disintegrate thoroughly. Available in standard sizes by mail from Seventh Generation, 10 Farrell Street, South Burlington, VT 05403; (800) 456-1177; $11.95 a box or $44.50 per case (four boxes) delivered to your doorstep.

---

**Action
27**      *Wrapped in Plastic*

In 1967 Dustin Hoffman playing *The Graduate* gets some advice on career direction. "Plastics, my boy. Plastics," he's told. Judging from the proliferation of plastic debris that washes up along on our beaches, a lot of people took this advice.

So many plastic tampon inserters litter some East Coast beaches that residents refer to them as "beach whistles." Plastic fishing gear, six-pack yokes, sandwich bags, and Styrofoam cups are so abundant in the ocean that they kill up to one million seabirds and 100,000 marine mammals each year.

The situation has gotten to the point where David Laist of the Marine Mammal Commission in Washington, D.C., says, "Plastics may be as great a source of mortality among marine mammals as oil spills, heavy metals, or other toxic materials."

Plastics disposal on land is also a big problem. Because the material resists the degrading action of sunlight and bacteria, it remains relatively intact for years.

When incinerated, chlorine-containing plastics contribute to the formation of dioxins, furans, and hydrogen chloride acid gas. Some of these molecules are considered highly toxic and are implicated in weakening the immune system, affecting fetal development, and causing a skin disorder called chloracne. Appropriately enough, the Japanese officially designate plastics "waste difficult to be disposed of."

Plastics are the fastest-growing share of the U.S. waste stream, and now account for 8 percent of household garbage by weight and as much as 30 percent by volume. Each American annually uses almost two hundred pounds of plastic, roughly sixty pounds of it consumed in the form of packaging.

According to Dr. Darrell R. Morrow, director of the Center for Plastics Recycling Research, "Some 20 billion pounds of plastics now find their way into the U.S. waste stream each year." This includes 1.6 billion disposable pens and 2.2 billion disposable razors.*

Unfortunately, plastic makes inroads at the expense of easily recycled glass and aluminum. Refillable glass bottles require only a steam bath before reuse, and more than half of all aluminum beverage cans are recycled. But according to Gretchen Brewer, recycling coordinator for the state of Massachusetts, only 20 percent of plastic soda bottles were recycled in 1987, representing 0.3 percent of all plastic produced.

In 1987 the United States used almost one billion barrels of petroleum—enough to meet the nation's demand for imported oil for five months—just to manufacture plastics.†

The top plastics manufacturers are companies we already know only too well: Dupont, Dow Chemical, Monsanto, Gulf Oil,

*New York Times, September 21, 1988.
†"Plastic Waste Proliferated," World Watch magazine, March-April 1988. Worldwatch Institute, Washington, D.C.

Goodyear, Mobil Oil, Union Carbide, and Occidental Petroleum. Fortunately, most of these companies, due to legislative and consumer pressure, are now beginning to explore how to recycle some of what they produce.

## WHAT YOU CAN DO:

1. Follow the suggestions in the table of "Do's and Don'ts for the Waste-Conscious Consumer," which features the simple rule —avoid plastics wherever possible, especially disposable items such as razors, pens, lighters, and packaging.

2. Purchase biodegradable garbage bags or, better yet, heavy-duty water-resistant paper garbage bags, both available by direct mail from Seventh Generation (800) 456-1177.

3. Take a tour through the drugstore or supermarket to see how the use of plastics has proliferated to include almost every imaginable form of packaging.

4. For a wide variety of commercial and industrial uses of plastic (where a nonplastic alternative isn't practical), contact the Manchester Packaging Company, 2000 East James Boulevard, St. James, MO 65559; (314) 265-3569. Manchester produces a wide variety of biodegradable plastic bags and films for commercial use, including custom color printing for retail stores.

---

**Action
28**
## *Don't Litter*

## WHAT YOU CAN DO:

Last, but not least, don't litter. It doesn't make sense to control acid rain, practice organic gardening, conserve water, and increase the energy efficiency of our homes if we also litter.

And, if you're willing to take the next step, consider picking up after a stranger or gently confronting your friends and neighbors who are less aware than you are. Often your willingness to retrieve someone else's trash will cause them to think twice about littering the second time around.

## *Recycling*

Simply recovering the print run of the Sunday edition of the
*New York Times* would leave 75,000 trees standing. A soda can
made from recycled aluminum uses 95 percent less energy than
one made from raw materials, reduces air pollution by 95 percent
and water pollution by 97 percent. Recycling creates jobs and
avoids the air pollution and toxic waste caused by incineration.

Action
29

# *Why Recycle and How to Get Started**

"Most of the products available to consumers are intended
for a one-night stand. They are purchased, consumed, and dis-
carded with little regard for their remaining value. The energy,
materials, and environmental losses associated with this consumption pattern are staggering."

David Morris of the Washington-based Institute for Local
Self-Reliance puts it well: "A city the size of San Francisco dis-
poses of more aluminum than is produced by a small bauxite
mine, more copper than a medium-sized copper mine and more
paper than a good-sized timber stand. San Francisco is a mine.
The question is how to mine it most effectively and how to get
the maximum value from the collected materials."

Recycling offers communities everywhere the opportunity to
trim their waste output, and thereby reduce disposal costs, while
simultaneously combating global environmental problems. Recycling metals, paper, glass, plastics, and organic wastes would
lessen the demand for energy and raw materials. Producing aluminum from scrap instead of bauxite cuts energy usage and air
pollution by 95 percent.[†] Making paper from discards instead of
virgin timber not only saves valuable forests, it reduces the energy used per ton by up to 75 percent and requires less than
half as much water.[‡] And since cutting fossil fuel consumption

---

[*] Excerpted from Cynthia Pollack Shea, "Realizing Recycling's Potential," *State of the World, 1987,* Worldwatch Institute, Washington, D.C.

[†] Robert Cowles Letcher and Mary T. Sheil, "Source Separation and Citizen Recycling,"
in William D. Robinson, ed., *The Solid Waste Handbook* (New York: John Wiley & Sons,
1986).

[‡] Ibid.

is one of the most effective actions people can take to slow the buildup of carbon dioxide that is warming the earth's atmosphere, recycling must be part of the effort to combat the greenhouse effect.

In many areas of the world, recycling has been hampered by a prejudice against used materials and the products that incorporate them. Currency is not considered worthless after it has been exchanged, but because refuse collection began as a measure to protect health, many people mistakenly believe that materials that have already been used are dangerous and dirty. On the contrary, most materials in use today are chosen for their durability. One wearing does not make a dress a rag, nor does one trip through the typewriter or the bottling plant render paper or glass unusable.

An inventory of the world's discards would reveal metal wastes more valuable than the richest veins of ore, paper wastes representing millions of acres of forests, and plastics wastes incorporating billions of dollars of highly refined petrochemicals. That these products rich in raw materials and concentrated energy are frequently considered worthless is indicative of a distorted economic system. We are literally throwing away our future.

Using recycled material in the manufacturing process has huge environmental benefits as the table below shows.

## ENVIRONMENTAL BENEFITS DERIVED FROM SUBSTITUTING RECYCLED MATERIALS FOR VIRGIN RESOURCES

| ENVIRONMENTAL BENEFIT | ALUMINUM | STEEL | PAPER | GLASS |
|---|---|---|---|---|
| Reduction of: | | | | |
| Energy Use | 90–97% | 47–74% | 23–74% | 4–32% |
| Air Pollution | 95% | 85% | 74% | 20% |
| Water Pollution | 97% | 76% | 35% | — |
| Mining Wastes | — | 97% | — | 80% |
| Water Use | — | 40% | 58% | 50% |

*Source:* Robert Cowles Letcher and Mary T. Sheil, "Source Separation and Citizen Recycling," in William D. Robinson, ed., *The Solid Waste Handbook* (New York: John Wiley & Sons, 1986).

The government, at the urging of environmentalists, is slowly beginning to encourage us through legislation and tax incentives to recycle waste—but we can't afford to wait for legislation to force us to change our disposal habits. As citizens we must take the lead to recycle garbage, demand that our local governments provide mechanisms for convenient collection, encourage industry to replace virgin resources with recycled ones, and then to complete the cycle by developing a strong awareness of and preference for the purchase of any and all products made with recycled materials.

## WHAT YOU CAN DO:

1. Call the Environmental Defense Fund for a free copy of their booklet *How to Recycle*; (800) 225-5333.

2. Read *Mining Urban Wastes: The Potential for Recycling,* by Cynthia Pollock, available for $4 from the Worldwatch Institute, 1776 Massachusetts Avenue, N.W., Washington, DC 20036.

3. Order a copy of *101 Practical Recycling Tips for the Home and Office* from the Windsor Foundation, EarthPulse Project, 2317 Snowmass Creek Road, Snowmass, CO 81654 (800) 669-4777, $3.95. This ninety-page guide is full of ideas beyond those covered here as well as additional resources.

4. Write to the Pennsylvania Resources Council, P.O. Box 88, Media, PA 19063-0088; (215) 565-9131, and request a free copy of their *Recycling Publications List.*

5. Get *BioCycle, The Journal of Waste Recycling.* It will keep you up to date on what's happening in the recycling industry. Published monthly by J. G. Press, Box 351, 18 South 7th Street, Emmaus, PA 18049; (215) 967-4135. Subscriptions are $46.

   To receive general information, specifics on legislation under consideration in your state, and find out about test recycling programs already under way in your neighborhood and how you can participate, contact:

6. Join the National Recycling Coalition, 17 M Street N.W., Suite 294, Washington, DC 20036; (202) 659-6883. NRC holds an annual conference on recycling and brings together individuals, industry, and environmental groups. They also publish *Resource Recycling*, 12 issues, $42.

7. The Environmental Defense Fund, 257 Park Avenue South, New York, NY 10010, (212) 505-2100. It has an excellent list of:

State Recycling Coordinators
Recycling Industry Associations
State Recycling Hotlines
Recycling Periodicals
A Recycling Bibliography

Plus a listing of key individuals in the industry. All are available in the appendices to their publication *Coming Full Circle—Successful Recycling Today*, $9.50. Also ask about their National Recycling Campaign.

Other sources for finding out about who to contact on recycling efforts in your neighborhood include: your county's solid waste authority; your state's recycling coordinator, who usually works in the state capital or in the Public Works Department; the Department of Environmental Protection, Solid Waste Management, or the Department of Natural Resources.

Also:

See your local Yellow Pages under headings such as "Paper," "Waste Paper," "Scrap Metals," "Salvaging," "Recycling" . . .

8. If you're ready to make a major investment, for $95 you can order *American Recycling Market,* which lists 14,000 companies that purchase recyclable materials. Call (800) 267-0707, or write Recoup, P.O. Box 577, Ogdensburg, NY 13669.

---

**Action 30**     *Soda and Beer Cans\**

Recycled aluminum requires 95 percent less energy than producing it from bauxite and each recycled can saves the equivalent of half a can of gasoline.

In 1985 more than 70 billion beverage cans were used—of which 66 billion, or 94 percent, were aluminum. The Beer Wholesalers Association found that in the first two years of New York State's deposit law, $50 million of clean-up costs, $19 million of solid waste disposal costs, and $50 to $100 million of energy costs were saved, while a net employment gain of 3,800 jobs was created.

\* *State of the World, 1987.*

Since 1981 over half of the 300 billion beverage cans sold in the United States have been returned for recycling; the average can that is returned is remelted and back on the supermarket shelf in six weeks.

## WHAT YOU CAN DO:

Reduce water and air pollution and cut energy costs. Recycle beer and soda cans and avoid all plastic beverage containers. For additional information contact the Aluminum Recycling Association, 1000 16th Street, N.W., Suite 603, Washington, DC 20036; (202) 785-0550.

---

**Action
31**
                              *Paper*

Not surprisingly, the U.S. leads the world in paper consumption per person and trails far behind in recycling. Each year our nation uses 67 million tons of paper or 580 pounds per person. Paper consumption has doubled since 1965 and continues to rapidly increase.*

—Simply recovering one print run of the Sunday edition of *The New York Times* would leave 75,000 trees standing.[†]
—If you recycled your own copy of *The New York Times* (or a newspaper of similar size) every day of the year, you'd save the equivalent of 4 trees, 15 pounds of air pollutants from being pumped into the atmosphere, 2,200 gallons of water, and 1.25 million BTUs of energy (or enough electricity to power a 100-watt light bulb for 152 days).
—Through the Maryland state recycling program, in place since 1977, $17 million of recycled paper have been purchased, saving enough energy to heat nearly nine thousand homes for one year.[‡]
—Newspaper, paperboard, cardboard and other types of paper make up 40 percent of garbage in the United States.

---

* *State of the World*, 1987.
[†] Ibid.
[‡] Earth Care Paper Company, Madison, WI.

—Logging tropical rain forests for paper pulp has helped contribute to the destruction of ninety-five acres of these forests every minute.

—In 1987 the United States exported 4.2 million tons of waste paper to nations such as Japan and Taiwan, which recycled it into products such as TV and stereo boxes, which were then shipped back to the United States.

## WHAT YOU CAN DO:

First, recycle newspapers, computer paper, and any other type of paper from both home and office that your local recycling center will accept. For more information contact the American Paper Institute, 260 Madison Avenue, New York, NY 10016; call (212) 340-0600, or contact your local recycling center.

Second, and of equal importance, purchase products made from recycled paper. The number one bottleneck to expanding the demand for waste paper is the lack of demand for recycled paper. Your purchases will help this developing industry get off the ground. Once you sample recycled paper products, you'll discover that their quality and aesthetic value are equivalent or superior to the paper you are currently using.

## SOURCES FOR RECYCLED PAPER PRODUCTS

—Earth Care Paper Company sells stationery, cards, pads, envelopes, giftwrap, Xerox paper, computer paper, and a full range of office paper supplies through their direct-mail catalog—available by calling (608) 256-5522, or writing P.O. Box 3355, Madison, WI 53704.

—Conservatree Paper Company wholesales a complete line of recycled paper products. It sells computer paper, high-speed Xerox paper, offset paper, linen text, and envelopes. Call (800) 522-9200 for a copy of the company's price list and sample book or write: 10 Lombard Street, Suite 250, San Francisco, CA 94111.

—Seventh Generation sells toilet paper made from 100 percent recycled paper. The company also sells paper towels, tissue paper, and napkins, all made from 100 percent recycled paper, as well as legal pads, stationery, notepads, and placemats. The address is 10 Farrell Street, South Burlington, VT 05403; (800) 456-1177.

## Action          *Glass*
### 32

For every ton of recycled crushed glass used in the manu-facturing process, some 1.2 tons of raw materials are saved. Recycled glass requires 50% less water and reduces air pollution by 20%.*

### WHAT YOU CAN DO:

Save all glass containers, separate clear from colored glass, wash, and take to your local recycling center.

## Action          *Plastics*
### 33

Plastics are by and large *not* recycled and in general it is preferable to purchase products packaged in either metal, alu-minum, glass or paper over those packaged in plastic [see Action 27 for additional information on the unnecessary and wasteful uses of plastic]. There is, however, a fledgling plastics recycling industry that is taking plastic (PET) soda bottles and (HOPE) milk jugs and shredding them for use as filler in sleeping bags and parkas as well as rug fiber and other textiles.

Some plastic waste is also being melted for refabrication, which saves 85 to 90 percent of the energy costs of using virgin materials. Refabrication also minimizes the release of toxic chemicals that become airborne when plastic is burned in an incinerator.

Currently only 1 to 2 percent of the plastic in the waste stream is recycled, only about 50 percent is even collectible using existing technology, and except for plastic PET bottles, it's still technically impossible or uneconomical to recycle the rest.

Wellman, Inc., is one of the few companies to recycle plastic consumer bottles successfully; about 80 percent of all PET con-

*The Solid Waste Handbook, 1986.

tainers processed by the whole industry are handled by them. Wellman manufactures polyester fiber and polyester-engineered resins used in making carpeting, fabrics, scouring pads, blankets, and as filling for apparel and furniture. For more information contact Wellman, Inc., 67 Walnut Avenue, Clark, NJ 07066; (201) 388-0120.

## WHAT YOU CAN DO:

For more information about plastics recycling in general, contact Center for Plastics Recycling Research, Building 3529, Busch Campus, Rutgers University, Piscataway, NJ 08855; (201) 932-4402; attention Dr. Morrow.

---

**Action 34**     *Automobile Tires*

About one-fifth of all vehicle tires produced in the United States are retreaded. These 45 million retreads have lifetimes up to 90 percent as long as those of new tires. If all new tires were retreaded once, the demand for synthetic rubber would be cut by about one-third, tire disposal problems would be cut in half and substantial energy savings would be realized.*

## WHAT YOU CAN DO:

Check the sources listed below for where to recycle used tires and, when you're in the market for new ones, buy retreads.
For additional information contact:

—Tire Retread Information Bureau, P.O. Box 811, Pebble Beach, CA 93953; (408) 649-0944

Or:

—Nation Tire Dealers and Retreaders, 1343 L Street, N.W., Washington, DC 20005; (202) 789-2300

---

*Cynthia Pollock, in *World Watch Paper #76,* Worldwatch Institute, Washington, D.C., 1988.

## Action
### 35
# *Metal*

Recycling of scrap metal by steel mills and foundries leads to an 86% reduction of air pollution, a 75% reduction in water pollution and a 40% reduction in water use.*

## *WHAT YOU CAN DO:*

Call your local recycling center or check the Yellow Pages under such headings as "Scrap Metals" or "Salvaging" to find out which metals are acceptable and in what form. Also contact:

—Institute of Scrap Recycling Industries, 1627 K Street, N.W., Washington, DC 20006; (202) 466-4050

Or:

—American Iron and Steel Institute, 1000 16th Street, N.W., Washington, DC 20036; (202) 452-7100

## Action
### 36
# *Batteries*

Each year we use and dispose of over 2.5 billion batteries.[†]

Almost half of all the mercury used in industry goes into the production of household dry-cell batteries. Batteries also contain heavy metals such as silver, nickel, cadmium, and lead, which if allowed to enter the household waste stream can pose a serious health risk to aquatic life, wildlife, and humans. Wet-cell automobile batteries contain a solution of sulfuric acid, another toxin.

## *WHAT YOU CAN DO:*

Few recyclers are presently handling batteries, but check the Yellow Pages or contact:

---

*Cynthia Pollock, in *World Watch Paper #76,* Worldwatch Institute, Washington, D.C., 1988.
[†] *The New York Times.*

—Environmental Action Coalition, 625 Broadway, 2nd Floor, New York, NY 10012; (212) 677-1601

Or:

—Household Hazardous Waste Project, Southwest Missouri State University, 901 South National Avenue, Box 87, Springfield, MO 65804; (417) 836-5777

When you buy new batteries, get rechargeables, which will last for up to one thousand charges and can also be recycled. While conclusive evidence isn't yet available, it would seem that rechargeable batteries can solve much of the short-term problem, at least until large-scale recycling gets under way.

---

**Action
37**
*Composting*

Twenty to thirty percent of the municipal waste stream is composed of organic kitchen and yard wastes. Many communities are establishing composting programs to reduce the volume of waste landfilled. Yard waste is collected separate from other wastes, then composted into a nutrient-rich mulch and soil conditioner which can be used to slow soil erosion, improve water retention, and increase agricultural yields.*

Composting is most advanced in Europe, where special composting plants speed up the natural breakdown rate by creating an optimal environment for waste decomposition. France alone has more than one hundred plants producing 800,000 tons of compost each year. In Sweden one fourth of all solid waste is composted.

In New Jersey a program of state-sponsored economic incentives has spurred more than eighty municipalities to develop leaf composting and mulch programs. Broome County, New York, banned leaves from the landfill to encourage local townships to establish composting programs.

## WHAT YOU CAN DO:

Composting is easy to do in your own backyard. For more information, order *Let It Rot! The Complete Home Gardener's Guide to Composting,* $5.95 from Gardeners Supply Company, 128 Intervale Road, Burlington, VT; (802) 863-1700.

* Earth Care Paper Company, 1988.

# 7

# Poisoning the Planet

## Controlling the Use of Toxic Chemicals in and Around Your Home

No information is available on the toxic effects of more than 79 percent of the 48,500 chemicals listed in the EPA inventory. We do, of course, know what happened in Bhopal, that in India and Nicaragua women produce toxic breast milk and that thirty out of fifty states already have contaminated groundwater.

Action
38

## Protecting Yourself and the Planet from Toxic Chemicals

Industry, agriculture, and a society determined to clean, disinfect, polish and deodorize as well as rid itself forever of the nasty little creatures that we believe are determined to invade our homes—are producing some unexpected results.

—Up to one million poisonings occur each year with as many as 20,000 resulting in death.

—Half a million fish were killed when pesticides accidentally spilled into the Rhine River.

—Two thousand people died in Bhopal, India, from a gas leak in a manufacturing facility.

—Consumers in industrial countries remain exposed to deadly chemicals when, even after their use has been banned at home, manufacturers continue to sell them to Third World countries. When industrial countries import food from their poorer neighbors, they end up consuming the same deadly chemicals that have supposedly been banned!

—Of course, we directly assault the Third World, too. Soap containing mercuric iodide, whose sale is forbidden in Europe, is sold freely to African distributors. This soap, used to "lighten the skin," can cause fetal damage, anemia, and renal failure.

—Worse, DDT and benzene hexachloride (BHC), both banned in the United States and much of Europe, account for about three quarters of the total pesticide use in India. Residues of these compounds, both suspected carcinogens, were found in all seventy-five samples of breast milk collected from women in India's Punjab region. Through their mothers' milk, babies were daily ingesting twenty-one times the amount of these chemicals considered acceptable. Similarly, samples of breast milk from Nicaraguan women have shown DDT levels that are an astounding forty-five times greater than tolerance limits set by the World Health Organization.

—Routine agricultural practice in the United States has contaminated groundwater with more than fifty pesticides in thirty states.

—At least one thousand and as many as ten thousand landfills and other waste sites may now cost more than $100 billion to clean up—the equivalent of $400 for every U.S. resident. Not surprising, since we dump the equivalent of one ton per person of hazardous waste into the ground every year.

—Our poisoned atmosphere is expected to cause up to one million additional cases of skin cancer over each seventy-year lifetime in the United States alone.

Not a pretty picture. Again, of course, the question is, What can we do? While admittedly most of our planet's toxic problems are caused by industrial agriculture and municipal waste-disposal practices, a careful look in the bathroom cabinet, under the sink, and the basement or garage would probably reveal a list of poisonous chemicals long enough to fill this page.

The consequences and risks of using many of these chemicals are not even known.

"The U.S. National Research Council estimates that no information on toxic effects is available for 79 percent of the more than 48,500 chemicals listed in the inventory prepared by the Environmental Protection Agency (EPA). Fewer than a fifth have been tested for acute effects, and fewer than a tenth for chronic (for example, cancer-causing), reproductive, or mutagenic effects. Pesticides generally have received more extensive testing, but there, too, serious gaps remain. By allowing the production and release of these compounds without understanding their damaging effects, society has set itself up for unpleasant surprises."*

Unfortunately, the list of toxins that can be found in typical consumer products is so diverse and at times so complex that a complete list can't even be presented here. The resource section that follows will direct you to a number of excellent publications and organizations from which you can obtain much more complete and detailed information.

## WHAT YOU CAN DO:

There are a few simple rules that do apply to minimizing the use of toxic chemicals. The first rule is to read the label of everything you purchase. If the label says POISON or DANGER, the contents are highly toxic. WARNING or CAUTION means the contents are toxic but probably less so than the former. NONTOXIC should mean safe—although use of the word is not controlled by any federal regulations.

Other commonsense rules include:

—Don't dispose of hazardous chemicals (such as automotive products, painting supplies, lawn-care products, and cleaning products) by pouring them down the drain or toilet.

—Don't mix toxic chemicals.

* *State of the World, 1988.* Research and statistics cited on pages 000 and 000 are also drawn from *State of the World, 1988.*

—Follow careful disposal instructions when dealing with all toxic products from batteries to used auto oil.

—Avoid buying toxic products in the first place if at all possible.

—Search for nontoxic substitutes to do the same job.

—If you must purchase a toxin do so in the smallest possible quantity.

---

**Action 39**
## Hazardous Household Products

Do you have any of the following products in your home: disinfectants, furniture polish, bleach, floor wax, drain cleaners, silver polish, rug cleaners, spot removers, paint thinner, car wax, or mothballs?

Most people have them all, and unfortunately each and every one contains toxic chemicals that are hazardous to the environment. Worse yet, this list is far from complete.

### WHAT YOU CAN DO:

**1.** The most constructive actions we can take as consumers is starting to replace toxic substances with nontoxic alternatives, such as:

| | |
|---|---|
| AIR FRESHENER | Set vinegar out in an open dish. |
| DRAIN CLEANER | Pour baking soda or salt down drain, follow with boiling water. |
| ALL-PURPOSE CLEANER | Use ammonia and water; soap and water; a little "elbow grease." |
| SPOT REMOVER | Old-fashioned laundry soap takes out spots on clothing; dishwashing detergent removes spots on rugs. |
| FURNITURE POLISH | Use 1 teaspoon lemon oil in 1 pint mineral oil. |

OVEN CLEANER            Use baking soda, salt, and water.

SILVER CLEANER          Soak silver in 1 quart warm water
                        containing 1 teaspoon baking soda,
                        1 teaspoon salt, and a piece of alu-
                        minum foil.

FLOOR CLEANER           Use white vinegar and water, or
                        soap and water.

WINDOW CLEANER          Use white vinegar and water, or
                        ammonia and water; wipe with
                        newspapers.


**2.** One of the best resources for nontoxic alternatives to dangerous household products and a detailed review of which toxins are in most household products is published by the Household Hazardous Waste Project. Their *Guide to Hazardous Products Around the Home* is available for $5 by writing to Box 87, 901 South National Avenue, Springfield, MO 65804; (417) 836-5777. The book also contains disposal guidelines, product-labeling information, and a host of other valuable tips.

**3.** A shorter four-page flyer, *Stepping Lightly on the Earth: Everyone's Guide to Toxics in the Home*, is available free from Greenpeace, 1436 U Street, N.W., Washington, DC 20009; (202) 462-1177.

**4.** For those who are not inclined to mix their own natural cleaning solutions, Ecover manufactures a line of 100 percent biodegradable phosphate-free, nontoxic household cleaning products, including a fabric softener, a wool wash, a general-purpose cleaner, a dishwashing product, a *laundry powder,* a *floor soap*, and a *toilet bowl cleaner*. Available from Seventh Generation, 10 Farrell Street, South Burlington, VT 05403.

---

## The Pesticide Problem

Toxic pesticides [the general term for such poisons as insecticides, herbicides, rodenticides, and fungicides] ultimately touch everyone's life. We are exposed daily to pesticides in the workplace, in the water we drink, through community and household spray programs, or as neighbors of dump sites, sprayed fields, forests and utility lines. While the chemical industry pushes these "wonder drugs," untold problems with long-term repercussions have already begun to develop.

## Myths of Safety

Myth 1: A pesticide is safe because it is registered by the U.S. Environmental Protection Agency and your state.
Myth 2: A pesticide is safe when it is used according to product label instructions.

"At the heart of any discussion of pesticide safety is the status of what we know and do not know about the pesticide product in question. While we may know something about the effects of one chemical, we may know almost nothing about another. In fact, a 1982 U.S. Congressional staff report indicates that: (i) between 79 and 84 percent of pesticides on the market have not been adequately tested for their capacity to cause cancer; (ii) between 90 and 93 percent of pesticides have not been adequately tested for their ability to cause genetic damage, and; (iii) between 60 and 70 percent have not been fully tested for their ability to cause birth defects."*

There are three main areas where we are most likely to use pesticides: (1) in our homes to kill bugs, flies, mosquitoes, spiders, and ants; (2) in our gardens to protect flowers, vegetables, trees, and plants; and (3) on our lawns. Consumer pesticide use is no small matter, amounting to a total of sixty-five million pounds of toxic nonagricultural chemicals in 1986 alone.

| Action 40 | *What You Can Do in Your Home*[†] |

Learn to control indoor pests the natural way and avoid using commercial toxic chemicals. Try natural alternatives for the following:

* Excerpted from *Pesticide Safety*, by the National Coalition Against the Misuse of Pesticides, Washington, D.C.
[†] Excerpted in part from Greenpeace's newsletter, *Toxics*.

**ANTS:** Locate the place of entry, squeeze the juice of a lemon onto it, and leave the peel. Ants will also retreat from lines of talcum powder, chalk, damp coffee grounds, bone meal, charcoal dust, and cayenne pepper.

**COCKROACHES:** Plug all small cracks along baseboards, wall shelves, and cupboards, as well as around pipes, sinks, and bathtub fixtures. A light dusting of borax sprinkled around the refrigerator, stove, and ductwork is effective in controlling cockroaches. For a trap, lightly grease the inner neck of a milk bottle and put a little stale beer or raw potato in the bottle.

**FRUIT FLIES:** Pour a small amount of beer into a wide-mouthed jar. Cut off one corner of a plastic bag and attach the bag to the jar with a rubber band. Flies will enter and be trapped. Change the beer when necessary.

**FLIES:** Sunny open windows are flies' most common entrance into your home, so close the windows before the sun hits them. Use ordinary sticky flypaper to catch unwelcome flying guests. You can make your own flypaper using honey and yellow paper.

**MOTHS:** Keep vulnerable clothes dry and well aired. Camphor —which is the major nontoxic ingredient in mothballs—may be used. To trap moths, mix one part molasses to two parts vinegar and place the mixture in a yellow container. Clean regularly.

**SPIDERS:** Under ideal conditions, do not destroy spiders because they help control pests.

**TICKS AND FLEAS:** If your pets are infested, wash them well with soap and warm water, dry them thoroughly, and use this herbal rinse: Add two tablespoons of fresh or dried rosemary to one-half pint of boiling water. Steep twenty minutes, strain, and allow to cool. Spray or sponge evenly onto pets and allow to air dry. Do not towel down, as this will remove the residue. Make sure pets are dry before letting go outside.

For more detailed information contact the National Coalition Against the Misuse of Pesticides (NCAMP)—its address, as well as that of other organizations, appears in the following resource section, Action 42.

Also, stop purchasing commercial bug sprays and pest strips. Natural nontoxic alternatives are available for those who don't care for homemade solutions.

—Green Ban is a natural and safe line of insect repellents, flea and tick powders, and plant insecticides. Write for a catalog,

P.O. Box 745, Longview, WA 98632, or check your local health food store. Green Ban is made in Australia by Mulgum Hollow Farm.

—Co-Op America sells Roach-Kil and Ant-Kil, boric-acid products that are much less toxic than other commercial pesticides. Call (802) 658-5507 for details, or write to them at 2100 M Street N.W., Suite 310, Washington, DC 20036.

---

| Action 41 | *What You Can Do in the Garden* |
| --- | --- |

Organic gardening—that is, without the use of toxic pesticides and chemical fertilizers—has long been established as an effective, economical, and environmentally sound way to grow vegetables, trees, bushes, and flowers. This huge field (dealt with more fully in Action 48) has an equally large number of resource providers from catalog companies like the Necessary Trading Company and Gardeners Supply Company.

Both catalogs sell almost everything imaginable for organic and environmentally sensitive gardening, from soil testing equipment and services to composts and fertilizers, potting soil, disease control formulas, insect traps, and lawn-care equipment.

The *Necessary Catalog* is also full of educational information, how-to publications, and a list of relevant books. The cost of the catalog is $2, which is refundable with your first order. Write 422 Salem Avenue, New Castle, VA 24127; or call (703) 864-5103. To get a copy of the Gardeners Supply Company catalog, call (802) 863-1700, or write to them at 128 Intervale Road, Burlington, VT 05401.

Rodale Press is an excellent source of how-to information with an extensive list of books and magazines, including *Rodale's Organic Gardening*. Write 33 East Minor Street, Emmaus, PA 18049; or call (215) 967-5171.

---

| Action 42 | *What You Can Do with Your Lawn* |
| --- | --- |

In 1987 eight million American homeowners spent over $1.5 billion to have chemical companies provide them with perfectly green lawns. The thirty to forty different pesticides used by these companies, such as ChemLawn the industry leader, can kill birds, endanger our water supply, and have proven to be a formidable threat to children, dogs, and the occasional adult who unsuspectingly wanders onto a freshly sprayed lawn. The chemicals, when sprayed, also become airborne and can drift to affect neighbors.

Nontoxic lawn maintenance can achieve equally effective results, and includes:

—planting well-adapted and pest-resistant grass varieties

—aerating the lawn regularly

—controlling thatch buildup

—balancing the lawn's pH level

—proper watering

—mowing the grass with sharp blades, with the mower set as high as possible

Equally important is avoiding the use of chemicals to kill weeds around the driveway, sidewalk, or deck. The worst and most powerful of these toxins, called "systemic weed killers," are designed to seep deep into the soil and kill plants from the roots up.

If you're a golfer or live near a public park, you might also inquire about lawn-care practices in these areas and voice your concern if toxins are being used.

Consult Rodale Press and the Necessary Trading Company catalog in Action 41.

---

**Action 43**     *Resources for Controlling and Reducing the Use of Toxic Chemicals*

1. *Citizens Clearinghouse for Hazardous Waste* (CCHW)
   P.O. Box 926
   Arlington, VA 22216 (703) 276-7070
The Citizens Clearinghouse will endeavor to answer any questions their members have about toxins over a special phone

line. They also publish two quarterly newsletters: *Action Bulletin*, which covers news items, state-by-state issues, legislation, events, and special resources; and *Everyone's Backyard,* which focuses on local organizing actions, legal issues, science and technical subjects, and news from local groups that are fighting toxic problems in their communities. CCHW also supports the efforts of more than 1,700 grass-roots organizations and 400 neighborhood groups through providing support, technical assistance, research, and educational programs. Membership is $15.

**2.** *Environmental Protection Agency (EPA)* (800) 424-9346
The EPA publishes *Household Hazardous Waste,* a free bibliography of useful references and a listing of state experts.

**3.** *National Coalition Against the Misuse of Pesticides*
(NCAMP)
530 7th Street, S.E.
Washington, DC 20003 (202) 543-5450
Comprising three hundred groups plus hundreds of individual members, NCAMP is the primary national organization working on pesticide issues. They promote public policy reform and provide referrals to local pesticide action groups and other contacts. A staff toxicologist helps answer pesticide questions. The quarterly newsletter, *Pesticides and You,* costs $20 (includes membership). Practical fact sheets will help you solve almost all your home, garden, and lawn-care problems.

**4.** *Bio-Integral Resource Center (BIRC)*
P.O. Box 7414
Berkeley, CA 94707 (415) 524-2567
BIRC prescribes integrated pest management (IPM) strategies for controlling pests that attack the human body, building structures, plants, or pets. Membership benefits include a detailed written consultation on a pest problem and a subscription to the *IPM Practitioner* or *Common Sense Pest Control Quarterly* for $25. For more details and a catalog of IPM publications and audiovisual materials, send $1 and a self-addressed, stamped envelope.

**5.** *Concern, Inc.*
1794 Columbia Road, N.W.
Washington, DC 20009 (202) 328-8160
An environmental education organization that publishes concise, readable community-action guides on pesticides, hazardous wastes, and ground- and drinking-water contamination.

They also provide answers to and referrals for pesticide questions.

**6.** *Rodale Press, Inc.*
  33 East Minor Street
  Emmaus, PA 18049 (215) 967-5171

Rodale is one of the best resources in the field. For $1, you can receive *Resources for Organic Pest Control*, which includes: practical steps you can take; a list of organic manufacturers and suppliers; pest control materials you can grow or make yourself; and resources for answering pesticide questions. Ask for a catalog and list of magazines, which will include such excellent publications as *Rodale's Organic Gardening*.

**7.** *NRDC Toxic Substances Information Line*
  (800) 648-NRDC, outside New York State
  (212) 687-6862, New York State

The hotline fields questions on toxic substances and their health effects. If NRDC doesn't have the answer, staff members will try to refer inquiries to appropriate organizations.

**8.** *Pesticide Hotline of the National Pesticide Telecommunications Network (NPTN)* (800) 858-7378

Funded by an EPA grant and located at Texas Tech University, NPTN answers pesticide questions twenty-four hours a day, seven days a week. It provides technical chemical and regulatory information; toxicity and health data; and referrals to residue testing labs, poison-control centers, and local doctors experienced with pesticide poisonings.

**9.** Check the listings under Action 19 for Environmental Action Letters you can write to support stronger pesticide legislation.

---

Action
44

# Water Pollution
## Citizen Suits Fight Industrial Polluters

Over the past four years, an estimated 600 citizen suits have been filed against scores of companies by individuals and environmental groups such as the *Natural Resources Defense Council* and the *Sierra Club*.*

---

*Natural Resources Defense Council, New York, N.Y.

In 1987 the U.S. Congress approved amendments to the Clean Water Act—the federal statute under which most citizen suits are filed—that increase daily fines for each violation to $25,000. Lawyers say that most citizen suits are brought under the act because it requires companies to file public reports listing pollutant discharges into public sewerage systems and to submit records showing discharges above permitted limits serve as a legal admission of guilt. If the government hasn't already moved to penalize the offender, private action can be taken. "It's like shooting fish in a barrel, and we've shot a lot of fish," says Mr. James Thornton of the Natural Resources Defense Council, who contends the suits are a way for citizens to plug a gap in federal and state enforcement.

Some of the settlements have been substantial. For example, Bethlehem Steel's participation in the Chesapeake Bay cleanup arose from a recent $1.5 million settlement of a citizen suit for 353 alleged pollution violations. Other companies that have been sued include Chrysler, for 750 violations; Ford, 351 violations; General Electric, 543 violations; and Pfizer, 339 violations.

## WHAT YOU CAN DO:

To find out how to bring your own citizen suit, contact James Thornton of the Natural Resources Defense Council at 122 East 42nd Street, New York, NY 10168; (212) 727-2700.

Also contact these organizations to find out how you can protect our oceans, rivers, lakes, and groundwater:*

**1. American Rivers, Inc.,** 801 Pennsylvania Avenue, S.E., Suite 303, Washington, DC 20003; (202) 547-6900. Works to protect a priority list of "wild, natural, and free-flowing" rivers and their landscapes, and acts as an information resource for river activists. Lobbies, drafts legislation, and assists local and state organizations in conservation projects. Newsletter updates members on river-related legislative action, provides contact names, and lists recreational opportunities.

**2. Clean Water Action Project,** 317 Pennsylvania Avenue, S.E., Washington, DC 20003; (202) 547-1196. Works for clean and safe water at an affordable cost, control of toxic chemicals, and the protection of natural resources. Techniques include

*Excerpted from "The 1989 Guide to New Age Living," *New Age* magazine.

door-to-door canvassing, petition drives, and meetings. A citizens' organization with locations throughout the United States.

**3. National Water Center,** P.O. Box 264, Eureka Springs, AR 72632; (501) 253-9755. Nonprofit volunteer organization promotes awareness of alternatives to contaminating water supplies with wastes (both human and industrial). Quarterly newsletter, *Water Center News*, facilitates networking and reviews new products (such as various "dry" toilet systems that don't use water), and provides news on developments in water issues. Also publishes *We All Live Downstream*, an eclectic catalog of water conservation and composting devices, funny poems, and conservation philosophy.

**4. Water Information Network,** P.O. Box 909, Ashland, OR 97520; (800) 533-6714. National organization provides consumer information on water contamination and pure drinking-water systems; offers training and support for start-up businesses in the field of water purification. All services are free.

**5. Conservation Law Foundation's Groundwater Protection Program**, 3 Joy Street, Boston, MA 02108; (617) 742-2540. This program focuses on education and the empowerment of communities to strengthen state and federal regulations to protect their water supply.

## Part 2

# FOOD, HUNGER, AND AGRICULTURE

*What you can do at your next meal, how to feed the hungry in your own neighborhood, solving the international food crisis, and getting legislative results*

# 8

# Eight Myths About Hunger

Hunger is perhaps the most urgent, compelling, and emotionally charged issue we confront as we explore how to make the world a better place. I will not repeat the facts and figures that are so saddening, especially for those of us who live in the midst of such plenty and waste.

Hunger haunts us everywhere—outside our homes, in faraway places, in the pages of magazines, in newspapers, on TV, and by strongly phrased fund-raising letters that greet us in the mail:

> In the ten seconds it took you to open and begin to read this letter, three children died from the effects of malnutrition somewhere in the world.
>
> No statistic can express what it's like to see even one child die that way . . . to see a mother sitting hour after hour, leaning her child's body against her own . . . to watch the small, feeble head movements that expend all the energy a youngster has left . . . to see the panic in a dying tot's innocent eyes . . . and then to know in a moment that life is gone.*

Before we begin to explore what each of us can do, it's important to examine eight of the most common misconceptions about what does and does not cause hunger. These myths have been unveiled by Frances Moore Lappé and the Institute for Food

---

*UNICEF direct-mail fund-raising letter, 1988.

and Development Policy. Over eighteen years ago, Ms. Lappé, in her first book *Diet for a Small Planet,* helped the world to see how diet is integrally related to hunger as well as to health. In her later work, she has explored how power and powerlessness underlie all of the issues that surround world hunger and food distribution problems.

---

## Eight Myths*

Hunger is not a myth, but myths keep us from ending hunger. Only by freeing ourselves from the grasp of these widely held beliefs can we understand the root causes of hunger and see how to bring it to an end.

### MYTH 1: *There's simply not enough food*

#### MYTH

With farmland and other food-producing resources stretched to their limits in so much of the world, there's not enough food to go around.

#### REALITY

Abundance, not scarcity, best describes the world's food supply. Enough wheat, rice, and other grains are produced to provide every human being with 3,600 calories a day—enough to make all of us fat.

Virtually every "hungry" country produces enough food for all its people. Redistribution of a tiny fraction of each country's food supply would wipe out hunger. For example, in Indonesia, with the second greatest number of undernourished people in the world, redistributing a mere 2 percent of the available food would make a healthy life possible for everyone.

Many "hungry" countries export more food and other farm products than they import. India, home to over a third of the world's hungry people, not only has mounting surpluses of wheat and rice—currently more than 32 million tons—but also ranks as one of the Third World's top agricultural exporters.

*Excerpted with permission from *Hunger Myths & Facts,* Food First, the Institute for Food and Development Policy, San Francisco, CA. For more information about Food First, including publications lists and membership information, see pages 159–160.

Here at home scarcity can hardly explain the lack of adequate diet for twenty million Americans. Not when overproduction is the American farmer's persistent headache.

In the United States, just as in the Third World, hunger is an outrage because it is profoundly needless.

Hunger is real; scarcity is not.

## MYTH 2: *Nature is to blame*

### *MYTH*

Droughts and other disasters beyond human control cause famine.

### *REALITY*

Deaths from natural disasters have leaped sixfold since the 1960s, but not because nature has become more cruel. Man-made forces are making more people increasingly *vulnerable* to nature's vagaries.

Millions live on the brink of disaster because they are deprived of land by the wealthy elite, trapped in the unremitting grip of debt, heavily taxed, or miserably paid. Natural events rarely explain death by starvation; they are the final push over the brink.

*Human* institutions and policies determine who eats and who starves. In Bangladesh during the 1974 floods, rich farmers hoarded rice to sell for greater profit while famine took 100,000 lives, mostly unemployed landless laborers and their families.

Famines are not natural disasters but social disasters. They result from unjust economic and political arrangements, not acts of God.

## MYTH 3: *Too many mouths to feed*

### *MYTH*

Hunger is caused by overpopulation. Reducing population growth is the best way to combat hunger.

### *REALITY*

Although rapid population growth is a serious concern in many countries, nowhere does population density explain hunger. In India over 300 million people are chronically hungry. Yet neighboring China, with only half the cropland per person as India, has eradicated widespread and severe hunger.

Rapid population growth is not the root cause of hunger. Like hunger itself, it results from underlying inequities that deprive poor people, especially women, of economic opportunity and security. Rapid population growth *and* hunger are endemic to societies where land ownership, jobs, education, health care, and old-age security are beyond the reach of most people.

## MYTH 4: *Food vs. our environment*

### *MYTH*

Pressured to feed the hungry, we are pushing crop and livestock production into marginal erosion-prone lands, clearing age-old rain forests, and poisoning the environment with pesticides. We cannot both feed the hungry and protect our environment.

### *REALITY*

That an environmental crisis is undercutting our food-producing resources and threatening our health is no myth. But efforts to feed the hungry are not causing the crisis.

In many countries, logging and ranching companies are leveling irreplaceable rain forests. The lumber and beef, however, are not for the hungry but for the well-off, often those abroad.

Global pesticide use has expanded from virtually nothing only forty years ago to more than five billion pounds a year. While the chemical companies would have us believe that pesticides help produce food for the hungry, in the Third World most pesticides are applied to crops for export.

## MYTH 5: *The Green Revolution is the answer*

### *MYTH*

Boosting food production through scientific advances is key to ending hunger.

### *REALITY*

In the very countries most touted as Green Revolution success stories—India, Indonesia, Mexico, and the Philippines—production of Green Revolution grains has increased while hunger has worsened.

Throughout much of the Third World today, the widening

control of the land by a powerful few deprives nearly one billion rural people of any land at all. And as an Indian farmworker once reminded us, "If you don't own the land, you never get enough to eat, no matter how much it is producing."

Hunger can be alleviated only by redistributing food-producing resources and purchasing power to the hungry.

### MYTH 6: *Land redistribution vs. production efficiency*

### *MYTH*

A fairer distribution of land, credit, and other food-producing resources would undercut production. Since only the big producers have the know-how to make the land produce efficiently, reforms that take away their land will lower food production.

### *REALITY*

Unjust farming systems leave land in the hands of the most *in*efficient producers. Owners who control most of the best land often leave much of it idle. By contrast, small farmers typically achieve four to five times greater output per acre, in part because they work their land more intensively.

### MYTH 7: *Increase foreign aid*

### *MYTH*

To help end world hunger, our primary responsibility as U.S. citizens is to increase and improve our government's foreign aid.

### *REALITY*

Foreign aid is only as good as the recipient government. The bulk of U.S. aid goes to only a handful of governments; most of them are dead set against reforms that would benefit those in need.

Where such governments answer only to elites, our aid not only fails to reach hungry people, it shores up the very forces working against them.

Two thirds of U.S. foreign aid is now "security assistance" —military aid and cash transfers to governments Washington policymakers support. The arms we send are often used by governments against their own citizens who oppose the structures responsible for their poverty and hunger.

As long as we allow Washington to define the national interest to mean keeping the lid on change in the Third World, our foreign aid cannot help end hunger. We cannot be both against change and for the hungry.

## MYTH 8: *The solution involves sacrifice*

### *MYTH*

To end world hunger, Americans would have to sacrifice much of their standard of living.

### *REALITY*

The biggest threat to the well-being of the vast majority of Americans is not the advancement but the continued deprivation of the hungry.

Enforced poverty in the Third World jeopardizes U.S. jobs, wages, and working conditions as corporations seek cheaper labor abroad. In a global economy, what American workers have achieved in employment, wage levels, and working conditions can be protected only when working people in *every* country are freed from economic desperation.

As we have seen, because the dispossessed majorities within Third World countries lack buying power, agricultural practices in those countries shift toward growing export crops. These exports further undercut markets for U.S. farmers, and America is made increasingly dependent on the outside world for its food.

What can we do to end hunger now that we better understand what does and does not cause it?

The following section of this book will cover actions you can take at every meal you eat and every time you shop, the importance of eating locally grown organic produce, how the food business endangers human health as well as the planet's, actions to help the hungry, and what you can do about the politics of hunger.

# 9

# Eating As a Political Act: Your Diet and a "Diet for a Small Planet"

---

**Action
45**

### *Twenty-eight Reasons to Stop Eating Meat*

While one less steak won't put food in the mouth of a hungry child, cattle raised for beef in the U.S. eat more than enough grain and soy beans to adequately feed the sixty million people that starve to death every year.

As Frances Moore Lappé said years ago, "Every decision we make about the food we eat is a vote for the kind of world we want to live in." No choice better exemplifies that truth than the decision to eat or not eat meat. The consumption of meat plays a major role in the balance of global food resources, the future of our environment, Third World economies, and the humane treatment of animals as well as our own health.

So, here goes—twenty eight-reasons not to eat meat!*

---

*Facts and statistics taken from *Diet for a New America,* by John Robbins, Stillpoint, P.O. Box 640, Walpole, NH 03608; (800) 847-4014, $12.95. Text excerpted from "How Our Food Choices Affect the World," by Ronald Kotzschand, reprinted with permission from *East West: The Journal of Natural Health and Living.* All rights reserved.

## Livestock Eat Better Than
## Many of the World's Poor

Livestock eat the grain and soybeans that could feed the hungry. In so doing, they inefficiently convert agricultural products to a very small amount of beef.

1. Number of human beings who could be fed annually by the grain and soybeans eaten by U.S. livestock: *1,300,000,000*

2. Number of people who will starve to death this year: *60,000,000*

3. Number of people who could be adequately fed by the grain saved if Americans reduced their intake of meat by 10 percent: *60,000,000*

4. Pounds of grain and soybeans needed to produce one pound of feedlot beef: *16*

5. Number of pure vegetarians who can be fed on the amount of land needed to feed one meat-eating person: *20*

6. Percentage of protein wasted by cycling grain through livestock: *90*

7. Percentage of carbohydrate wasted by cycling grain through livestock: *99*

8. Percentage of dietary fiber wasted by cycling grain through livestock: *100*

9. Pounds of potatoes that can be grown on 1 acre of land: *20,000*. Pounds of beef that can be produced on 1 acre of land: *165*.

## Animal Rights

Eating meat, of course, involves killing animals. A single visit to a slaughterhouse has been enough to convert many to vegetarianism.

10. Reason veal is so tender: *Calves are never allowed to take a single step.*

**11.** Reason veal is a whitish pink: *Calves are force-fed an anemia-producing diet.*

**12.** The McDonald's clown, Ronald McDonald, tells children: "Hamburgers grow in hamburger patches and love to be eaten." Ronald McDonald doesn't tell children: "Hamburgers are ground-up cows who've had their throats slit by machetes or their brains bashed in by sledgehammers."

**13.** Number of animals killed for meat per hour in the United States: *500,000*

**14.** Occupation with highest employee-turnover rate in the United States: *slaughterhouse worker*

**15.** Occupation with highest employee rate of injury in the United States: *slaughterhouse worker*

**16.** Cost to render an animal unconscious prior to slaughter so that process is done humanely: *1 cent*. Reason given by meat industry for not utilizing captive bolt pistol: *too expensive*

Even if we have no qualms about the slaughter of animals for food, there are serious environmental and other ethical issues involved.

The grazing of cattle, sheep, and goats for meat can have a valid place in an ecologically balanced food economy. For one thing, not all land is fit for the cultivation of food crops such as grains and beans; the soil may be poor and there may be inadequate water.

However, the number of animals raised exclusively on rangelands in America is small. Most spend a good part of their lives in feedlots. These are enclosed areas where thousands of animals are crowded together and fattened with a diet of corn, soybeans, and other potential human foods. These feedlots amount to animal concentration camps. *Life in the feedlots is so unhealthy that the animals are constantly dosed with antibiotics, which poses health risks for humans.*

**17.** Percentage of antibiotics produced in this country used in livestock feeds: *55*

*The animals produce manure*—literally mountains of it, which if properly treated might be used as fertilizer or even as a source of methane fuel. Unfortunately, it usually is treated as a waste product. *It is allowed to wash away into streams, rivers, and lakes, where its high concentrations of nitrates and phosphates upset the natural ecology.* The Chesapeake

Bay, for example, long a major source of fish and shellfish, has become almost barren due to animal-waste runoff from farms along its source rivers.

18. Production of excrement by total U.S. human population: *12,000 pounds per second*. Production of excrement by U.S. livestock: *250,000 pounds per second*.

19. Percentage of harmful organic waste-water pollution attributable to U.S. human population: *10*. Percentage of harmful organic waste-water pollution attributable to U.S. livestock: *90*

---

## Wasted Water

Not only are vast amounts of water polluted by livestock— but even larger amounts are consumed in the breeding process.

20. Enough water goes into the feeding and care of the average cow to: *float a destroyer*.

21. Water needed to produce a pound of wheat: *25 gallons*. Water needed to produce a pound of meat: *2,500 gallons*

---

## Protecting Our Forests

If we eat beef, especially the cheaper varieties used in fast-food outlets, there is another fact to consider. A substantial amount of this beef comes from Central American countries where the cattle industry has been involved in the wholesale destruction of the *tropical rain forests*. Huge tracts of forest are cleared by bulldozers and are sown with grasses for grazing. Cattle are pastured in these areas and the meat sold at low prices to American companies. In a few years the fragile topsoil becomes depleted and the area is abandoned. The bands of massive rain forests that gird the equator is a key factor in the ecology and climate of the earth. It is being devastated in the noble cause of the cheap hamburger. A similar problem exists in the United States.

22. Number of acres of U.S. forest that have been cleared to create cropland to produce a meat-centered diet: *260,000,000*

**23.** How often an acre of trees disappears in this country: *every 5 seconds*

**24.** At the present rate of deforestation, number of years before not a single tree will remain standing in the United States: *50*

**25.** Amount of trees spared per year by each individual who switches to a pure vegetarian diet: *1 acre*

---

## Protecting Our Own Lives

Lastly, we all have our own health, and that of our friends and family to consider.

**26.** Most common cause of death in the United States: *heart attack*. Risk of death from heart attack by average American man: *50 percent*. Risk of death from heart attack by average American man consuming a pure vegetarian diet: *4 percent*

**27.** Increased risk of breast cancer for women who eat meat daily compared to women who eat meat less than once a week: *four times higher*

**28.** Leading source of pesticide residues in the U.S. diet: *meat —55 percent*. Total pesticide residues in U.S. diet supplied by vegetables: *6 percent*. Total pesticide residues in U.S. diet supplied by fruits: *4 percent*. Total pesticide residues in U.S. diet supplied by grains: *1 percent*

Finally, if you're wondering how to select the lesser evil—beef, pork, turkey, eggs, or chicken—let the illustration on page 124 be your guide.*

### WHAT YOU CAN DO:

Stop eating meat or reduce your consumption. If and when you do eat meat, select organically fed, humanely treated, range-free beef or poultry. See the actions in the next section on Farmers' Markets and Food Co-ops for more details.

For answers to questions about raising your children as

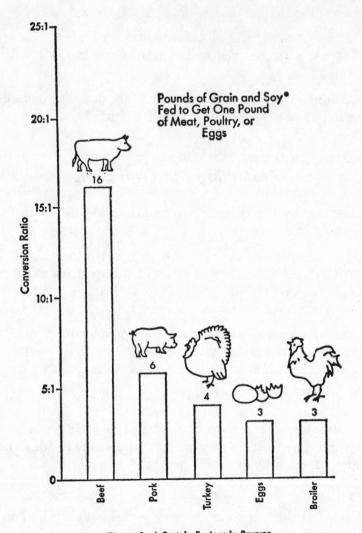

**Figure 1. A Protein Factory in Reverse**

Sources: USDA, Economic Research Service, Beltsville, Maryland.
*Soy constitutes only 12% of steer food and 20–25% of poultry.

vegetarians, which fast-food restaurants use *only* vegetable oil, and how best to replace the iron and protein found in meat, consider subscribing to the *Vegetarian Journal,* monthly, for $18. Write P.O. Box 1463, Baltimore, MD 21203.

# Action 46    *Dairy Products: A Fate Worse Than Death\**

Unfortunately dairy products don't come from happy farm animals who would rather produce milk, eggs and cheese than be sent to the slaughterhouse!

We would like to think we are doing livestock a good turn by not eating meat, and by substituting cheese, yogurt, and milk in our diet. But to the compassionate observer, many dairy farms have little to recommend them over the feedlot and the slaughterhouse.

In an earlier, more innocent age, milk cows led a quiet, bucolic life. Ole Bessie roamed hillside pastures and twice a day was hand-milked in the barn by her owner. She performed a useful service by changing seeds and forage into food.

Today, this is largely a thing of the past. Very likely, Ole Bessie is chained for most of her life in an enormous barn with several hundred other cows. She can do little more than eat, lactate, and defecate. This makes her prone to infection, so she receives antibiotics. At milking time, vacuum hoses are attached to her teats as her udders are pumped dry. Like her brothers and sisters in the feedlot, Bessie is treated as little more than a biological machine. As soon as her milk production falls below a certain level, she is sent to the slaughterhouse.

Clearly, the consumption of dairy products raises some issues for the humane and environmentally aware consumer. Bessie may not be the smartest of God's creatures, but she probably knows the difference between life in a stall and in a pasture. With our glass of milk, bit of cheese, even our wholesome bowl of yogurt, we are contributing to her life of incarceration.

*Eggs:* There is something appealing in thinking of a flock of hens clucking about the yard, trysting with the rooster behind the willow tree, and laying an occasional egg to nourish their human caretakers. Again this pleasant image is a thing of the past. Most chickens (both egg layers and those destined for the frying pan) are raised in conditions that make a feedlot or dairy barn look like a four-star luxury hotel.

---

\* Reprinted with permission from *East West: The Journal of Natural Health and Living.* All rights reserved.

The typical chicken spends her life in a windowless "factory," inside a cage that is one foot high and one foot long. She eats, defecates, and lays her eggs in the same spot. She is fed hormones and doused with antibiotics. The factory lighting is manipulated so the "day" passes quickly and the chicken lays more frequently. The bird is lucky to survive a single year under such conditions.

## WHAT YOU CAN DO:

Shop in health food stores, food co-ops, and farmers' markets, and look for eggs from free-range chickens. These are the best places to find dairy products from small farms, which are more likely to treat animals humanely.

---

Action    *Tales of Coffee, Coconuts,*
47          *Cashews, and Cocoa*

Imported food items are often to blame for the poverty and destruction of local agriculture in much of Central and South America.

Given the current level of regular and massive consumption of such items as sugar, coffee, cocoa, tea, and tropical fruits, like pineapples and bananas, it's hard to believe these products were foreign to American diets barely one hundred years ago. Once we acquired a taste for these luxuries, nothing stopped us in our pursuit of them, including the near-total destruction of local agricultural practice in much of Central and South America.

"In some regions plantations were immediately established to raise these products on a massive scale. In others, taxation forced small farmers to cultivate export cash crops, and eventually, in hard times, they were forced to sell off their land to large owners. In most areas the net result was the same. The agricultural land was concentrated in the hands of a few native or foreign concerns, and most of it was used for the cultivation of export cash crops. Land used for domestic food production decreased. Many peasants who were once self-sufficient farmers, ended up deprived of even a garden plot and became dependent for survival on imported foods, which could be acquired with cash earned by employment on the plantations. Our powerful agricultural interests bound these peasants to a life of poverty and hunger.

"Although most of these countries are now independent, little has changed. In the 'banana republics' of Central America, in the coffee-growing nations of sub-Saharan Africa, in the sugar-producing areas of the Philippines, the agricultural, social and economic situation is essentially the same. Most of the land is used for cash crops and is controlled by a native elite or by multinational corporations.

"The problems of social and economic justice, poverty, hunger and famine in the Third World are complex ones. But, at least, we should be aware that our choices in the supermarket are intimately related to them."*

## WHAT YOU CAN DO:

Purchase luxury items from small businesses and worker-owned cooperatives in Third World countries. These businesses are represented in the United States primarily by the nonprofit alternative trade organizations listed on page 222–224. Many products are available, from coffee and sugar to tea, vanilla, sesame tahini, and nuts. Fruit is usually not handled by these organizations, and it is best to purchase only locally grown, in-season products.

*Reprinted with permission from *East West: The Journal of Natural Health and Living.* All rights reserved.

# 10

# Eat Locally—Act Globally

## An Introduction

"Most of the agricultural produce that Americans consume are produced by standard commercial agricultural techniques. This system involves the use of chemical fertilizers and petroleum-based pesticides and herbicides. Thus, American commercial agriculture is often a major polluter of the environment. Fertilizer run-off is a major cause of water pollution. Broadcast spraying puts agricultural poisons into the air and water as well as the soil.

"In addition, this is not a sustainable agriculture. It is steadily destroying the topsoil and the living organisms within it. Some observers say that by the turn of the century much of the farmland now in use will be infertile. We may be approaching another 'Dust Bowl' era, with disastrous consequences for ourselves and for the rest of the world.

"Almost every time we buy a loaf of bread, a can of beans, or a head of lettuce, we are supporting this system of agriculture. And while we may oppose industrial polluters on the one hand, we're abetting agricultural polluters on the other if we purchase their products on supermarket shelves. While we're concerned about food scarcity in other parts of the world, we may be contributing to an eventual shortage closer to home."*

The alternative to this environmentally destructive scenario is close at hand. The following actions examine how purchasing organic produce—through the mail, in local greenmarkets, or from a food co-op—can make a big difference. We'll also look at growing your own food and at community gardens as ways to help you become a socially responsible eater.

---

| Action<br>48 | *Organic Farming*[†]<br>**Regenerating the Earth** |
|---|---|

On the menu tonight is chicken with gentian violet, potatoes a la chlorothalonil, carrots in triflurolin, and for dessert, grapes with methyl bromide.[‡]

"Farmers now spend nearly $1 billion on agricultural chemicals each year. Meanwhile, damage from insects, weeds and disease has increased by 40 percent. Pesticides applied to farmland in California's San Joaquin Valley, the nation's richest agricultural region, have seeped into underground reservoirs over a 7,000 square-mile corridor, contaminating the drinking water of one million residents.

"Across the country, valuable topsoil is eroding at dangerous rates. Streams are poisoned by chemicals washing off the land. Underground reservoirs are being depleted by farmers irrigating fragile drylands that experts say should not have been farmed at all.

"Yet amid this tableau of human pain and ecological damage, a dramatic and strategic change in production practices is appearing. Since the start of the decade, new and increasingly effective techniques for growing food have been developed that could turn out to be the best hope for saving the family farm.

---

[†]Excerpted with permission from "The Re-Greening of America," by Keith Schneider with Dick Russell and Noel Weyrich," *New Age Journal*, March 1986, pp. 50–93.
[‡]Known or suspected carcinogens often found in these commercially grown foods.

"From Virginia to Oregon, tens of thousands of farmers have reduced their costs and increased their profits by replacing conventional industrialized farming techniques with sophisticated organic ones. They are not, however, just the backyard gardeners usually associated with back-to-the-land organic movements. They also include some of the biggest farms and some of the largest users of petrochemical pesticides and fertilizers.

"This new farming method, called *regenerative agriculture,* will not solve such critical farm problems as crippling interest rates, dwindling export trade, or fluctuations of the dollar overseas. Yet a growing body of state, federal, and private experts agree that modern organic cultivation practices can restore the natural biological balance to vast stretches of once-depleted farmland while reducing the soil erosion, groundwater depletion, and pest damage caused in large part by over-dependence on farm chemicals."

As consumers, once again we have a vital role to play in the future direction of agriculture, the survival of these organic farms, and the protection of our groundwater, lakes, and rivers.

Faced with growing evidence about the dangers of pesticides, waxes, drugs, and preservatives commonly used by the food industry, selecting organic food becomes an even more compelling action as we also seek to protect our own health.


## WHAT YOU CAN DO:

**1.** Buy organic food whenever you can. Shop in farmers' markets, in natural food stores, or join a food co-op (see Actions 49–53).

**2.** Call or write for a free copy of *Organic Food Mail Order Supplies* from Americans for Safe Food, 1501 16th Street, N.W., Washington, DC 20036; (202) 332-9110. This listing will help you find everything from garlic, olive oil, walnuts, almonds, and pecans to kiwi fruit and sun-dried tomatoes, beef and chicken, even organic potato chips.

**3.** For more information call Rodale Press at (215) 967-5171, for a list of relevant books and magazines. Order a copy of *Pesticide Alert: A Guide to Pesticides in Fruits and Vegetables* from Sierra Club Books, 1987, $6.95. Their address is The Sierra Club, 730 Polk Street, San Francisco, CA 94109.

Action
49

## *Farmers' Markets*
## Revitalizing Local
## Agriculture

Tired of long, quiet, narrow supermarket aisles; of produce packed in plastic, frozen into little brickettes or caked with wax? Depressed by the sight of those sad, tired, droopy heads of lettuce; rock-hard, anemic-looking tomatoes or apples that glare back at you under the hum of fluorescent lights? If you are, then farmers' markets are definitely what you're looking for.

The New York City Greenmarket, one of thousands across the nation, provides a direct outlet for about 170 farmers from four states who sell fruits, vegetables, flowers, homemade baked goods, herbs, and wines. The majority of the produce sold at the greenmarket is harvested a day before it's sold and is likely to include more than 350 varieties of fruits and vegetables. Prices during the peak season can be 30 percent less than those of produce found in supermarkets.

Shopping at farmers' markets helps revitalize local agriculture, save family farms, and boost production of organic produce. A recent study of Stockton, California farmers by the state Department of Food and Agriculture showed that while consumers saved money at farmers' markets, farmers earned a 52 percent greater return on produce sold directly to consumers than they obtained by selling to middlemen in the commercial marketing system. These markets also allowed farmers to sell an average of 22 percent of their total crop that would otherwise have gone to waste, since it would have failed to meet sizing, container, and labeling requirements for commercial sale. This is perfectly good food that supermarkets might reject for a minor blemish.

The Texas Department of Agriculture has assisted in the opening of farmers' markets in over seventy cities. These markets earn the three thousand participating farmers more than $25 million annually and an additional cash income of $8,000 or more per grower.

Since small family farms are the major producers of organic food, are more likely to treat their animals humanely and their land with respect, and are a critical part of our nation's heritage and economic stability, shopping in farmers' markets does help to make the world a much better place.

### WHAT YOU CAN DO:

Shop in your local farmers' market. To find out where the closest one is, contact the Project for Public Spaces, Inc., 153 Waverly Place, New York, NY 10014; (212) 620-5660. PPS can provide you with a list of local markets and additional information about how to start a market if your neighborhood lacks one.

---

**Action 50**
## The New York—L.A. Broccoli Shuffle*
## More Reasons to Buy Local Produce!

"Last year New York area residents bought 24,000 tons of broccoli—importing almost all of it from the West Coast, nearly 2,700 miles away. The cost: $6 million for transportation alone.

"What's more, refrigerated broccoli loses 19 percent of its vitamin C in 24 hours, 34 percent in two days.

"The absurdity is this: Broccoli prefers cool weather and could have been grown at home, providing additional jobs and income for New York residents.

"Robert Rodale, publisher of *Prevention* magazine, and founder of the Cornucopia Project, says, *'For every two dollars we spend to grow food, we spend another dollar to move it around. Not just to New York. Massachusetts imports more than 80 percent of its food, and Pennsylvania—a leading agricultural state in the U.S.—more than 70 percent!'*

Here are some startling facts that turned up in the Cornucopia report:

"Last year New Yorkers spent $1 billion on food transportation. New York State imports 77 percent of its celery, 95 percent of its pork, 84 percent of its lettuce, 93 percent of its peaches, 97 percent of its chicken, and 87 percent of its green peppers. This is a typical example of what goes on in other states. And

*Excerpted from *The Tarrytown Letter*, September 1984.

consider that the cost of shipping one truckload of greens from California averages $2,400 today."

Local economies suffer, family farmers go out of business, the quality of the food we eat declines, and our environment suffers as huge corporate farms burden the earth with massive amounts of pesticides and careless farming techniques that cause tremendous soil erosion.

## WHAT YOU CAN DO:

Eat a "local diet." It creates jobs in the region, reduces transportation costs and energy consumption, ensures higher nutritional value, and encourages local small-scale agriculture that protects land from developers.

For more information write The Cornucopia Project, Rodale Press, 33 East Minor Street, Emmaus, PA 18098.

---

## Action 51       *Join Your Local Food Co-op*

Another way to support local agriculture, purchase a vast array of organic produce and avoid the New York–L.A. broccoli shuffle.

According to Paul Hazen of the National Cooperative Business Institute, there are roughly four thousand food co-ops and buying clubs in the United States, eighty percent of them carry organic produce and their prices are likely to be 5 to 30 percent less than supermarkets'. Co-ops utilize the volunteer labor of their members, so in some cases you'll have to pitch in and help out a few hours a month.

Don't worry; you won't have to compromise variety. North East Co-ops in Vermont, for example, supplies regional food co-ops with a selection of more than 1,300 items plus a full line of dairy products.

## WHAT YOU CAN DO:

Join your local food co-op. For the name and address of the one closest to you, contact the National Cooperative Business Institute, 1401 New York Avenue, N.W., Suite 1100, Washington, DC 20005; (202) 638-6222. They have listings on-line in their computer and are ready to help. They also publish a national directory of more than 20,000 different kinds of co-ops. The directory, which costs $4.95, is called *Finding Co-ops*, but since it was published in 1984, much of its information is out of date.

---

**Action**      *Grow Your Own\**
**52**

Growing your own food, while not a solution for everyone, is one way to eat organic products that are environmentally sound and untainted by social injustice.

The suburbs have the ideal ratio between humans and land for permaculture, a land-use system designed to feed a family on a small plot of land while protecting the environment. *Amateur gardeners can routinely produce four to six times the yield per square foot of professional farmers because of the close attention they can give their plants.* Your backyard just may be America's future breadbasket.

Today *53 percent of the households in the United States garden. Using only about six hundred square feet on the average, they produce 18 percent of the food in this country.*

As a social institution, the lawn originated as a petty imitation of the grand parks of the landed English gentry. To own a bit of park was to be a little bit noble. Food was not produced on the lawn, for that implied an embarrassing need to provide for oneself.

*Today, in the United States, there are thirty million acres of lawn—a patch of grass equivalent in area to the state of Indiana. This amounts to about one twelfth the area of all U.S. farmland.* Almost all these lawns are watered, and they consume significant amounts of other agricultural materials. For example, the phosphate used on American lawns each year is equal to about one third of that used to grow food for the population of India.

Why not redesign these lawns as small farms? Since they are irrigated, we should be able to at least double the national yield if edible crops were planted. Thus, we could produce 100 percent of the American food supply, with ample capacity for

\*Excerpted with permission from *Whole Life* magazine, March 1984.

raising small animals like rabbits and poultry (including their eggs) at most suburban and rural homes.

## WHAT YOU CAN DO:

Turn your lawn into a breadbasket—grow your own food.

For detailed information, contact Rodale Press, 33 East Minor Street, Emmaus, PA 18098; (215) 967-5171. Of special interest is *Organic Gardening* magazine, twelve issues, $13.97. They also publish a number of books, including *How to Grow Vegetables Organically,* $21.95; *High Yield Gardening,* $24.95; *Greenhouse Gardening,* $16.95; and *The 60-Minute Garden,* $24.95. Also see Actions 40 to 42 on pesticide-free gardening and organic gardening supplies.

---

**Action 53**   *Cooperative or Community Gardens\**

Whether you live in the city or country, cooperative gardening is an enjoyable and effective way to provide the hungry with food while building a community and empowering yourself and others. You can start almost anywhere; on the grounds of a church, in a friend's backyard, an abandoned lot, or on land contributed by local officials.

Some cities set aside land for community gardens. Utility companies may make power-line rights-of-way available. Senior citizens' centers, youth clubs, and schools also have potential garden sites.

Some gardens are subdivided into separate plots that are planted, tended, and harvested by individuals and families. Others encourage members to work cooperatively and send produce to needy families, a local soup kitchen, or a food bank. One church terraced the hill behind its building and provided more than one thousand pounds of greens a year for a downtown soup kitchen. Another alternative is to sell the food on Saturday mornings and use the proceeds to feed hungry people.

A group of churches in Waco, Texas, gardens cooperatively.

---

\* Excerpted with permission from "Hunger Action Handbook," *Seeds* magazine; see page 146 for ordering information.

Each church concentrates on growing one vegetable; one grows potatoes, another beans, and another tomatoes. With this focus on a specialty, each church provides larger quantities of food.

Be clear about who bears responsibility for the garden: the church committee, a gardening club at the senior citizens center, or an independent organization. Decisions to be made include choosing a garden site, what will be done with the produce, what sort of participation is expected, and who will take on tasks such as hauling the produce to the food bank. Decide whether plots will be assigned to individuals and families or whether the whole garden will be a cooperative venture. Consider cooperative purchasing of seeds, tools, fertilizer, lime, and gardening books. The garden may be hand dug, or a rototiller can be rented. Your local county agricultural extension service will probably be able to give advice and practical help even if you live in a city.

### WHAT YOU CAN DO:

Join a community gardening effort already under way in your neighborhood (they're usually easy to spot), or put together a group of your own and contact the American Community Gardening Association, (213) 744-4341, for details on how to get started. The association publishes a quarterly called *Journal of Community Gardening*.

---

Action
54
## The Seikatsu Club
## A Look into the Future

The Seikatsu Club is a Japanese cooperative, or buying club on a grand scale. With over 300,000 members it's founded on the principles of protecting the environment, the empowerment of women, improving conditions for workers, political activism, quality and simplicity, and the elimination of both nuclear weapons and nuclear power.

A full-time staff of more than seven hundred people manages the orders, delivery, accounting, and warehousing of over four hundred different food products. Each product is available only in one size and one type. By limiting variety and increasing the volume on each item, the club is able to make special demands on producers—such as the elimination of all chemicals and preservatives. The club will not sell products such as salad dressing because it believes that members should be creative enough to make their own.

Products with adverse environmental or health effects are strictly avoided. Members would rather assist farmers with harvesting produce than have chemical fertilizers used in the growing process. Club members subsidize the cost of products with their own labor—and at the same time establish a strong bond with the producer. When the club is unable to find products that meet its standards, it starts its own production enterprises to meet the members' demands.

Club members are predominantly housewives, many of whom have now gone into politics under the slogan *Political Reform from the Kitchen*. As a political force they have succeeded in banning synthetic detergents from supermarket shelves and are engaged in banning other unsafe products, stimulating local recycling projects, and developing plans for renewable energy use.

When the Seikatsu Club suspected that fallout from the Chernobyl nuclear accident had drifted over Japan, it commissioned a major electronics firm to manufacture small, highly sensitive Geiger counters for its members. These members then went out into the farmers' fields to check crops for radioactivity. Finding widespread contamination of the green tea crop, they then proceeded to harvest the crop and package it with a special label announcing that this tea was radioactive and had been contaminated by Chernobyl. The sole purpose of this exercise was to build consumer awareness about the dangers of nuclear energy.

The club has also been active outside the areas of politics and agriculture, having started its own not-for-profit insurance company, the Mutual Benefit Fund, which provides members with monetary assistance in the event of accident or illness. The Seikatsu Club is a truly democratic organization and "empowers each and every member with a voice and role in participatory politics."

The Seikatsu Club is eager to work with other local, national, and international groups that share its concerns. It is also willing to assist others in starting their own buying clubs.

## WHAT YOU CAN DO:

For more information, write the Seikatsu Club Consumers Cooperative, 2-26-17, Miyasaka, Setagaya-Ku, Tokyo, Japan, or call (03) 706-0031.

# 11

# The Business of Food

---

## *Be a Supermarket Activist*

### *WHAT YOU CAN DO:*

Next time you visit the supermarket make the following suggestions to the manager:

1. Ask that sugared cereals be placed on high shelves, out of reach of children.

2. Do the same with cookies and candy.

3. Ask that more shelf space be devoted to natural, salt- and sugar-free food.

4. Say that you're interested in local, especially organic, produce, and that you'd like to see it displayed in the produce section.

5. Ask that in-season fruits and vegetables be specially noted.

6. Request that foreign produce be labeled so that consumers are aware of the food's origins.

7. Ask that all prepackaged fruits and vegetables be phased out of the produce section.

**8.** Suggest that paper bags rather than plastic ones be available in the produce section.

**9.** Recommend that bulk buying of grains, pasta, and other dried foods be available.

If the above sounds too difficult, pick only one suggestion and start with the assistant manager!

---

Action
56
*Socially Responsible Food*

Now you can shop for a better world with an easy-to-use guide that rates 1,300 brand-name products.

How can you tell that the company that makes Grey Poupon mustard does business in South Africa, that Jiffy-Pop's parent corporation tests products on animals, or that the makers of Jell-O have a consistently poor record for polluting the environment? *Shopping for a Better World,* published by the Council on Economic Priorities, will direct you to products made by companies that give generously to charities, promote equal opportunity employment, support their communities, and work to keep the environment clean, while helping us avoid munching on foods that put money in the pockets of major defense contractors, supporters of nuclear power, and those who unnecessarily test products on animals.

The guide covers 1,300 brand-name products, all of which are rated according to ten social issues.

**WHAT YOU CAN DO:**

Order a copy of *Shopping for a Better World* from the Council on Economic Priorities, 30 Irving Place, New York, NY 10003; or call (800) U-CAN-HELP, or (212) 420-1133. It costs only $4.95 and fits into your pocket!

Action          *Stopping the Spread of*
57                 *Food Irradiation\**

Food irradiation is the nuclear industry's latest solution to
the nuclear waste disposal problem.

## What Is Food Irradiation?

On April 18, 1986, the federal Food and Drug Administration (FDA) adopted a regulation allowing the sale of irradiated
fruits, vegetables, and meats to the general public. The FDA
claims food irradiation will help prevent food spoilage, solve post-
harvest infestation, and control bacterial growth.

Food irradiation is a preservative process that uses the radioactive isotopes cobalt-60 or cesium-137 from *nuclear waste.*
These isotopes emit gamma rays, which pass through the food.
As they do, electrons are ripped from the individual atoms, cell
division is disrupted, and the ripening process slows down. If
the radiation is at high enough levels, bacteria and even viruses
can be destroyed. Ionizing radiation can also kill organisms or
destroy their genetic material. The FDA allows radiation ab-
sorbed doses (rads) of up to 100,000 for fruits and vegetables.
Spices can be irradiated at levels of up to 3,000,000 rads. At the
levels currently allowed by the FDA, the food itself does not
become radioactive.

## What Are the Risks and Dangers to People?

1. The process of food irradiation causes chemical changes in
   food, leading to the formation of "radiolytic products." These
   include formaldehyde, peroxide, and others still unknown.

2. Aflatoxins—potent, cancer-causing chemicals created by fungi
   that occur naturally in some foods—have a tendency to grow
   more abundantly on foods after they have been irradiated.

3. Some laboratory tests done on animals fed irradiated food
   show significant increases in the incidence of birth defects,

---

*Excerpted from the "Food Irradiation Fact Sheet," by NYPIRG, and the *Workbook*, Vol.
13, No. 2.

kidney disease, reduced life span, and loss of fertility. In one study, children and animals fed freshly irradiated wheat developed "polyploidy," an abnormality that causes the cells in the body to develop more than the normal set of chromosomes.

4. Gamma radiation, depending on the dose, depletes or destroys essential nutrients in foods, including vitamins A, C, E, and especially B, nucleic acids, and enzymes.

5. Most microorganisms that cause decomposing food to smell bad would be destroyed by the irradiation process. Irradiation could make food appear fresh that is in fact contaminated.

6. While some irradiated fruits and vegetables might have a longer shelf life, studies have shown that they are more likely to lose their taste, their fresh smell, and general appeal.

## What About the Environment?

The U.S. Department of Energy envisions the construction of more than one thousand radiation plants over the next ten years. Large-scale food irradiation will cause a quantum leap in the amount of nuclear waste transported on highways and located near large urban centers. If a major explosion, a fire, or sabotage were to occur at a single large commercial food irradiation plant, the potential damage would be roughly comparable to the estimates for the long-term health effects and premature deaths from cancer forecast over the next seventy years as a result of the Chernobyl accident. Indeed, the possibility of a severe accident in these facilities may be far greater than in reactors; irradiation plants are far less restrictively designed, constructed, safeguarded, or regulated than are nuclear power plants.

Cesium-137 has a thirty-year half-life; regulators assign it a hazardous life ten to twenty times longer; with an estimated three hundred to six hundred years needed until it decays to what they consider to be "innocuous levels." Therefore, the true damage from an nuclear accident must be calculated for centuries in terms of the uptake of radioactive cesium by growing plants, its concentration in the food chain (e.g., in meat from animals consuming contaminated grass or water), and ultimately its ingestion by human beings.

## WHAT YOU CAN DO:

Treated with Radiation

Environmental Protection Agency

**1.** Don't be misled by the confusing symbols!

Avoid the purchase of all irradiated foods and let your supermarket manager know you'd prefer he didn't carry any irradiated products.

**2.** Write letters to your congressional representatives to support legislation that opposes food irradiation. For information on legislation that needs your help, see the publications listed in Actions 19 and 43.

**3.** Contact NYPIRG's (New York Public Interest Research Group) Food Irradiation Project, 9 Murray Street, New York, NY 10007; (212) 349-6460, for more information.

---

**Action 58**          *Eat Brown Eggs\**

Protect the diversity of species and fight reduction of the gene pool at breakfast!

One hundred species disappear from the planet every day of every year. This reduction in the number of species shrinks the world's genetic pool. Since diversity is a requisite of survival, this is a sad and dangerous trend.

One example of this problem is that while there are hundreds of species of chickens, 95 percent of people in the United States eat eggs from only one kind. If that particular strain of bird were attacked by a disease to which it had no resistance, we would be out of eggs overnight. And since all egg-laying chickens are raised by just nine large chicken producers, the chances of such

*Excerpted with permission from "Activism in Everyday Life," Marty Teitel, *UTNE Reader*, March-April 1988.

a catastrophe are real: All our eggs are literally in one (genetic) basket.

If you're a passionate or even occasional egg lover there's no reason to quit your job and launch a twenty-four-hour-a-day vigil outside the nearest chicken farm. The problem of a declining egg gene pool can be addressed simply by buying brown eggs. Inside their shells, white and brown eggs are the same—the only difference is in the packaging. If a fair number of people were to make just one small adjustment in their lives and buy brown eggs, they could drastically alter the gene pool. Since the White Leghorn hens that produce most of our eggs cannot lay anything but white eggs, buying brown eggs will create a new market that justifies farmers raising another breed to produce brown eggs. Then at least we would have two major breeds of chickens producing eggs in this country instead of one. It wouldn't make a huge change in the gene pool or in the world, but wouldn't you rather sail on a ship with two lifeboats instead of one?

## WHAT YOU CAN DO:

Eat brown eggs (packaged in cardboard, not Styrofoam)— preferably from a farmers' market, your local food co-op, or a natural food store.

# 12

# Helping the Hungry

| Action | *Taking the First Step* |
|---|---|
| 59 | **Feeding the Hungry in Your Community\*** |

*Getting Started:* Working to end hunger and learning to play a musical instrument have one thing in common: It's hard to get started. In both cases we need discipline—a deliberate effort to turn old habits and patterns into new ones. Once we're in the habit of seeing the needs of poor and hungry people and responding to those needs, we usually find more and better ways to be helpful. Just increasing our awareness of the problem can lead to guilt and paralysis. *Acting* on our concern—playing the instrument even though our first attempts are more painful than pleasant—moves us from guilt to responsibility. Habits of active compassion have to be deliberately established.

Musicians set up routine disciplines more easily when others around them are doing the same. Likewise, we will be more effective when surrounded with the support and example of others who share our concerns and are acting on them. We don't need to find a hundred committed people before we begin, but we do need a few.

*Excerpted with permission from the "Hunger Action Handbook," © *Seeds* magazine 1987.

We don't have to be child prodigies to play the piano. Nor do we have to be a saint like Mother Teresa or Dorothy Day to help the hungry. People fighting hunger are just plain folks. Trace the roots of almost any hunger group and you'll find a single, ordinary person with a passionate concern that sparked the compassion of others.

*Selecting an Action:* Hunger is being fought on many fronts—from short-term solutions, helping provide a hot meal to someone who doesn't know where their next meal is coming from, to medium-term solutions, organizing to open a soup kitchen or doing food stamp outreach, to long-term solutions, supporting legislation, creating jobs and building low-income housing. Though it might sound a bit overwhelming at first, the following list describes some simple actions that make it easy to get started. Once you find an action that appeals to you, the next step is to hook up with a local hunger group that needs your help.

## WHAT YOU CAN DO:

1. Volunteer two to three hours a week in a soup kitchen serving and cooking food.

2. Volunteer to pick up donated food.

3. Offer the use of your car or van to those working in a soup kitchen to assist with food deliveries.

4. Donate kitchen equipment: Coffeemakers, cutting boards, pots and pans, and utensils are often welcome.

5. Donate food (see Action 61, Food Banks).

6. Offer to help out in an office, answering phones, writing letters, or raising funds.

7. If you have special skills, such as in public relations, computer operations, grant writing, or warehouse management, you might be able to provide a group with technical assistance.

8. If you're interested in writing letters, supporting legislation, or meeting with local politicians, see Action 64.

9. If you're in printing, restaurant management, advertising, or transportation, your business can probably help you play an important role too.

*Taking the Next Step:* Now you're ready to pick up the phone
and get a list of the local hunger groups in your area. Start by
calling your church or synagogue, the mayor's office, or check
the Yellow Pages under "Social Service Agencies." If you don't
have any luck, there are many national organizations that will
be happy to help you locate a local group. Some of them include:

National Student Campaign Against Hunger
29 Temple Place, Boston, MA 02111
(617) 292-4823

Network of student hunger activists organized through Public Interest Research Groups (PIRG) in twenty states. Promotes a major event each semester, assists students starting
hunger groups, and serves as a clearinghouse for new project ideas and activities of local groups.

The Salvation Army
799 Bloomfield Avenue, Verona, NJ 07044
(201) 239-0606

Local offices in communities across the country provide direct assistance to poor and hungry people. Can advise groups
on ways to organize effectively.

Seeds
222 East Lake Drive, Decatur, GA 30030
(404) 378-3566

Magazine contains background information on domestic and
international hunger and poverty and what individual groups
are doing to help.

World Hunger Year
261 West 35th Street, Room 1402, New York, NY 10001
(212) 629-8850

Dedicated to the reality that "every year is world hunger
year until hunger is ended." Publishes *Food Monitor*, a bimonthly magazine on hunger and *Hungerline Reports*.

or contact these denominational hunger programs:

American Baptist Churches in the U.S.A.
Hunger Office, P.O. Box 851, Valley Forge, PA 19482-0851
(215) 768-2245

National Council of the Churches of Christ in the U.S.A.
Ecumenical Domestic Hunger Network
Division of Hunger and Poverty
475 Riverside Drive, Room 572, New York, NY 10115
(212) 870-2307

The Episcopal Church
Episcopal Hunger Office
815 Second Avenue, New York, NY 10017
(212) 867-8400; ext. 451

The Evangelical Lutheran Church in America
Lutheran Hunger Program
8765 West Higgins Road, Chicago, IL 60631
(312) 380-2700

The Presbyterian Hunger Program
100 Witherspoon, Louisville, KY 40202-1396
(502) 569-5000

Religious Society of Friends (Quakers)
American Friends Service Committee
1501 Cherry Street, Philadelphia, PA 19102
(215) 241-7000

United Church of Christ
Hunger Action Office
475 Riverside Drive, 16th Floor, New York, NY 10115
(212) 870-2951

Let the group know that you want to help and tell them a bit about what you might like to do, or feel free to ask them for suggestions. Let them know the amount of time you're willing to invest and what, if any, resources you're willing to contribute.

---

**Action 60**     *Starting Your Own Hunger Group*

Admittedly this involves making a major commitment. And obviously it's no small undertaking—but it's not as difficult as you might think. These activities are some of the best ones to begin with:

—Starting a Food Pantry

—Starting a Soup Kitchen

—Opening a Shelter

—Doing a Food Stamp Outreach

—Holding a Hunger Walk

—Surveying the Needs of the Poor in Your Community

## WHAT YOU CAN DO:

Order a copy of Seeds' *Hunger Action Handbook—What You Can Do and How to Do It*. It's available for $9.15 from Seeds, 222 East Lake Drive, Decatur, GA 30030. This outstanding handbook will provide you with both the knowledge and inspiration to get started.

Seeds is a ten-year old nonprofit organization that also publishes a magazine by the same name that covers the struggle to end hunger. The magazine is filled with moving stories, domestic and international analyses, plus profiles, news updates, and book reviews; six issues—$16. Write to the above address.

---

**Action
61**

## *Food Banks*
## A Second Harvest for the Hungry*

When the Parker Meridien Hotel in New York City offered Helen Palit a two-ton chocolate Statue of Liberty left over from the bicentennial celebration, Ms. Palit knew exactly what to do.

She telephoned one of her co-workers to "come at midnight with a crowbar." Within hours, the chocolate was broken up and delivered to a drug-rehabilitation program for patients in the New York region who required large doses of sugar as part of their treatment.

*Reprinted by permission from the New York Times Company.

Ms. Palit is the founder and executive director of City Harvest, a nonprofit food bank that collects excess food and distributes it to soup kitchens, drug-rehabilitation centers, homeless shelters, and other programs for the hungry in New York.

While donations of giant chocolate statues are rare, for the first six years the agency's vans have picked up and distributed more than five thousand pounds a day of New York City's choicest leftovers to the hungry.

Much of the leftover food comes from upscale restaurants and their suppliers. But there are other sources as well: 50,000 bottles of orange juice from a failed orange juice enterprise; five hundred live chickens, left over from a commercial photography shoot; and one hundred boxed lunches from a brokerage firm luncheon that was canceled.

"The United States Department of Agriculture estimates that twenty percent of all food produced in the United States is wasted," Ms. Palit said. "There is enough food in this city to feed every hungry person, it is just a matter of logistics."

Local food banks are connected nationally by an organization named Second Harvest. Second Harvest has taken the cause of the hungry one step further. It has convinced the nation's largest food manufacturers and supermarket chains to contribute their surplus stock, production overruns, and mislabeled merchandise to its national distribution system. At a retail value of over $700 million in 1987, Second Harvest's food-collection efforts make it the nation's largest nongovernmental food service program for the hungry.

With a network of 87 local food banks and 118 affiliates, food is distributed to over 38,000 charitable agencies. Second Harvest makes good business sense, for the food industry as well as its supporters. Every dollar it spends or receives as a contribution enables it to distribute $157 worth of food.

## WHAT YOU CAN DO:

Your local food bank needs your help. To locate the food bank nearest you, call or write Second Harvest, 116 South Michigan Avenue, Suite 4, Chicago, IL 60603; (312) 263-2303. Consider volunteering in the warehouse, sorting contributed food, assisting with pickups or deliveries, and, of course, donating food yourself.

Action          ***Help Feed the Hungry***
  62          ***Every Time You Go Out to***
                          ***Eat***

Share Our Strength (SOS) is a non-profit organization of chefs and restaurateurs who have banded together to dedicate themselves to fighting hunger. Those who spend their days working diligently to feed the often not so hungry and frequently overfed have now taken a stand for those truly in need. *USA Today* called SOS "The Most Civilized Food Fight in History."

## WHAT YOU CAN DO:

Support restaurants that display the SOS logo, and participate in special fund-raising events. Contact SOS for a free list of its member restaurants at 733 15th Street, N.W., Suite 700, Washington, DC 20005, or call toll-free (800) 222-1767, or in DC, call (202) 393-2925. When you eat at an SOS restaurant make sure you let the chef or manager know the reason for your patronage. Bold customers can also assist by encouraging non-members to call the SOS office to find out about joining as well as participating in SOS's Fight Food Waste program that provides local food banks with surplus food.

## *Ending Hunger Around the World*

There are many organizations working to end hunger around the world. Most of them are doing good work and deserve your support, but are simply too numerous to be listed here. Many of them offer volunteer opportunities if you're willing to commit an extended period of time and are able to travel outside the country. *Seeds* magazine publishes a special *Volunteer Opportunities* guide for $2.50 (see Action 59 for the mailing address).

While in general we have avoided focusing on actions that involve contributing money, the options for eliminating hunger outside the United States are limited. The Freedom from Hunger Foundation, discussed in the next action, presents us with a unique opportunity to play a somewhat more active role.

---

**Action 63**       *Freedom from Hunger*

Feed a man a fish and he'll eat for a day. Teach him to fish and he'll eat for a lifetime.

This Chinese proverb expresses the philosophy of the Freedom from Hunger Foundation (FFH). FFH is conducting a worldwide effort through self-help programs that enable families to eliminate the causes of hunger, chronic malnutrition, and death among their children.

Instead of providing food to hungry people, the Freedom from Hunger Foundation offers a helping hand—not a handout—through comprehensive training programs and self-help projects, which include:

—assisting mothers improve nutrition and hygiene to reduce the death rate among their children;

—showing farmers new ways to improve crop yields so that more food will be available for their families;

—teaching village health workers about community sanitation and water purification to help prevent sickness and death;

—making seeds and the know-how to grow productive home gardens available to families; and

—helping people, through revolving loan funds, obtain start-up money needed for income-producing activities in agriculture or small business.

Freedom from Hunger has a unique "gift catalog" that allows you to provide a very specific, and in fact longlasting, form of assistance. The gifts listed below can be targeted to any of the following countries:

Freedom from Hunger has a unique "gift catalog" that allows you to provide a very specific, and in fact longlasting, form of assistance. The gifts listed below can be targeted to any of the following countries:

| AFRICA | ASIA | LATIN AMERICA |
|---|---|---|
| Togo | Nepal | Honduras |
| Sierra Leone | Thailand–Khorat | Bolivia |
| Mali | Thailand–Lampang | Ecuador–Esmeraldas |
| Ghana | | Ecuador–Santa Elena |
| Kenya–Embu | | Antigua |
| Kenya–Siaya | | |

**1.** *Watermelon seeds to produce food and income*
Watermelons are a great income-producing crop for poor families in Latin America. The melons are also full of vitamins and minerals —ideal nourishment for hungry children.
NEEDED:—$32 to provide enough seeds for one acre

**2.** *Bicycles for health workers*
In Africa, Freedom from Hunger community health workers need bicycles to bring lifesaving health care and nutrition information to remote villages and settlements. These bikes make it possible for health workers to reach many more people.
NEEDED:—$200 for one sturdy trail bicycle

**3.** *Little chicks for poultry raising*
Poor families find poultry production a great and continual source of good food. Eggs provide the protein and calories their children need to grow up healthy and strong. Mature birds can be sold for income or used for food.
NEEDED:—$25 to provide enough chicks for two families

**4.** *Grain silos to protect food supplies*
Families in Latin America need a safe, dry place to store grains. In this way they'll have a food source for the entire year. Metal grain silos keep rodents out of their food supplies and reduce insect infestation and spoilage.

NEEDED:—$60 to build one small silo for a single family
   —$75 to build a large silo shared by extended families

**5.** *Clean water for a needy family*

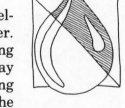

Much of the disease and suffering in developing nations is related to contaminated water. People often spend hours every day just getting water for their families. That's time taken away from growing food, earning a living, and caring for their children. You can help a family get the clean, safe water it needs to live a healthy, productive life.

NEEDED:—$10 for one ten-gallon water filtration tank
   —$30 for one 260-gallon tank to store clean rainwater
   —$48 to help teach parents how to free their families of water-related diseases

**6.** *Rabbits and fish for nutritious food*

Hunger and malnutrition can sometimes be overcome with gifts as simple as rabbits and fish. Families can be taught to raise them for food and to sell them for income. Through these sources of high protein, their children can become strong and healthy and better able to fight off the diseases that are killing so many of them.

NEEDED:—$37.25 to provide three rabbits and a rabbit hutch
   —$62.50 to provide 500 fingerlings for a family fishpond

## WHAT YOU CAN DO:

Mail your check to Freedom from Hunger Foundation, P.O. Box 2000, Davis, CA 95617-9982. If you wish, you can specify the gift and country. Donations of any size are welcome and all contributions are tax-deductible.

# 13

# The Politics of Hunger and the Future of Food

---

**Action
64**  **Getting Results**

Sam Harris gets results every day. His organization of volunteers, spread out across the nation and in four other countries, is a vital link to the passage of legislation in Washington that is helping to end hunger.

Not unlike the Miami music teacher he used to be, Sam Harris, thirty-eight, wearing his dark blue tie, paces back and forth in front of the twenty-one unusually attentive Washington, D.C., residents who have come to hear him speak about RESULTS, the "citizens' lobby on hunger" he founded and directs (for something like ninety hours every week).

It's a hot June evening, and people are still straggling in. They're meeting in the basement of a church that could be anywhere: fake wood on the walls, faded rug on the floor. But it's two and a half blocks from the U.S. Capitol Building. Like Harris's blue tie, the site was chosen to make a point.

Sam Harris smiles. "My first purpose," he tells the assembled health professionals, lawyers, secretaries, activists, and city administrators (who include two representatives from the mayor's office), "is to inspire you about the impact you can have working with others to create the political will to end hunger."

RESULTS is a nine-year-old, international grass-roots organization dedicated to generating a commitment from our political leaders to end world hunger. In the process, RESULTS teaches us all that we can and do make a difference and, if determined, we will have a profound impact.

Members of local groups, such as the Washington, D.C., gathering described above, meet to study the issues, learn how to speak effectively with local elected officials, participate in educational discussions via telephone conference calls (with experts like the executive director of UNICEF), and work tirelessly with the media in seeking coverage of vital legislative initiatives.

*The Results:* In 1985, a two-year-old funding squabble between the United States and OPEC (Organization of the Petroleum Exporting Countries) jeopardized the work by the International Fund for Agricultural Development (IFAD) to increase food production and income among small landholders and the landless poor in the Third World. After RESULTS volunteers initiated editorials in forty-six newspapers supporting continued funding and after the agreement was reached, Idriss Jazairy, president of IFAD, said: "The fact that the United States was prepared in the end to join in a consensus which allowed the negotiations to come to a successful close was very much related to the efforts of RESULTS."

—In 1986, RESULTS volunteers were responsible for more than ninety editorials supporting increased funding for immunizing the world's children by 1990. James Grant, executive director of UNICEF, wrote RESULTS at the beginning of 1987: "I want to convey my heartfelt thanks for the unflagging and satisfying successful efforts of RESULTS on behalf of vulnerable children and mothers everywhere."

—During 1987, RESULTS volunteers played a key role in the passage of legislation that mandated that $50 million be set aside for microenterprise loans to the poorest people (see Actions 83–86). During the campaign for this bill, volunteers initiated more than one hundred editorials and hundreds of letters to the editor. Representative Edward Feighan, one of the two House leaders proposing legislation, said in an article in the *Christian Science Monitor* (1988): "I attribute the success of the 'Self Sufficiency for the Poor' Act almost exclusively to RESULTS. They generated over one hundred editorials throughout the country in support of the bill that did not have high visibility on its own. That was a remarkable effort."

—In 1988, RESULTS' main legislative focus was the Global Poverty Reduction Act. This act directs the president to consult with other countries and groups that work with the poor to establish a plan for U.S. foreign development assistance to contribute measurably to eliminating the worst aspects of absolute poverty by the year 2000. Though the act did not pass in 1988, RESULTS volunteers generated more than 220 congressional co-sponsors and editorial support in more than sixty newspapers. An article in the *Christian Science Monitor* said: "Elegant in its simplicity, the bill cuts through decades of confusion and focuses on the core of the problem." The bill was reintroduced in January 1989.

Participation in RESULTS does require a significant time commitment —even a certain amount of discipline. "We're trying to shift the model," says Harris, "from traditional Washington-based lobbying to a model that says, 'If you bring the right structure and a sense of genuine empowerment to Denver, Kansas City, wherever, you'll end up with the best lobbyists in the country—citizens acting responsibly in their hometowns."

"If we look around," says Harris, "we see that very few of the people we know spend any time communicating with their elected representatives about their concerns. Against the background of this silent indifference, the voices of committed citizens can make an enormous difference."

## WHAT YOU CAN DO:

If you'd like to help Sam Harris get results, contact RESULTS, 245 Second Street, N.E., Washington, DC 20002; (202) 543-9340.

Action
65
### *Bread for the World*
## Passing Legislation to End
## World Hunger

Bread for the World does *not* provide direct relief or development assistance. Rather, much like RESULTS, it works to persuade Congress and the administration to implement policies that deal with the root causes of hunger and poverty.

How does it do this?

Each year, the group conducts a letter-writing campaign in which thousands of letters are sent to senators and congresspeople about a specific piece of legislation. As of 1989, over fifty thousand individuals across the country respond to monthly "Action Alert" mailings advising them on legislation before Congress. Additional suggestions on other, effective actions are also included.

In addition to a letter-writing campaign, a "Quickline" network enables all members to flood congressional offices with telephone calls in rapid response to critical events in the legislative process.

In the last five years alone, this national movement of citizen advocates has achieved impressive results. Among its accomplishments:

—In 1983, long before the African food crisis received media attention, Bread for the World helped obtain a U.S. response to emerging famine conditions.

—In 1984, Bread for the World persuaded the U.S. Congress to establish the Child Survival Fund, which has saved the lives of millions of children worldwide.

—In 1986, Bread for the World members were instrumental in getting tax-reform legislation passed so that six million of America's lowest-income working families and individuals were relieved from the burden of unjust taxes.

—In 1987, Bread for the World played a key role in helping to pass legislation for a $73 million increase in funding for the women, infants, and children's food and nutrition program.

## *WHAT YOU CAN DO:*

Join Bread for the World in its fight to pass legislation to ensure that we feed the hungry as well as educate children about nutrition and provide Americans with jobs that pay adequate wages. Contact them at 802 Rhode Island Avenue, N.E., Washington, DC 20018; (202) 269-0200.

Bread for the World also has an excellent publications catalog of books, information on how to organize in your own community, plus easy tips on how to write effective letters, work with the media, and speak with your local elected officials. Request the catalog when you contact the organization.

# Additional Resources to Help End Hunger

---

**Action
66**                              *Food First*

Food First, also known as the Institute for Food and Development Policy Study, is a nonprofit research and education center dedicated to investigating and exposing the root causes of hunger. It was founded in 1975 by Frances Moore Lappé, author of the best-selling *Diet for a Small Planet,* and Dr. Joseph Collins. Food First research has documented how hunger is created by concentrated economic and political power, not by scarcity. Resources and decision making in the hands of a wealthy few deprive the majority of land, jobs, and therefore food.

Hailed by *The New York Times* as "one of the most established food think tanks in the country," the institute has profoundly shaped the debate about hunger and Third World development.

The institute is, however, more than a think tank. Through books, reports, school curricula, audiovisual materials, media appearances, and speaking engagements, Food First experts not only reveal the often hidden roots of hunger, they show the public how we can all get involved in bringing an end to the problem. Food First inspires action by highlighting the courageous efforts of people around the world who are creating farming and food systems that effectively feed the poor. As a member of Food First, you can join a worldwide network of people working for a world free of hunger and injustice.

Two books of note, *Diet for a Small Planet* (paperback, $3.95) and *Food First, Beyond the Myth of Scarcity* (paperback, $4.95), have literally provided the background and conceptual framework for much of the best work being done today on hunger issues. These books are essential reading for anyone who wants a deeper understanding of the problem.

Other publications include:

—*Betraying the National Interest: How U.S. Foreign Aid Threatens Global Security by Undermining the Economic Stability of the Third World,* paperback, $8.95

—*World Hunger: Twelve Myths,* upon which the introduction to this section of the book is based, paperback, $9.95

—*Action Alerts* on Brazil, Central America, Honduras, Nicaragua, South Africa, foreign aid, the debt crisis, and family farming are available for fifty cents each.

Food First provides a constant flow of information and ideas for action to ensure that you can play an effective role in the struggle to end hunger and fight injustice in the Third World.

## WHAT YOU CAN DO:

Become a member of Food First today. Send $25 to 145 Ninth Street, San Francisco, CA 94103; (415) 864-8555. You won't regret it! (Your membership fee is tax-deductible.)

---

**Action 67**          *World Hunger Year*

Founded in 1975 by singer-songwriter Harry Chapin and present World Hunger Year (WHY) director Bill Ayres, WHY informs the American people about domestic and international hunger and its causes. WHY also works in coalition with other groups to develop programs and policies that combat hunger in the world and in the U.S.A.

Current projects include:

—The Reinvesting in America Campaign: a two-year effort to help interconnect and publicize the heroic efforts of thousands of grass-roots groups concerned with hunger, poverty, homelessness, health care, jobs, agriculture, and the environment, and to find the most replicable and sustainable programs in each area

—The International Campaign Against Hunger, Poverty, and Injustice: an international effort to develop alternate policies for the Third World debt crisis, foreign aid, trade, and development models

—Hungerline: provides up-to-date information on hunger to the media, U.S. Congress, and hunger activists through monthly *Hungerline Reports* and a speakers' bureau

—*WHY*: World Hunger Year's internationally acclaimed quarterly magazine (formerly known as *Food Monitor*), which provides in-depth analysis of and practical information on hunger and poverty

Membership of $25 entitles you to a year's subscription to *WHY, Hungerline Reports,* and *WHY* brochures.

## WHAT YOU CAN DO:

Become a member or write for more information: World Hunger Year, 261 West 35th Street, Suite 1402, New York, NY 10001-1906; (212) 629-8850.

---

**Action 68**      *Other Organizations Working to Fight Hunger\**

The following is a select list of only a small number of the many organizations working to fight hunger:

*CROP*
c/o Church World Service
P.O. Box 968, Elkhart, IN 46515
(219) 264-3102
[For recorded activities update, call (800) 223-1310; in New York: (800) 535-2713]

*Excerpted from *New Age Journal,* March-April, 1988.

162                How to Make the World a Better Place

A division of the National Council of the Churches of Christ. Twenty-seven regional offices in the United States coordinate community involvement in hunger walks, fasts, and other events to help finance both soup kitchens and food pantries in this country and such international relief efforts as community gardening projects in Senegal and the distribution of food and blankets to flood victims in South Africa. Members receive regional newsletters three times a year, the CWS annual report, and quarterly updates.

## End World Hunger
1460 West McNab Road, Fort Lauderdale, FL 33309
(303) 977-9700

Runs the Liberty Food Gardens program, which supplies seeds, materials, tools, and technical advice to residents of public-housing projects so they can grow their own food. Clubs now exist in housing projects in South Florida, New Orleans, and Los Angeles, with others planned for Chicago, Washington, and Baltimore.

## Food for the Hungry
7729 East Greenway Road, Scottsdale, AZ 85260
(800) 2HUNGER; in Arizona: (602) 998-3100

Christian organization founded to combat hunger and famine internationally through a four-part program: (1) Hunger Corps volunteers receive two-year assignments in Peru, Bolivia, Thailand, and Ethiopia, and work on food distribution, health care, long-range development programs, and education projects; (2) Every-child Program sponsors pay $18 each month for a needy child's food, clothing, education, and medical care; (3) Hunger Helpers support emergency relief projects through monthly donations and receive the member newsletter; and (4) church programs provide local churches with fund-raising ideas and speakers on hunger-related topics.

## Food Research and Action Center
1319 F Street, N.W., Washington, DC 20004
(202) 393-5060

Nonprofit, nonpartisan center works with individuals, elected officials, religious groups, and civic leaders to improve federal food programs, to seek greater opportunities for low-income people, and to protect the rights of the poor. Grass-roots network of volunteers works on such projects as starting school breakfast programs and monitoring food-stamp violations. Publishes a monthly newsletter, *Foodlines*.

*Interfaith Hunger Appeal*
468 Park Avenue South, Room 904A, New York, NY 10016
(212) 689-8460

Hunger-awareness project, sponsored by Catholic Relief Services, Church World Services, Lutheran World Relief, and the American Jewish Joint Committee, conducts hunger and development programs in 109 countries, including the United States. Members of the IHA Hunger Watch lobby Congress, assist local food banks, and help their communities or corporations host a "lunchless lunch" (spending a lunch hour before an empty plate listening to a speaker discuss a hunger issue of local or international concern).

*National Student Campaign Against Hunger*
29 Temple Place, Boston, MA 02111
(617) 292-4823

Largest network of student hunger activists in the United States. Launched by the Public Interest Research Groups (PIRGs) in cooperation with USA for Africa. Works with colleges and high schools to sponsor programs that offer immediate relief to the hungry and homeless, as well as longer-term projects that address the root causes of hunger.

# Part 3

# SOCIALLY RESPONSIBLE BANKING AND INVESTMENT

*Putting your money to work on the world's problems*

# 15

# It's 9:00 P.M., Do You Know Where Your Money Is?*

Money carries the values of the person whose pocket it happens to be sitting in—for as long as it sits there. When a dollar passes out of your hand to purchase a product, acquire a service, make an investment, contribute to a worthy cause, or even to be parked briefly in your checking account—you are casting a vote. Casting a vote for a particular company or institution, the quality of its product or service, its management, the way it treats its employees, whether or not it chooses to protect the environment, accept government defense contracts, or purchase supplies from minority businesses.

There is a direct and tangible connection between every investment or financial transaction you make and the values that are promoted throughout the world. While we may not all own stocks and bonds, most of us have a checking account, some type of insurance, and perhaps an IRA. When you pay your premiums, deposit your paycheck, or purchase something with a credit card, you are selecting a temporary custodian of your money. The moment a dollar leaves your hand, it can be used to make the world a more dangerous place for generations to come or it can be invested in your dreams and hopes for the world your children will grow up in.

*Headline from a *Working Assets* advertisement

## *Your Local Bank*

Let's examine this a bit more closely, taking for example your local bank. Assuming that you deposit your paycheck on a Friday, by Tuesday or Wednesday you might have access to those funds. While the screen on the Automatic Teller Machine confirms that the money's in your account, and you might think that your hard-earned dollars are sitting safely in the bank's vault—this is far from the real story. Before the money is even available to you, your bank has collected the funds and put your paycheck to work. It may have loaned your money out to a local McDonald's franchise or to a real estate developer, purchased General Electric corporate bonds to help build "Star Wars" components, or financed the military purchases of a repressive Third World government—all without your knowledge or consent. While it's true that federal regulations and the bank's own need for cash might cause 15 percent of your paycheck to be kept on hand, the other 85 percent is usually hard at work within one day of your deposit.

If you don't know where your money is, what it's financing or who it's being loaned to, there's a very good chance some of it is being used to destroy the environment, build weapons, or put to some other use that would offend your values and ethics. But the moment it leaves your hands, you've effectively surrendered control and given up responsibility for it.

"Socially responsible investing" is a way to retain control over your money—even after it leaves your hands. It's a way to make sure that your money isn't used by someone else (a bank, insurance company, money or mutual fund, stockbroker, etc.) to do anything that conflicts with your own values. In fact, socially responsible investing even helps you channel funds to constructive ventures such as low-income housing, creating jobs for minorities, or providing food for the hungry.

## *Responsible Business or*
## *Social Purchasing*

This concept can be expanded to cover business management as well as product selection and purchasing. Certain companies have elected to operate with a responsible set of values and ethics that work in concert with their desired level of profitability. Values and profit are in fact not necessarily conflicting ideas, as we'll explore in the following section on responsible consumerism.

A growing number of companies are striving to protect the environment, encourage world peace, treat their workers fairly, and support the responsible development of their own communities. They make products we can purchase at the supermarket, drugstore, through the mail, or over the phone. When we buy from these companies, we support their values, their workers, our environment, and our own beliefs.

At the same time, of course, we can boycott corporations that are destroying our natural resources, discriminating against minorities, manufacturing weapons, and abandoning their own neighborhoods.

# 16

# Socially Responsible Banking —Financing Housing and Small Businesses

---

**Action
69**

*South Shore Bank*

Enjoy the service of a caring, well-run commercial bank that puts your money to work in Chicago's poorest neighborhoods building housing and financing small minority-owned businesses. You'll earn competitive interest income and are insured by the FDIC up to $100,000.

Describe your classic low-income neighborhood—high unemployment, abandoned and deteriorating housing, failing small businesses—and no one bank willing to make an investment in the community to try and turn the situation around. Money and resources moved out of these communities. Even projects that could be financed by using funds deposited by local residents appear too risky a proposition to be worth consideration. This was the South Shore area of Chicago in 1975, until a group of social entrepreneurs purchased the local bank and began to change the face of community development banking. Today the South Shore Bank has almost $100 million in loans outstanding to local residents, businesses, and community groups. Twenty-five percent of the local housing has been renovated; 250 small businesses have been financed, creating local jobs, expanding retail services and improving the area's physical appearance; $4.4 mil-

lion in student loans have been made to build a stronger and
better-educated community; and almost $2 million has been loaned
to local nonprofit agencies to assure that needed human services
will be provided to local residents. South Shore is a special bank,
committed to serving its community. Clearly, it has accom-
plished a feat no other bank ever has—the revitalization of a
neighborhood that everyone thought was beyond hope.

Beyond South Shore's social achievements, the bank has
also proved that community development banking is sound banking. With over $150 million in deposits, an astounding 18 per-
cent return on equity, loan losses that were one tenth the amount
of the other banks, and a net income of over $1.5 million, 1988
was yet another year that South Shore defied popular banking
wisdom.

Today the bank has reached out to other Chicago neighborhoods, and even to rural Arkansas as well to a number of other
United States cities through its consulting work. Wherever you
live around the country you can open an account at South Shore,
at no cost or risk, that will work to renew urban neighborhoods.
All funds you deposit in the bank are protected and insured by
the FDIC up to $100,000.

## WHAT YOU CAN DO:

Call South Shore Bank at (312) 288-1000, ext. 312, or (312)
288-7017; or write the bank at 71st and Jeffrey Boulevard, Chicago, IL 60649-2096. They'll send you an application to open up
a money market fund with or without checking privileges, a
certificate of deposit for the length of time you select, a special
rehabilitation CD, commercial, personal, or NOW checking, or
a straight savings account. They'll include with the application
all current interest rates.

---

**Action
70**  *Community Capital Bank*

Modeled on the South Shore Bank, the Community Capital
Bank in Brooklyn, New York, focuses on lending to developers
of low- and moderate-income housing, to small businesses that
provide quality employment to lower-income workers, and to
businesses that provide products and services that are beneficial

to the community, such as home health care. Community Capital is also FDIC insured, and its stock is publicly traded, so you can support its efforts as either a depositor or investor.

### WHAT YOU CAN DO:

Call the Community Capital Bank at (718) 768-9344 or write to them at P.O. Box 404920, Brooklyn, NY 11240, to receive information and application forms for NOW checking, savings accounts, money market accounts, CDs, and other banking services.

| Action 71 | Community Development Credit Unions (CDCUs) |
|---|---|

CDCUs are financial cooperatives that service and are owned by the residents of low-income communities. Their goal is to revitalize America's poorest neighborhoods.

Community Development Credit Unions have a banking philosophy similar to that of the South Shore Bank. Unlike traditional banks, credit unions are owned entirely by their depositors—they are financial cooperatives. CDCUs serve low-income neighborhoods. They recycle their members' insured savings for loans that promote neighborhood revitalization. They finance housing rehabilitation and acquisition, small and minority businesses, cooperatives, and lending for traditional family needs. Unlike a traditional bank that might invest only 10 percent or less of its deposits back into its local low-income neighborhood, a CDCU is likely to reinvest 80 percent or more.

CDCUs confront the Catch-22 of low-income borrowers who can't get loans because they lack a credit history—and can't build credit records because they can't get loans. CDCUs stem the flow of money that usually runs out of low-income areas to nonresident, wealthier owners of land, housing, retail stores, and large businesses. CDCUs empower local residents to take an ownership position in their own communities.

Most CDCUs offer federally insured deposits up to $100,000 and have not experienced the problems confronting the savings-and-loan industry. Rates paid on deposits vary by credit union, ranging from a low of three to four percent at poorer institutions to rates that are *higher* than those of commercial banks. Assets range in size from a few thousand dollars to over $50 million in the more than three hundred national CDCUs. These CDCUs serve upwards of a million people and have total combined assets of more than $500 million.

The National Federation of Community Development Credit Unions (NFCDCU) is the national membership association of credit unions serving predominately low-income communities. NFCDCU is a national clearinghouse for information on these special credit unions and publishes a quarterly newsletter that is available to individuals for $12 annually. Approximately one third of the three hundred CDCUs belong to NFCDCU.

## WHAT YOU CAN DO:

Find out about the CDCU nearest you, the CDCU movement in general, and how you can become involved and open up an account. Contact the National Federation of Community Development Credit Unions at 29 John Street, Room 903, New York, NY 10038; (212) 513-5191.

Action
72
## Community Development Loan Funds (CDLFs)

Poverty, despite popular misconceptions, results not so much from a lack of resources or capabilities as from the patterns of ownership of land, housing, businesses and financial institutions that drain the resources out of lower income communities.— *National Association of CDLFs*

Community Development Loan Funds (CDLFs) represent another approach to confronting the same problems that the South Shore Bank of Chicago and the Community Development Credit Unions seek to address. CDLFs are unique in both structure and mode of operation. They are designed quite specifically as vehicles for socially responsible investors to lend money indirectly to community land trusts, housing cooperatives, community development corporations, worker-owned/cooperative businesses, and other projects involving low-income individuals who would otherwise have no access to credit or capital. A CDLF is committed to building social and economic justice in a specific community by promoting the development of businesses and institutions that strengthen the economic base of that community.

A CDLF provides the social investor with the experience, contacts, expertise, and time needed to identify these investment opportunities, and then to manage and oversee the loans to community groups. It acts as an intermediary for the investor, and also provides the loan recipient with advice and technical assistance.

Lenders usually propose the terms of their loan within certain boundaries set by the CDLF; this is clearly a unique and original structure. Loans may range in size from $500 to $1 million, made for a few months or as long as twenty years. The funds are not insured, and all lenders usually have a claim on all of the funds' assets. In addition there is usually some endowment of a permanent capital, which provides an additional loan-loss reserve.

CDLFs are often "lenders of last resort," providing capital when no other financial institution will do so, or at least providing funds at rates that are affordable to the recipient. Often CDLF funds are able to leverage loans from other sources that are five to ten times greater than their own financial commitment. As of January 1989, no investor has ever lost a penny from a loan made to a CDLF.

Since 1979 the growth and development of revolving loan funds has been catalyzed by the work of Chuck Matthei and the Institute for Community Economics, founders of the National Association of Community Development Loan Funds (NACDLFs). Chuck and the institute have done some of the most important and inspiring work in the field of community economic development.

Currently the National Association of Community Development Loan Funds has forty active members and twenty-four associates. As of January 1989, NACDLF members were managing $50 million. These funds had over 1,100 loan recipients. Individual funds, many in the start-up phase, were growing at an average rate of 40 percent annually.

### WHAT YOU CAN DO:

To find out how to make a loan, receive additional information about Community Development Loan Funds, and obtain a listing of the individual funds nearest to you, contact the NACDLF, 151 Montague City Road, Greenfield, MA 01301; (413) 774-7956.

| Action | ***Community Land Trusts*** |
|--------|-----------------------------|
| **73** | ***(CLTs)*** |

A community land trust is a nonprofit corporation created to acquire and hold land for the benefit of a local community. Land trusts ensure the availability of housing for low- and moderate-income residents and also provide general access to and preservation of undeveloped land.

Take a low-income family living in the worst substandard housing and add up how much rent they will pay over their lifetime. Even at today's prices, unadjusted for inflation, over forty years they would pay ten to fifteen times the current market value of the housing they occupy. A middle- or upper-income person with a bank mortgage loan will pay only three or four times the market value of the home he or she owns (as a result of mortgage interest). That is what housing advocates describe as gross injustice! Community Land Trusts (CLTs) try to provide poor people with an alternative. There are currently more than sixty-five CLTs that have been set up around the nation, mostly in New England. Each owns about 100 to 150 units of housing.

Once formed, a typical CLT will purchase rundown homes in neighborhoods that appear destined for gentrification, commercialization, or other kinds of development. Volunteer work by CLT members brings the dwellings up to habitable standards. The dwelling will then be sold to a low-income applicant, but the deed to the land will be held by the trust. Often, the CLT will rent the home for a few months to the buyer, with the accumulated rental fees put toward a down payment. Unlike traditional buyers moving into the neighborhood, the CLT homeowner benefits little if prices begin to soar.

"The theory is that the owner gets back whatever he puts in, plus an adjustment for inflation during the period, but does not receive the added value that the community has given the home," says Chuck Matthei, director of the Institute for Community Economics. In that way, formerly distressed properties in now-rehabilitated neighborhoods can be kept for low- and middle-income people. Each CLT sets its own formula for maximum allowable income and family size to qualify for a home. Often consideration is given to people who already live in the neighborhood or who have recently been displaced from it.

The following principles usually guide the structure and operation of a Community Land Trust. A CLT:

—is a democratically structured nonprofit corporation with an open membership, created to hold land permanently for the benefit of a local community.

—provides access to land and housing at affordable rates, and maintains its affordability for future users.

—assures long-term security for those who occupy the land, a fair equity for their investment, and protection for future generations.

—gives communities greater control over their own long-term development.

—enables communities to preserve farmland, open space, and other natural resources through community ownership and careful land-use planning.

—allows the community as a whole, rather than special interests or absentee owners, to benefit from grass-roots development efforts and increases in land value.

—builds technical expertise and an economic base for community development.

—is *not* a utopian vision, but a *practical* model that is being successfully implemented in a growing number of urban and rural communities.

## *WHAT YOU CAN DO:*

Contact the Institute for Community Economics at (413) 774-7956, or write to them at 151 Montague City Road, Greenfield, MA 01301, for a list of CLTs, news on local and national meetings, technical literature on how to start a CLT, information on how to make a loan to a CLT, or to subscribe to their newsletter, *Community Economics*.

# 17

# Socially Responsible Investing

## Socially Responsible Money Market and Mutual Funds

The financial performance of socially responsible money market funds has been as good and often better than industry averages. These funds have shown that the avoidance of unethical corporations and the support of responsible businesses makes social as well as financial sense.

*Money Market Funds:* Most money market funds are likely to invest in business and government activities that conflict with your own social concerns and values. Whether it's Dow Chemical's destruction of the ozone, General Electric's nuclear-weapons production, or Scott Paper's assault on Indonesian rain forests, most funds own stocks in companies whose policies will offend almost anyone. The following money funds are screened so they do not invest in companies engaged in a variety of negative activities, and in some cases they are designed to pursue specifically positive social and economic goals.

Action               *The Calvert*
  74          *Social Investment*
            *Money Market Fund*

Started in 1982, the Calvert Fund grew from $36 million in in 1984 to $92.5 million as of January 1989. The fund *will not* invest in companies that are primarily involved in the production of nuclear energy or the manufacture of equipment to produce nuclear energy, in companies with business activities in South Africa, or corporations that manufacture weapons systems. The fund *seeks to invest in companies* that "enhance the human condition and the traditional American values of individual initiative, equality of opportunity, and cooperative effort." Specifically, they look for corporations that:

**1.** Deliver safe products and services.

**2.** Sustain the environment.

**3.** Negotiate fairly with workers.

**4.** Do not discriminate and provide opportunities for women and disadvantaged minorities.

**5.** Manage their business in a participatory style.

**6.** Show a commitment to human goals such as creativity, productivity, self-respect, and responsibility, both within and outside of the organization.

The fund views these standards as goals that few companies are able to satisfy fully. Calvert also recognizes the highly subjective element of judgment that goes into their own evaluations. While these criteria may sound lofty and a bit vague, it's highly commendable that Calvert has been willing to take such a value-oriented position, and—equally important—earn a respectable rate of return for the fund's investors.

## WHAT YOU CAN DO:

Call (800) 368-2748 for a prospectus or write to Calvert Fund, 1700 Pennsylvania Avenue, N.W., Washington, DC 20006. The minimum investment is $1,000. See Actions 79 and 80 for information about Calvert's mutual funds.

**Action
75**
## *Working Assets
Money Fund*

From 1985 to 1986, the Working Assets Money Fund, grew from $50 to $80 million. By January 1989, the fund had grown to over $136.6 million. About half of the assets are invested in government securities and commercial banks. Treasury bills are not purchased, since they finance defense spending. The types of government securities that are selected are student, home-owner, small business, and farm loans. Commercial bank loans focus on banks with a strong community involvement, like South Shore. The investment portfolio also includes alternative-energy companies, cooperatively owned businesses, child-care providers, and companies with an overall record for social responsibility. Companies are avoided if their principal business activity is weapons production, if they consistently harm the environment, have a substantial presence in a country dominated by a repressive regime, generate nuclear power, or manufacture nuclear equipment or materials.

### *WHAT YOU CAN DO:*

Call (800) 543-8800 for a prospectus, or (415) 989-3200 if you have additional questions, or write to Working Assets, 230 California Street, San Francisco, CA 94111. The minimum investment is $1,000. See Actions 87 and 88 for other Working Assets services.

## *Mutual Funds*

Mutual funds differ greatly in financial goals and investment strategies, unlike money market funds, which earn relatively similar rates of return. Mutual funds may be conservative or aggressive; they may invest in stocks, bonds, or a mixture of both. While all the funds described below are socially responsible in one way or another, make sure you review their prospectuses to understand their specific investment strategies. The reason to purchase a mutual fund rather than directly investing in stocks and bonds is the professional management of the fund

180 How to Make the World a Better Place

and the somewhat lower risk created by the fund since it buys a wide variety of stocks or bonds instead of only a few as you might do as an individual investor.

---

### Action 76 *New Alternatives Fund, Inc.*

New Alternatives, started in 1982, focuses on alternative-energy investments. A small fund, as of January 1989, it had $6.1 million under management. During 1986, when the average of all funds was up 15.9 percent, New Alternatives surpassed the industry with a healthy 22.27 percent growth rate. There are currently 850 shareholders.

New Alternatives has a unique approach to social responsibility, which it fulfills by investing in alternative energy, waste recovery, conservation, and environmentally oriented companies. While the fund makes financially conservative investments, including utilities generating energy hydroelectrically and geothermally, it also invests in new technologies such as solar cells and superconductivity. Additionally, its portfolio includes companies that make products like insulation, energy-conserving glass, and cogeneration plants.

The fund does not invest in companies doing business in South Africa, or that are involved in nuclear utilities, nor in weapons manufacturers or corporations building Star Wars components.

### WHAT YOU CAN DO:

Call (516) 466-0808 for a prospectus or write to New Alternatives Fund, 295 Northern Boulevard, Great Neck, NY 11021. The minimum investment is $2,650.

---

### Action 77 *The Parnassus Fund*

The Parnassus Fund was initiated in 1984, and as of January 1989, it had $11.3 million under management. While the focus of the fund's investment strategy is contrarian (investing in stocks that are out of favor with the financial community), it "also *prefers* to invest in companies that practice corporate responsibility." This rather weak statement is supported by the consideration of what it calls "Renaissance Factors," which cover some aspects of socially responsible investing but are *less* stringent than other funds. These "Renaissance Factors" are designed to help select "enlightened and progressive" corporate management. They include: (1) the quality of a company's products and services; (2) the degree to which a company is marketing-oriented and stays close to the customer; (3) the sensitivity of a company to the communities in which it operates; (4) the company's treatment of its employees; and (5) the company's ability to innovate and respond well to change.

The problem with this list of factors is that it uses only highly subjective variables. While The Parnassus Fund claims that these companies will have a positive social impact on the economy and society, it is not always clear how the "five factors" above, not all of which are applied to each company invested in, will ensure the social agenda the fund seems to aspire to. Of note is the fund's outstanding "post-crash" performance. During 1988 its average rate of return was *42.9 percent,* making it one of the top four performing mutual funds in the country out of the more than 1,500 funds followed by Lipper Analytical Services.

## WHAT YOU CAN DO:

Call (415) 362-3505 for a prospectus or write The Parnassus Fund, 244 California Street, San Francisco, CA 94111. The minimum investment is $2,000; additional investments must be at least $500.

---

**Action 78**        *Pax World Fund*

Started in 1971 by Methodist clergy, the firm had $73.6 million in assets as of December 30, 1988. From 1979 to 1988, the fund's average annual return was 13.11 percent. For the past five fiscal years the average fell to 11.07 percent.

Pax endeavors to make a contribution to world peace through investing in companies producing life-supportive goods and services. General criteria include non-war—related industries,* firms with fair-employment practices, and companies exercising reasonable pollution control. Pax avoids companies in the liquor, tobacco, and gambling businesses.

The fund invests in health care, education, food, retail, housing, renewable energy, and leisuretime businesses. It offers special programs, including Keogh plans, IRAs, IRA-SEP, and Section 403(b) plans.

### WHAT YOU CAN DO:

Call (603) 431-8022 for a prospectus or write to Pax World Fund, 224 State Street, Portsmouth, NH 03801. The minimum initial investment is $250, with subsequent investments of $50.

---

**Action 79**      *Calvert Social Investment— Managed Growth Portfolio*

This fund was started in 1982. As of January 1989, assets were $174 million. The fund "seeks to provide an economic return to its investors and an economic and social return to society that will contribute to the quality of life for all." (See the Calvert Social Investment Money Market Fund for a description of its social investment criteria, Action 74.)

The minimum investment is $1,000.

---

**Action 80**      *Calvert Social Investment Equity and Bond Portfolios*

These are Calvert's two newest socially oriented mutual funds. Both were started in late 1987 and have similar criteria to those of the Calvert Social Investment Money Market Fund. As of January 1989, the equity funds' assets stood at $2.4 million, substantially all of which are invested in the stock market, and the bond funds assets stood at $6.4 million, invested primarily in corporate bonds.

*Defined as companies on the U.S. Department of Defense's list of top one hundred contractors, or those companies that do more than 5 percent of gross sales volume with the Department of Defense.

## WHAT YOU CAN DO:

Call (800) 362-2748 for a prospectus. The minimum investment for each fund is $1,000.

---

Action
81

# Socially Responsible
# Investment Advisors and
# Newsletters

Guidance in selecting socially responsible investments that
support your values and meet your financial needs.

The socially responsible investment movement has spawned
a fairly large group of advisors who specialize in selecting investment opportunities that can meet both social and financial
goals. Each of the companies and individuals has a different fee
schedule, widely varying track records, and should be carefully
investigated before you select one.

The best way to proceed with the selection is to join The
Social Investment Forum, a national association of professional
financial advisors, brokers, managers, bankers, analysts, and
investors. The forum publishes a variety of information that will
help you begin the selection process, including *A Guide to Social
Investment Services,* which lists all of its professional members
and the services they provide as well as a quarterly newsletter
with updates on socially responsible investment trends.

It's significant that since around 1982, the total amount of
money invested in the United States with some type of social
screen grew from less than $500 million to more than $450 billion
by the end of 1988. This includes substantial funds controlled
by some of the nation's most respected colleges and universities,
pension funds, and insurance companies, as well as many funds
controlled by city and state governments.

## WHAT YOU CAN DO:

Become an individual member for only $35. For information
write to The Social Investment Forum, 711 Atlantic Avenue,
Boston, MA 02111; or call (617) 451-3252. Additional benefits
include seminars and national quarterly meetings.

And:

Subscribe to one or more of the newsletters that monitor the socially responsible investment industry, the social performance of American businesses, and strategies for managing your investments in a responsible manner. Some of the best of these publications include:

1. *Good Money: The Newsletter for Socially Concerned Investors*: Published bimonthly, it helps investors explore the relationship between corporate ethics, social responsibility, and the selection of investment opportunities with strong financial returns. Focus is on large, publicly traded corporations. *Good Money* also tracks its own list of socially responsible utilities and industrials against the Dow Jones average. Issue papers are available on investments for individuals concerned with abortion, animal rights, environmental pollution, labor unions, and women's issues. Highly recommended. Available for $75 annually from Good Money Publications, Inc., P.O. Box 363, Worcester, VT 05682; (800) 535-3551.

2. *Catalyst:* Published bimonthly, this newsletter focuses on alternative financial institutions, small businesses, nonprofit organizations, and other socially responsible investment opportunities not explored by many other publications. It also covers international investments, book reviews, and the basic how-tos of alternative investing. *Catalyst* provides an excellent way to stay in touch with small-scale grass-roots activities, from worker cooperatives and low-income housing to enterprises managed by women and Native Americans that are in the start-up phase and looking for capital. Available for $20 annually from Catalyst, 64 Main Street, 2nd Floor, Montpelier, VT 05602; (802) 223-7943.

3. *Clean Yield:* A monthly newsletter that focuses on publically traded companies and makes "buy, sell, or hold" recommendations based upon the companies' financial performance, future outlook, and socially responsible behavior. It also discusses major trends in the marketplace and the impact these trends are expected to have on the stock market. *Clean Yield* also publishes a model portfolio of recommended stocks. From March 1985 to December 1988, these stocks had outperformed the Standard & Poor 500 stock index by more than 100 percent! Available for $75 from Clean Yield, P.O. Box 1880, Greensboro Bend, VT 05842; (802) 533-7178.

4. *Investing for a Better World*: This Franklin Research Development Corporation newsletter focuses on specific topics such as "Women and Investing" and covers other general news related to the socially responsible investment industry. Available for $19.95 from Franklin Management, 711 Atlantic Avenue, 5th Floor, Boston, MA 02111; (617) 423-6655.

5. *Economics as If the Earth Really Mattered—A Catalyst Guide to Socially Conscious Investing,* by Susan Meeker-Lowry, is the best book on the subject. Available for $11.45 from New Society Publishers, P.O. Box 582, Santa Cruz, CA 95061.

---

**Action 82**   *Shareholder Activism\**

Shareholder resolutions utilize your ownership of stock in a corporation to encourage management to change unjust or destructive corporate policies and practices.

In 1971 the Episcopal Church boldly made business history when it filed the first church-sponsored shareholder resolution calling on General Motors to withdraw from South Africa. Twenty-six years later, in 1989, the corporate responsibility movement had grown to include other churches, public and private pension funds, and private citizens representing total investments of over $450 billion. The movement has clearly demonstrated its ability to make a tangible difference in corporate behavior.

The churches, together with conscientious people from across the United States, have convinced over eighty U.S. corporations to sell their South African assets and U.S. banks to stop loans to the apartheid government. They persuaded numerous corporations to publish equal employment opportunity reports, withdraw harmful and ineffective drugs from the market, change labor practices in Guatemala, and partially discontinue the marketing of dangerous infant formula in the Third World, to name but a few of their accomplishments.

Shareholder resolutions have addressed such issues as nuclear weapons production; Star Wars; affirmative action and equal employment opportunity; support of repressive govern-

---

\* Excerpted from the brochure of the Interfaith Center on Corporate Responsibility, New York, N.Y.

ments; capital flight and the world debt crisis; pharmaceutical marketing abuses; toxic waste, and nuclear and chemical plant safety. The Interfaith Center on Corporate Responsibility (ICCR) coordinates more than seventy-five stockholder resolutions each year.

## WHAT YOU CAN DO:

Read and vote on all corporate proxies you receive. To find out about other activities related to stocks you own, contact the Interfaith Center on Corporate Responsibility at (212) 870-2936, or write to them at 475 Riverside Drive, New York, NY 10115. Their newsletter, *The Corporate Examiner* (ten issues, $35), analyzes general issues and developments in the field. A package of proxy resolutions you might consider initiating is available for $7.

# 18

# Bootstrap Banking for Third World Entrepreneurs

With loans of $50 to $100, hundreds of thousands of the world's poorest people are starting businesses, feeding their families, and developing independence and self-esteem they could never have imagined possible. An incredible 97 percent of these loans are repaid in full and on time. From Bangladesh to El Salvador, microenterprise loans are eliminating poverty and challenging all of our assumptions about what the poor are capable of, if only given the chance.

In 1976 Muhammad Yunus, an economics professor, began an experiment. He decided he would try to lend money to the poorest people of his native Bangladesh. He would lend the money mostly to women, since he believed women's fierce determination to improve the lives of their children would make them better credit risks than men. He would lend money to women in a country where fewer than 5 percent of them were employed. The borrowers had to be poor, owning no more than a half acre of land. Still, that meant 50 percent of the country would qualify, since the average annual income is only $150. He would lend each person an average of only $67.

Today Muhammad Yunus is the founder of the Grameen Bank, which has over four hundred branches servicing more than eight thousand villages. The bank has made more than $54 million of loans to over 400,000 borrowers—75 percent of whom are women. There are no loan documents; in fact, borrowers need not even know how to read. Their signature alone satisfies any and all credit security. At the rate of $3 million a month in 1987, the Grameen Bank continued to maintain an average loan size of less than $100, with a repayment rate of 98 percent.

As a result of the bank's efforts, by 1986 the average family income of borrowers had increased at least 32 percent since they had first borrowed. Because of a forced savings program that requires borrowers to put aside three cents a week into a special account, those same borrowers (who now actually own 75 percent of the bank) had saved a total of $4.3 million.

The secret? The Grameen Bank uses a powerful alternative to collateral—the solidarity principle (what we would call peer pressure). To apply for a loan, fifty people of the same sex, in groups of five, must form a support group. They, together with bank personnel, evaluate the strength of each individual loan request. When agreement is reached on a request, two of the five group members receive their loans. After six weeks, if repayments have been made on schedule, the second two group members receive their money, and six weeks later, the last member of the group receives the loan.

The Grameen Bank was the beginning of what has become known as microenterprise development. To date, over a dozen other organizations have begun to offer similar loans. Here are some of the results:

—money that was previously available only from loan sharks at 10 to 20 percent interest *a day* is now available at 1 to 4 percent a month.

—a $30 loan to a small merchant can double a family's income in six months.

—$60 is enough to start over five hundred different types of small businesses.

—Santos Hernandez of El Salvador, at thirty-four, with four children, no husband, and who never attended school, moved out of her refugee camp with a $40 loan and went into business. With $35 she bought a tiny shack to live in, and with $5 she bought vegetables to resell in the local market. Out of her $2.40 profit she saved forty cents. She repaid her loan in six months.

There are at least 100,000 more stories, just as compelling as Santos Hernandez's, that prove beyond doubt that microenterprise development works!*

---

## Action 83  Accion International
## Creating Employment and Economic Opportunities in the Americas

Founded in 1961, ACCION is a private, nonprofit organization dedicated to promoting grass-roots economic development in the poorest urban and rural communities of the Americas. ACCION believes that even on the smallest scale owning one's own business can be a passport out of poverty and the establishment of economic self-sufficiency. Field staff are currently active in over a dozen countries in Latin America, the Caribbean, and the southwest United States.

Each year, ACCION facilitates short-term credit and basic business training for more than 16,000 tiny businesses, and through them it reaches nearly 100,000 people in the neediest communities in Latin America and the Caribbean.

With a small loan, business owners can take advantage of bulk purchasing, expand their markets, and operate more efficiently. Improved business skills translate into greater productivity, increased profits, and more savings for even the most marginal entrepreneurs. In turn, they provide much-needed goods and services for others in the community.

### WHAT YOU CAN DO:

To make a tax-deductible contribution, to find out about making a loan of your own, or to receive more information, call ACCION International at (617) 492-4930 or write to them at 1385 Cambridge Street, Cambridge, MA 02139.

---

*Sources include: *Multinational Monitor,* June 1988, p. 6; *INC.,* August 1987, pp. 70–72; *The Economist,* October 19, 1986, p. 26; *Christian Science Monitor,* September 30, 1987, pp. 16–17.

Action       *Foundation for International*
84             *Community Assistance*
                        *(FINCA)*

The Foundation for International Community Assistance (FINCA) is a nonprofit organization that supports efforts by low-income families to lift themselves out of poverty. FINCA provides technical assistance and funding to capitalize community revolving loan funds. These self-managed "village banks" make available to participating families an increasing line of credit for funding self-chosen productive investments by villagers.

Since its inception in 1984, FINCA has assisted over 750 villages and 32,000 of Latin America's poorest families with its empowering credit and savings model. No collateral of any kind is required, only the borrower's word of honor. This bond of trust—combined with the honesty, responsibility, and hard work of villagers themselves—has resulted in an overall loan repayment rate of 94 percent, and family savings averaging 20 percent of the value of every loan.

### WHAT YOU CAN DO:

To make a tax-deductible contribution ($60 sponsors one family loan, $2,500 sponsors a one-village banking program—any amount is welcome), to request more information, or to receive their newsletter, call FINCA at (602) 325-5044 or write to them at P.O. Box 1992, Tucson, AZ 85702-1992.

Action            *Trickle Up Program*
85

Trickle Up "seed money" turns landless peasants and impoverished slum dwellers into entrepreneurs who create bakeries, fruit stands, and dress stalls; sell milk, sugarcane juice, and ginger wine; raise poultry; keep bees; weave mats; and make shoes, hats, and mosquito nets.

In ten years the Trickle Up program has started more than 8,500 businesses with grants of $100 each to groups of five or more in ninety-three countries, affecting the lives of over 50,000 people.

A hundred dollars will help one group of people start its own business enterprise.

## WHAT YOU CAN DO:

To make a tax-deductible contribution or obtain additional information, call Trickle Up at (212) 362-7958 or write to them at 54 Riverside Drive, Penthouse, New York, NY 10024.

---

| Action 86 | Other Microenterprise Programs |
|---|---|

To find out more about other providers of small loans to poor people contact any of the following:

| ORGANIZATION | COUNTRY OR REGION OF LOAN RECIPIENTS | ENTERPRISES FUNDED |
|---|---|---|
| BADAN KREDIT KECAMATAN Jakarta, Indonesia 011-62-24-227-541 | Indonesia | Sewing, bamboo weaving, ceramics, vehicle repair, garbage collecting, vending, agricultural processing |
| CARE New York, N.Y. (212) 686-3110 | Bolivia, Ecuador, Peru, Philippines, Sri Lanka, Togo | Shoemaking, blacksmithing, carpentry, clothing production, fruit and vegetable drying |
| THE GRAMEEN BANK Dacca, Bangladesh 011-880-326-619 | Bangladesh | Food processing, farming, crafts, barbershop equipment, rickshaws, retailing, fishing |
| THE INSTITUTE FOR INTERNATIONAL DEVELOPMENT Oak Brook, IL (312) 279-9300 | 14 countries in Latin America, Asia, and Africa | Primarily small manufacturing and service businesses |

| ORGANIZATION | COUNTRY OR REGION OF LOAN RECIPIENTS | ENTERPRISES FUNDED |
|---|---|---|
| MENNONITE ECONOMIC DEVELOPMENT ASSOCIATES Winnipeg, Man. (204) 944-1995 | Bolivia, Haiti, Jamaica | Tailoring, leatherwork, food preparation, artisanship, manufacturing, retailing |
| OVERSEAS EDUCATION FUND INTERNATIONAL Washington, DC (202) 466-3430 | Central America, East and West Africa | Women only: food processing, agriculture, small livestock operations |
| SAVE THE CHILDREN FEDERATION Westport, CT (203) 226-7272 | 22 countries in Asia, Latin America, the Middle East, and Africa | Agricultural production, food processing, retailing, small industry, house building |
| SELF-EMPLOYED WOMEN'S ASSOCIATION Ahmadabad, India 011-91-11-390-329 | Ahmadabad region of India | Small-scale street vending, clothing production, food processing |
| WORKING WOMEN'S FORUM Madras, India (202) 879-2900 (in Washington) | India | Women only: street vending, baking, cigarette rolling, making cardboard boxes |

# Part 4

# THE RESPONSIBLE CONSUMER

*Buying your way into a better world through ethical services, responsible business, concerned shopping, and constructive trade with and travel in the Third World*

# 19

# Ethical Services—Credit Cards, Health Insurance, and Long-Distance Phone Calls

---

**Action 87**   *Working Assets Visa Card*

Every time you use this credit card Working Assets contributes five cents to a progressive organization committed to solving society's major problems—at no cost to you.

The Working Assets Visa card advertises itself quite aggressively as the first *socially responsible credit card*. When you become a cardholder, Working Assets contributes $2 to a nonprofit organization working for peace, human rights, the environment, or the hungry. Every time you use the card an additional five cents is contributed at no cost to you. In 1986, $32,000 and by 1988, more than *$200,000* were donated in amounts of $3,000 to $4,000 each to more than thirty-two organizations, including the National Coalition for the Homeless, Oxfam America, the Environmental Defense Fund, Sane Freeze, and Planned Parenthood.

This card, however, does not make every purchase a socially responsible one and is currently competing with cards that provide the same type of support to specific organizations such as the Audubon Society and the Environmental Defense Fund. MasterCard and Visa also run their own "cause-related marketing" programs. For example, MasterCard in 1986 generated $500,000 for the National Committee for the Prevention of Child Abuse. The main difference between the MasterCard program and the Working Assets program, other than the size of funds generated, is that Working Assets as a company is committed to social responsibility, whereas it appears that MasterCard uses social causes as a marketing tool.

The Working Assets Visa card has a $20 annual fee, which is deferred for the first six months; it charges 17.5 percent interest on balances not paid within twenty-five days; carries an initial credit line of $500 to $5,000 that can be increased to $10,000; offers cash advances at 150,000 banks, and provides all the standard benefits that most Visa cards offer. As of January 1989, Working Assets had more than 100,000 cardholders.

### WHAT YOU CAN DO:

Call for an application today! Working Assets can be reached at (800) 522-7759.

---

| Action 88 | ***Working Assets Long Distance: The responsible way to make long-distance phone calls*** |
|---|---|

Sponsored by Working Assets (see Actions 75 and 87), Long Distance contributes 1 percent of your long-distance phone charges to the same progressive nonprofit groups supported by the Working Assets Visa card. Rates are 10 to 30 percent less than AT&T's. Service is offered direct through U.S. Sprint, and you receive a free FONCARD for use away from home.

### WHAT YOU CAN DO:

Call (800) 669-8585, to sign up or to request additional information.

Action
89

## *Consumers United*
## *Insurance Company (CUIC)*
## Healthy Insurance

There is simply no other insurance company in America with Consumers United's track record and commitment to social justice, community development, and quality health care. They truly put people before profits.

The premiums you pay (or your employer pays) to your insurance company are invested in a socially indiscriminate manner to yield the highest return for the insurance provider. In any given year, premiums paid are likely to exceed claims. As long as this is the case, the insurance carrier uses excess premiums (your money and his profits) in a wide variety of ways, including investing in a nuclear arms manufacturer or a corporation that endangers the lives of its workers through inadequate safety precautions. You have no control over how these premiums are invested and whether those investments are consistent with your values.

There is an alternative. By purchasing health insurance through the Consumers United Insurance Company (CUIC) not only will your premiums be used in a socially responsible manner but you can be assured that they'll help finance low-income housing, aid food production for the poor, support cooperative businesses, and assist in the economic regeneration of low-income communities.

CUIC is a unique worker-owned, cooperatively managed company. It has a work force that is 80 percent female and 60 percent black; it maintains a no-layoff policy and keeps the salary range between the lowest- and highest-paid employees at a three-to-one ratio (and this includes James Gibbons, the founder and president of the company). With $52 million in annual premiums, it is the only insurance company committed to fulfilling a social purpose rather than simply making a profit. Its rate of asset growth in the past decade is nearly three times that of the twenty-five largest insurance companies in this country.

Premiums have been used to finance $16 million of low-income cooperative housing in Washington, D.C., St. Louis, and Youngstown, Ohio; produce food at below-market rates for the poor through the operation of a three-hundred-acre farm; open a community health clinic; provide low-income neighborhoods with loans at 50 percent below the market rate, and organize a small-business-venture company that provides seed capital for start-up businesses. The fact that $463 out of every $1,000 CUIC receives is invested in these types of projects, compared to only sixteen cents out of every $1,000 going to similar projects by any one of America's largest seven insurance companies, makes the effectiveness of Consumers United even more compelling.

CUIC's health insurance policy provides all standard coverage, with the added benefits of unisex rates, well baby care, alternative health care coverage, $10,000 of term life insurance, comprehensive maternity benefits, mental health coverage, and a one-year money-back guarantee (less claims paid).

## WHAT YOU CAN DO:

Call (800) 424-9711 for information about the Consumers United Health Insurance Plan.

# 20

# Responsible Business
# "Redefining the Bottom Line"*

Business is no longer what it used to be. Led by a growing group of corporate visionaries and entrepreneurial heroes (yes, we have some—but not nearly enough), America is discovering that personal values and social ethics can be successfully combined with reasonable profit.

This group includes such individuals as:

*Nancy Abraham*, a Shearson Lehman executive who used her financial leverage to convert a five-story building into housing for homeless families

*Harrison Owen*, consultant in organizational transformation for Fortune 500 companies, who uses myth and ritual to create organizational spirit

*William Norris*, retired CEO of Control Data, who had the visionary belief that social problems offered valuable business opportunities

*Anita Roddick*, whose franchised Body Shops sponsor employees to participate in community projects and pay them for the time they give

*Ben Cohen and Jerry Greenfield* of Ben & Jerry's Homemade Ice Cream, who limit salaries from the lowest- to the highest-paid worker to a five-to-one ratio (Action 90)

* Quote from Ben Cohen of Ben & Jerry's Homemade Ice Cream.

And corporations:

*South Shore Bank* in Chicago (Action 69), whose investment program in low-income housing and small business has led it to profits that exceed most of those of its peers

*Johnson & Johnson*, whose "Live for Life" employee health care program provides exercise facilities; stop-smoking, stress-reduction, and nutritional and weight-loss clinics, and healthful food in its cafeterias

*Cummins Engine Company* in Columbus, Indiana, which employs a full-time ethicist, with the title of Corporate Responsibility Director

*Herman Miller, Inc.,* which offers its workers "Silver Parachutes," promising a year's salary or more if a hostile takeover eliminates their jobs

*Detroit Edison*, which encourages employee whistleblowing at nuclear power plants through its Safeteam program, which brings in impartial experts to investigate employee complaints.

These businesses and individuals need our support as consumers. Purchasing their products is a vote for their values. And while we can't profile them all, what follows is a sampling of a few of the best, with a focus on the values and ethics that make them America's real business leaders.

For more inspiring examples subscribe to *Business Ethics*, 1107 Hazeltine Boulevard, Chaska, MN 55318; (612) 448-8864.

---

**Action
90**
## *Ben & Jerry's Homemade
(Ice Cream), Inc.*

Rarely does such a delicious and pleasurable opportunity to "make the world a better place" present itself. Ben and Jerry have proved that making money, having fun, and creating positive social change can all be done at the same time.

Ben Cohen and Jerry Greenfield have brought to life what perhaps can best be described as a business that creates social change, a challenging and unique goal in a world where few businesses even attempt to be socially responsible. Your support of their products encourages a critically important business vision which believes that it's impossible to:

—make money and satisfy shareholders;

—share prosperity with your labor force and keep your employees happy;

—be a responsible and supportive member of the community;

—produce the highest-quality products in an environmentally sound manner; and

—have fun—all at the same time.

How do they do it?

*They make money:* Over the past five years company revenues have grown thirtyfold—to sales exceeding $32 million. Shareholders' equity has risen from $20,000 to more than $9 million, profits have increased from $57,000 in 1983 to $1.4 million in 1988, and the stock has increased in value from $10.50 per share in 1984 to more than $16 per share in 1989. Not bad!

*They keep employees happy and treat them fairly:* Perhaps one of Ben & Jerry's most innovative business practices is to limit the salary spread from the lowest- to the highest-paid worker (including Ben and Jerry) to a five-to-one ratio. This means that if executives raise their salaries, they must bring the lowest-paid workers up along with them at twenty cents on the dollar. This, however, is just the beginning. Five percent of all company profits are distributed as a bonus for employees, and distribution is based purely on their length of service. The company hires the handicapped, provides free therapy—including anonymous drug and alcohol counseling—and takes its workers on trips to Montreal for hockey and baseball games. There are changing tables for babies in the men's bathrooms as well as the women's. Once a month everyone attends a staff meeting complete with coffee and cider doughnuts. No dress code, other than the frequently seen combination of jeans and workshirts, is apparent even in the executive offices, and, best of all, during heavy overtime on the ice cream packing line, Jerry has been known to bring in a masseuse to revive tired workers. Who wouldn't want to work there?

*They support their community:* Ben & Jerry's contributes 7.5 percent of its pretax profits directly to its own foundation, which, in the company's words, helps "projects that are models for social change; infused with a spirit of generosity and hopefulness; those that enhance people's quality of life; which exhibit creative problem solving; and projects which are involved with community celebrations." In 1987 the company awarded a total of $280,000 in grants to more than ninety organizations. The company also gives away $120,000-a-year worth of ice cream to food banks (see Action 61) throughout the Northeast and to nonprofit organizations for fund-raising and celebrations.

*They produce a quality product:* Only natural, preservative-free ingredients are used in their ice cream (with the exception of some of the fillings—Heath Bars and Oreos).

*They have fun:* Ben & Jerry's is the only business in the country to have an "Undersecretary of Joy." In that capacity Jerry is the company's spiritual leader, sometime comedian, and keeper of the heart. Often Ben joins in. They perform "The Dramatic Sledgehammer Smashing" of a cinder block on the bare stomach of the noted Indian mystic Habeeni Ben Coheeni. Suspended between two chairs with a cinder block on his stomach, held in place by volunteers who try to counter the effects of too much product sampling, Ben awaits Jerry who, wearing a pith helmet, is carried onto the scene. Ben lifts a conventional sledgehammer high in the air and with one powerful swing disintegrates the cinder block on his partner's rounded belly, without harm to Habeeni Ben Coheeni.

### WHAT YOU CAN DO:

Ben & Jerry's Homemade challenges the greed, injustice, and narrow-mindedness that is still so rampant in corporate America. Your support can help prove that there is another way to do business. Your support may even help open a few new eyes and perhaps move other business leaders to question some of the values that are impoverishing our nation.

Eat Ben & Jerry's Homemade Ice Cream wherever it's sold. If you can't find it in your local grocer's freezer, suggest that he place an order for you and your friends!

---

**Action
91**               *The Body Shop*

Would you believe that one of the world's most successful new cosmetics companies doesn't advertise, allows customers to refill old product containers rather than purchase new ones, prints its sales literature on recycled paper, promotes human rights in its store windows, and pays employees to work on community projects during store hours?

In 1976 Anita Roddick opened the first Body Shop in Brighton, England. She started with $6,500 after her husband had departed to pursue his lifetime goal of riding from Buenos Aires to New York on horseback. Today, there are over three hundred franchised shops selling 350 products from Dubai to Denmark, the Arctic to Australia, Sweden to Singapore, and Holland to Hong Kong. When the company went public in 1984, its stock climbed 50 percent on the first day of trading. Employees who spent $1,600 exercising stock options when the shares were issued can now sell them for over $100,000. Roddick's stock was worth more than $120 million at the end of 1988.

However, the real point is that the financial success is in most ways a by-product of Anita Roddick's passion, vision, and commitment to make the world a better place. The fact that so many people have been attracted by her vision is a small but growing bright spot in the corporate world, where most companies believe they can't afford to put values ahead of profits.

*What Does the Body Shop Sell?* "Products that cleanse, polish, and protect the skin and hair," or what is more commonly known as cosmetics. But the Body Shop is clearly not part of the cosmetics industry. "The entire industry appears to be run by men: they create needs that don't exist [such as vaginal deodorants], make women feel dissatisfied with their bodies and then sell them a hope and a promise and lots of packaging," Roddick says. The Body Shop sells soaps, scents, lotions, and shampoos that don't promise beauty or youth, but do promise they are made from natural vegetable ingredients, or even based on an ancient Third World formula, have never been tested on animals, and are packaged in refillable containers.

*How Does the Body Shop Sell Its Products?* Without advertising or elaborate packaging—virtually unheard of in an industry that spends 85 percent of its budget on those two items alone. All shops are self-service with no salespeople pushing customers to buy products they don't want in sizes that are larger than they really need. Often window displays focus on human rights or environmental problems. Suggestion boxes solicit customer ideas.

***How Does the Body Shop Protect the Environment?*** The Body Shop uses biodegradable shopping bags, prints sales literature and labels on recycled paper (it even uses toilet paper that's made from recycled paper pulp), and it offers refills for most products instead of forcing containers into the waste cycle. The Body Shop has joined forces with Greenpeace UK to help "Save the Whales," and with Friends of the Earth UK to raise public awareness of the dangers of acid rain. The company evaluates every action taken with its environmental impact in mind—no small task—but one that Anita Roddick pursues with great passion.

***The Body Shop and the Third World*** In 1988 a Body Shop Boys' Town opened in Athoor, India. Eighty-five homeless boys live there and are supported through school as they learn a skill or trade. The Body Shop has been supporting other Boys' Towns for many years. Many ingredients for products are purchased from local communities in developing countries, encouraging trade and employment. In its nonexploitative way the Body Shop pays first world prices for these products, often four times what is offered by other purchasers. In Nepal the company helped a small town set up a plant to make natural paper from banana plants. The Body Shop uses the paper in its shops.

***Community Service*** "It's understood that when you come in as a franchisee you should be involved in community projects—a battered women's shelter, an AIDS program, whatever—and that your staff should participate (and be paid) during working hours," Anita Roddick says. The goal is to have each shop appreciate, understand, and help solve the problems of its own community whether it's helping educate the young or providing massage therapy for the elderly.

The Body Shop vision continues to embrace all aspects of the business operation—from the way the staff is trained to educational programs on topics including drugs and urban survival.

## WHAT YOU CAN DO:

To support Anita's vision—look for a shop opening near you or write to The Body Shop, Inc., 45 Horsehill Road, Hanover

Technical Center, Cedar Knolls, NJ 07927-2003, for a direct-mail catalog, or call (800) 541-2535.

---

## Action 92    *Employee-Owned Business*

It's striking that someone who has worked 20 years for a company has no legitimate claim on it, while somebody who recently purchased its stock has total control.—ROBERT KUTT-NER, *The New Republic,* June 17, 1985

"Ever since 1974, when Congress enacted the first of a series of tax measures designed to encourage employee stock ownership plans (ESOPs), the number of employee-owned (or partially owned) companies has grown from about 1,600 to 8,100, and the number of employees owning stock has jumped from 250,000 to more than eight million. Employee-owners publish the *Milwaukee Journal,* bag groceries at Public Supermarkets, roll tin plate at Weirton Steel, and create high-tech products at W. L. Gore Associates.

"Underlying worker ownership is a radically democratic, Jeffersonian ideal. Every American wants to own some property, to have a stake. We all want to know that we are working 'for ourselves.' Studies of worker-owned companies clearly show both increased growth and performance as compared with the period prior to stock ownership and as compared with non–worker-owned competitors.

"The lessons for American management are clear. Give employees an opportunity to acquire a significant share of the company and develop opportunities for them to participate as owners. This course is remarkably effective, remarkably exciting, and remarkably different from the one the vast majority of American companies travel."*

Unfortunately, not all employee-owned businesses are equal. Of the estimated total, which as of 1986 numbered 8,100, covering some eight million employees—seven percent of the total work force—there were only seven hundred companies whose employees controlled a majority of the stock, and even fewer where workers effectively have democratic control of the com-

---

*Excerpted from *Harvard Business Review*, September-October 1987.

pany. Three issues are critical to real employee participation: (1) stock should not be held in a trust where employees are unable to vote their own shares; (2) employees should be able to elect the board of directors; (3) employees should be able to have input into the management and operation of the company.

The best sources of information on worker-owned businesses are:

—National Center for Employee Ownership, 426 17th Street, Suite 650, Oakland, CA 94612; (415) 272-9461

—Industrial Cooperative Association, 58 Day Street, Suite 200, Somerville, MA 02144; (617) 629-2700

—The Association for a Democratic Workplace, 1400 High Street, Suite A, Eugene, OR 97401; (503) 683-8184

Of the one hundred largest companies that are at least 20 percent owned by employees, the following table gives you a sample of those you're most likely to have an opportunity to do business with. Also noted are those that are more than 50 percent employee owned, and those where employees elect the board of directors and participate in management decisions.

| COMPANY (AT LEAST 20% EMPLOYEE OWNED) | MAJORITY EMPLOYEE OWNERSHIP | EMPLOYEES ELECT BOARD | EMPLOYEES PARTICIPATE IN MANAGEMENT |
|---|---|---|---|
| Avis Rent-a-Car | X | | X |
| Hallmark Cards | | | X |
| Dan River Textiles | X | | |
| W. L. Gore (makers of Gore-Tex Fabrics) | X | | X |
| Herman Miller Furniture | | | X |
| Anderson Windows | | | X |
| Tony Lama Boots | | | |
| Arthur D. Little Consulting | X | | |
| The Journal Company | X | X | X |
| Thompson-McKinnon Brokerage | X | | |
| Emery Air Freight | | | |
| Harcourt Brace Jovanovich Publishers | | | |

| COMPANY (AT LEAST 20% EMPLOYEE OWNED) | MAJORITY EMPLOYEE OWNERSHIP | EMPLOYEES ELECT BOARD | EMPLOYEES PARTICIPATE IN MANAGEMENT |
|---|---|---|---|
| American Standard Plumbing | | | |
| Carter Hawley Hale | | | |
| Ryder Trucks | | | |
| Fireman's Fund Insurance | | | |

*Source:* National Center for Employee Ownership

## WHAT YOU CAN DO:

Support employee-owned businesses through your purchasing. Ask the smaller companies you do business with whether they provide opportunities for worker ownership and consider asking your employer to explore such a program with you.

---

**Action 93**     ## Worker and Consumer Cooperatives

Here's how you can help support America's workers to support themselves. Here's your opportunity to do business with people who care, because they own it. Here's your chance to encourage participation and responsibility rather than businesses who train their workers to say "it's not my job."

Cooperatives operate for the benefit of member-owners. In a cooperative, those with similar needs act together and pool their resources for mutual gain. The returns are not just monetary. Members ensure that their cooperative business provides the best-quality products and services at the lowest possible cost. Members control the business through an elected board of directors. Through their own participation, members extend the democratic practice into their own economic lives.

Nearly sixty million people have organized forty thousand U.S. cooperatives to provide themselves with goods and services in nearly every sector of our economy.

*Consumer-owned cooperatives* enable members to secure a

wide array of goods and services. For example, they may offer health care, utilities, insurance, or housing. They may buy and sell food, heating fuel, hardware, and other consumer goods. Or they may operate credit unions, funeral and memorial societies, and child-care facilities. Almost all consumer needs can be met by a cooperative.

*Worker-owned cooperatives* are businesses owned and controlled by their employees. Worker cooperatives may be found in almost any industry, including employee-owned food stores, processing companies, restaurants, taxicab companies, sewing companies, timber processors, and light and heavy industries.

The following principles govern the structure of most cooperatives:*

1. *Open and voluntary membership.* A cooperative is open to anyone who can use its services and is willing to accept the responsibilities of membership.

2. *One member, one vote.* Members are equal co-owners in the business and have a say on a one-member, one-vote basis (in contrast to one share, one vote in private enterprises).

3. *Limited interest on shares.* Investments in the cooperative pay limited interest to insulate the membership from those who would invest purely for speculative return.

4. *Return of surplus to members.* All net earnings (profits) are returned to members proportionally to their patronage with the business. These returns are commonly made partially in cash and partially in cooperative dividends.

5. *Cooperation among cooperatives.* Cooperatives work together at the local, regional, national, and international levels to further economic democracy.

## WHAT YOU CAN DO:

### To Support Worker-Owned Cooperatives

The Industrial Cooperative Association (ICA) provides a list of more than eight hundred worker-owned cooperatives, divided by type of product and service and geographical location—so you can support cooperative businesses in your town or city. List can

---

*Excerpted from *Cooperatives Are . . . ,* National Cooperative Business Institute.

be ordered for $2 from ICA, 58 Day Street, Suite 203, Somerville, MA 02144; (617) 629-2700.

ICA also provides workshops, technical assistance, and financing for worker cooperatives and employee-owned businesses as well as putting out a wealth of publications and a newsletter.

Other resources:

—Institute for Community Economics, see Actions 72 and 73.

—Cooperative Enterprise, published quarterly by the National Cooperative Bank, 1630 Connecticut Avenue, Suite 201, Washington, DC 20009; (202) 745-4670, no charge.


## WHAT YOU CAN DO:

### To Support Consumer Cooperatives

Housing cooperatives (often dependent on municipal, state, or federal funding) provide more than half a million families with low-cost housing; health care cooperatives serve a quarter of a million families; 22,000 credit unions, with over $52 billion on deposit, serve more than 41 million individuals; and other co-ops provide child care, preschool programs, auto repair, legal services, oil and gas, insurance, and products ranging from furniture and sports equipment to medications and hardware.

For information on how to join a cooperative in your community, contact:

—The National Cooperative Business Association (NCBA), 1401 New York Avenue, N.W., Suite 1100, Washington, DC 20005; (202) 638-6222. Their publication *Finding Co-ops: A Resource Guide and Directory 1983*, $9.95, will help you find over 20,000 producer and consumer cooperatives (although the publication is dated, it's the only one of its kind).

NCBA also provides material on how to start a wide variety of co-ops and buying clubs as well as material on the history of the co-op movement and inspirational models such as Mondragon in Spain.

Additionally, contact:

—NASCO (North American Students of Cooperation), P.O. Box 7715, Ann Arbor, MI 48107; (313) 663-0889. NASCO has an excellent publications department and goes out of its way to answer questions and suggest resources.

---

**Action
94**
## *Co-Op America*
## Mail-Order Activism

The Co-Op America Catalog helps the conscientious person become an ethical buyer in a marketplace of ethical sellers.—RALPH NADER

"Co-Op America is trying to build a more cooperative economy. An economy based on equality and cooperation, a world of peace and justice, a clean and healthy environment and an economic system that shares the planet's resources." Quite a tall order for a mail-order company! But in fact when you purchase the Nut Lover's Gift Box from Once Again Nut Butter, Inc., a worker-owned and -operated food-processing company in Nunda, New York, or wild rice from the White Earth Reservation in Minnesota, or a Womanswork Sweatshirt, fine oak furniture, a Gro-Dome greenhouse, natural organic skin-care products, or even luggage and jewelry—you'll be participating in and supporting Co-Op America's vision.

Co-Op America, in addition to an eighty-page catalog of socially responsible products, also publishes an excellent quarterly magazine, *Building Economic Alternatives*, which provides access to socially responsible investment services, information on boycotts, collective health insurance coverage, and reports on the progress of ethical business ventures.

### WHAT YOU CAN DO:

Become a member of Co-Op America by calling (800) 424-COOP, or write to the company at 2100 M Street, N.W., Suite 310, Washington, DC 20063. Membership is $20; individual copies of the catalog are $1.

# 21

# The Socially Conscious Consumer Casting Your Vote in the Marketplace

| Action | *Rating America's Corporate* |
|:---:|:---:|
| **95** | *Conscience\** |

Purchasing General Electric light bulbs helps fund the nation's fourth largest defense contractor to lobby the government for greater defense spending. Purchasing 3M products supports innovative pollution prevention programs. The choice is yours! Here's how to get the information you need to make the best decision.

Every product you buy is a vote for the company that made it. By purchasing from companies whose policies are socially, ethically, and environmentally responsible, you can support your vision of how to make the world a better place. Or—unknowingly—you can support corporations that are pursuing a path that causes pain, war, social injustice, and environmental degradation.

**As a consumer you have the power to:**

—buy a camera from a company that stopped selling to South Africa because it did not want to support apartheid;

---

*Excerpted from Lyndenberg/Marlin/Strub/Council on Economic Priorities, *Rating America's Corporate Conscience*, Addison-Wesley Publishing Co., Inc., Reading, Mass. Reprinted with permission.

—purchase a breakfast cereal made by a company that pledges a generous 2 percent of its pretax earnings to charity;

—cook your supper on a kitchen range made by a company that is not involved in the manufacture of nuclear weapons;

—snack on peanut butter made by one of the first major U.S. corporations to institute a comprehensive child-care network for its employees;

—invest in companies that have supported the advancement of women and minorities in management; and

—avoid buying from corporations whose policies you feel reflect a disregard for the public good.

The question of course is, How can you tell the good from the bad? In that moment of indecision of choosing between Pepperidge Farm and Thomas's English Muffins, how do you know which one does business in South Africa and which doesn't? (Pepperidge Farm doesn't; Thomas's does.) Or—on Sunday morning when you rush out to the supermarket for some pancake mix—do you choose Downyflake or Aunt Jemima? (If you want to avoid supporting a weapons manufacturer, select Aunt Jemima.)

Fortunately, there's one source you can turn to for almost all the answers. *Rating America's Corporate Conscience,* by the Council on Economic Priorities, has rated the social performance of 130 companies that dominate the market in the food, health and personal care, home appliance, oil, airline, hotel, and automobile industries. The large companies, major advertisers, and frequently purchased, nationally distributed brand-name products listed in this book are familiar to most consumers.

### The data and ratings are presented in two ways:

Product charts, organized by brand name, highlight and compare corporate performance on selected social issues. These charts provide a handy checklist on how companies are rated on issues of vital concern:

—charitable contributions;

—representation of women and minorities on boards of directors and in top management;

—social disclosure;

—South Africa; and

—nuclear and conventional arms contracting.

Company profiles specify and discuss data on each company's social record. These profiles present a more detailed portrait of individual companies and their programs as well as give you a look at selected issues and controversies not covered in the product charts.

"FACT: While many people may have trouble choosing among brands of pain relievers, it might interest you to know that Norwich and Encaprin come from one of the only major manufacturers of pain relievers with no operations in South Africa—Procter & Gamble.

"FACT: Common brand-name cold or cough remedies such as Robitussin, Dimetapp, and Chap Stick are produced by A. H. Robbins, the same company that sold over two million Dalkon Shield intrauterine contraceptive devices to American women in the early 1970s. Robbins now faces over 300,000 lawsuits and claims alleging the Dalkon Shield causes grave health effects and even death."

## WHAT YOU CAN DO:

Order a copy of *Rating America's Corporate Conscience* by Steven D. Lydenberg, Alice Tepper Marlin, and Sean O'Brien Strub, published by Addison-Wesley. Send $14.95 (plus $2 postage and handling) to the Council on Economic Priorities, 30 Irving Place, New York, NY 10003; (212) 420-1133. Or, for $35, you can become a member of the council and receive its monthly newsletter plus a copy of *Rating America's Corporate Conscience*, free.

Also see Action 56 for information about the Council's newest project, "Shopping for a Better World."

---

**Action
96**　　　　　*Boycotts*

Boycotts present all consumers with another option for casting your vote against irresponsible corporate behavior every time you step up to the cash register.

Consumer boycotts are organized programs designed to place financial pressure on a corporation to change a given policy. Some boycotts have lasted years and become well known, such as INFACT's boycott of Nestle to protest the use of its infant formula in Third World countries. But there are literally hundreds of smaller, local, and less publicized boycotts going on at any one time. They've included those against:

—*California Grapes*, organized by the United Farm Workers of America against pesticide use in the fields

—*Hormel*, organized by union workers to protest wage cuts and unsafe working conditions

—*Exxon*, for its failure to clean up the mess from the Valdez spill and its other antienvironmental policies

—*Guess Jeans*, for its use of violent and sexual images in national advertising

—*Morrell*, for greatly increasing the speed of its production line, which has caused an unacceptably high level of worker injuries

—*Scott Paper*, for its harmful forestry practices and its destruction of the rain forest

—*H. W. Heinz, Ralston Purina*, and all canned tuna companies, for fishing methods that knowingly drown over 100,000 dolphins a year

—*Morton Salt* (a division of Morton Thiokol), to protest its role as a top nuclear weapons contractor

Boycotts are a simple way for you to play an active role in supporting issues that concern you most, and they allow you to cast your vote against a corporate practice that you find offensive.

## WHAT YOU CAN DO:

**1.** *The Nation Boycott Newsletter*, though published irregularly, is the boycotter's bible. With issues that range from forty to two hundred pages long, the newsletter will provide you with the most detailed and accurate information, including responses from boycotted companies. Boycotts are organized in several categories, including human rights, peace, labor, the environment, and animal rights. The newsletter is almost completely put together by one person—Todd Putnam—who desperately can use your help, support, or subscription dollars.

Contact Todd at 6506 28th Avenue, N.E., Seattle, WA 98115; (206) 523-0421. As of 1989, subscriptions were $10 annually for an unpredictable number of issues.

**2.** *Building Economic Alternatives*, published quarterly by Co-Op America, carries a two-page summary of major boycott activities. See page 000 for subscription information.

**3.** See Action 117 for information about INFACT's boycott of General Electric, and contact Action for Corporate Accountability, 3255 Hennepin Avenue South, Suite 230, Minneapolis, MN 55408; (612) 823-1571, about its ongoing boycott of the Nestle Company and American Home Products for their refusal to abide by the World Health Organization's code for marketing infant formula. This is a reactivation of the boycott that was settled in 1984.

# 22

# Trade and Travel in the Third World

---

<table>
<tr><td>Action<br>97</td><td>Socially Responsible<br>Travel*</td></tr>
</table>

Rather than an unending source of sun, sand and sex—alternative travel sees the Third World as struggling societies in need of understanding and support from the people of industrialized nations.

Every hour more than five thousand tourists from industrialized countries set out on a Third World adventure. Tourism has become the leading source of income for many developing countries. North Americans flock to Mexico and the Caribbean every winter; Europeans descend on the Canary Islands, North Africa, and the South Pacific; and planeloads of Japanese converge on the Philippines.

While tourism had been touted as a quick way for poor countries to earn foreign exchange, many countries have begun to wonder if they've been sold a bill of goods. Most tourist dollars unfortunately end up right back in the coffers of the countries from which the tourists came, since the industrialized nations

* Excerpted by permission from *Seeds* magazine, February 1988, and *Bridging the Global Gap: A Handbook for Linking the First and Third Worlds,* by Medea Benjamin and Andrea Freedman, Seven Locks Press, Md./Washington, D.C., 1989.

control the hotels, airlines, tour operators, and agencies that collect most of the money.

Native communities are pushed aside to make way for high-rise hotels and private beaches. Fishermen and farmers and craftswomen are turned into barmen and hotel maids. Prostitution becomes a new growth industry, and disease spreads quickly through local populations.

Natural environments are often laid to ruin, and while some low-paying menial jobs are created, most of the well-paying, managerial positions are reserved for foreigners. The tourist who spends more in one night at a luxury hotel than the average local citizen earns in one month has dulled his or her sensitivity to the life, and often the suffering, of the people he might have otherwise have come to know.

At the same time that the benefits of Third World tourism began to be reexamined, a different kind of tourism emerged. The new brand of travel—called "alternative tourism," "socially responsible tourism," "social tourism," or "ecotourism"—gained tremendous momentum during the 1980s. Today more than one hundred groups in the United States alone are organizing alternative travel with an astounding range: bicycle treks through China, peace tours to the Pacific Islands, study tours to Cuba and Nicaragua, socially conscious pilgrimages to the Holy Land, locally run village resorts in West Africa, environmentally responsible beach resorts in Bali.

Work brigades and delegations have already taken more than 100,000 U.S. citizens to Central America. Environmental groups promote vacations that attempt to save whales in the Virgin Islands and study tropical rain forests in Ecuador. Groups such as Journeys International even channel a portion of the tour cost to fund seed distribution in Nepal or reforestation in Peru. The women's movement has given birth to alternative tours that link women in industrialized countries to women's struggles in the Third World. Mujer a Mujer (Woman to Woman), for example, takes U.S. women to meet with Mexican women to discuss land reform, union organizing, sexism, and forced sterilization.

## WHAT YOU CAN DO:

For specific travel information, contact the following groups, or send $10.95 to Global Exchange, 2940 16th Street, Suite 307, San Francisco, CA 94103, for a copy of *Bridging the Global Gap*, which covers alternative travel and other international people-to-people ties more extensively.

Specific travel arrangements can be made directly by all of the following:

LEARNING ALLIANCE
494 Broadway
New York, NY 10012
(212) 226-7171

CENTER FOR GLOBAL
SERVICE IN EDUCATION
c/o Augsburg College
731 21st Avenue South
Minneapolis, MN 55454
(612) 330-1159

ELDERS FOR SURVIVAL
P.O. Box 9057
Berkeley, CA 94709

TRAVELERS SOCIETY/
SCHILLING
722 Second Avenue South
Minneapolis, MN 55402
(800) 328-0302

MARAZUL TRAVEL
AGENCY
250 West 57th Street, #1311
New York, NY 10107
(212) 586-3847

PLOWSHARES
P.O. Box 243
Simsbury, CT 06070

AMAZONIA EXPEDITIONS
18323 Gulf Boulevard
Indian Shores, FL 33535
(813) 391-6211

BICYCLE AFRICA
(International Bicycle Fund)
4247 135th Place, S.E.
Bellevue, WA 98006
(206) 746-1028

CASA NICARAGUENSE
DE ESPAÑOL
853 Broadway, #1105
New York, NY 10003
(212) 777-1197

CIRCLE PINES CO-OP
CAMP
8650 Mullen Road
Delton, MI 49046
(616) 623-5555

FRIENDSHIP TOURS
(INT'L)
1508 Coffee Road
Modesto, CA 95355
(209) 576-7775

HAWAII CENTER FOR
ECOLOGICAL LIVING
Star Route 13008
Keaau, HI 96749
(808) 966-3592

MAHO BAY CAMPS (U.S. VIRGIN ISLANDS)
17 East 73rd Street
New York, NY 10021
(800) 392-9004

ODYSSEY TOURS (ASIA)
1821 Wilshire Boulevard
Santa Monica, CA 90403
(800) 654-7975

SHELTER INTERNATIONAL (TIBET)
2230 Sixth Street
Boulder, CO 80302
(303) 449-0677

CHARTER SAILBOAT *STRANGER*
Captain Mac Jernigan
Route 3, Box 46
Lexington, VA 24450
(703) 463-1539

TROPICAL TOURS (NICARAGUA)
2330 West Third Street, #4
Los Angeles, CA 90057
(800) 421-5040

NICA (NICARAGUA)
P.O. Box 1409-CO
Cambridge, MA 02238
(617) 497-7142

SERVAS (HOMESTAYS-INT'L)
11 John Street, Suite 706
New York, NY 10038
(212) 267-0252

SOON COME TRAVEL (JAMAICA)
1644 East Cactus Wren
Phoenix, AZ 85020
(602) 944-3654

GLOBAL EXCHANGE
2940 16th Street, #307
San Francisco, CA 94103
(415) 255-7296

WILDERNESS EXPEDITIONS
(Peruvian Amazon)
310 Washington Avenue, S.W.
Roanoke, VA 24016
(703) 342-5630

WILDLAND JOURNEYS
(Earth Preservation Fund)
904 West Highland Drive
Seattle, WA 98119
1-800-345-HIKE

### For further reading on alternative travel:

*The Directory of Low-Cost Vacations with a Difference*
J. Crawford

Contains hundreds of listings on everything from bed-and-breakfasts to farm vacations. Available only from Pilot Books, 103

Cooper Street, Babylon, NY 11702, for $4.95 plus $1 postage and handling.

*Directory of Alternative Travel Resources*
D. Brause/One World Family Travel

An informative directory of up-to-date listings on alternative travel in the United States and abroad. Includes adventure travel, citizen diplomacy, crosscultural exchange programs, volunteering, and guidebooks. P.O. Box 146130, San Francisco, CA 94114, for $5.

*Alternative Tourism—A Resource Book*
Ecumenical Coalition on Third World Tourism (ECTWT)

Provides an overview of the worldwide "just" tourism network with a focus on Asia. Includes action guide-contact listings. Available through the Center for Responsible Tourism—S.F.T.S., 2 Kensington Road, San Anselmo, CA 94960, for $6. CRT newsletter and membership available for $10 per year.

---

## Action 98      *Fair Trade with the Third World*

Alternative trade organizations assist the Third World's poorest producers to market their crafts and commodities directly to American consumers allowing them to earn up to 300 percent more than exporters traditionally pay them, while still delivering these products to American consumers at a competitive price.

The goal is to return as much money as possible back to local Third World producers, and to create a more equitable system of trade with the people of debt-ridden, nonindustrial nations. Alternative Trade Organizations, or ATOs, offer Third World producers the sense of self-worth and confidence that comes from earning a fair living instead of relying on gifts, handouts, or demeaning employment that fails to generate enough income for basic food and shelter.

For consumers, ATOs provide an opportunity to support the

poor in a way that goes beyond charity and generates respect and understanding for people of other cultures.

ATOs struggle to keep their costs and overhead low, often on a nonprofit basis, so they can return the bulk of consumers' dollars to Third World producers. ATOs pay such producers up to 300 percent more than commercial importers do, often raising the base or market price for a given craft or commodity. At times, ATOs can even break a crippling monopoly held by a multinational corporation that has forced Third World producers to work for wages too low to feed their families and provide decent clothing and shelter.

The goal of the ATOs is to help local producers become sophisticated enough so that they can go beyond selling raw cocoa beans to manufacturing finished chocolate products, and earn the substantial value-added income that the importing nation usually keeps. Stichting Ideele, an ATO in Holland, has developed such a program in Zimbabwe; it also works in Mozambique, Angola, Cuba, Nicaragua, and Vietnam.

Pueblo to People, operating out of Houston, Texas, helps villagers in the Third World learn to process and package cashew nuts themselves so they can earn 100 percent more than the raw unprocessed nuts would normally sell for. In Finland New Wind developed a simple teabag machine so Tanzanians could export higher-priced teabags instead of loose tea.

ATOs often sell through mail order, using catalogs to educate consumers about the countries products come from, the conditions under which they were produced, as well as some of the economic and political issues currently facing the producers.

While the international ATO movement accounts for only $75 million of Third World food and craft exports, it has an impact that goes well beyond. Your support and purchase of these products helps create decent jobs, self-respect, and hope for many who have become hopeless, and it builds trust between the industrial world and our fellow human beings in the Third World.

## WHAT YOU CAN DO:

To order coffee, cashews, clothing, jewelry, crafts, and much, much more, request catalogs from the ATOs listed below:

CO-OP AMERICA
2100 M Street,
N.W.
Suite 310
Washington, DC
20063
(800) 424-COOP

Catalog covers a
variety of products
from Third World
cooperatives and
socially responsible
businesses in
the U.S. and
throughout the
world.

COVENANT
CRAFTS, INC.
2722 Frankfort
Avenue
Louisville, KY
40206
(502) 897-7319

Nonprofit
organization that
imports and sells
crafts from co-ops
in developing
countries.

GLOBAL
EXCHANGE, INC.
37 South Detroit
Street
P.O. Box 261
Xenia, OH 45385
(513) 376-8233

Provides technical
and marketing
assistance to
Bolivians for
knitware.

JUBILEE CRAFTS
300 West Apsley
Street
Philadelphia, PA
19144
(215) 849-2178

Christian
organization sells
crafts from church
groups and co-ops
in the Third World
and impoverished
areas of the United
States.

PUEBLO TO
PEOPLE
1616 Montrose
Boulevard
Houston, TX 77006
(713) 523-1197

Focuses on Central
and South
American
cooperatives.
Supports grass-
roots social
change, provides
markets for
handcrafts, and
offers technical
assistance.

SAVE THE
CHILDREN
CRAFT SHOP
54 Wilton Road
Westport, CT
06880
(203) 226-7271

Runs two craft
shops and issues
a catalog of
handcrafts from
communities
around the world.

DRY CREEK CO-
OP TRADING
c/o Route 2,
Box 11A
Woodbury, TN
37190
(615) 563-8207

Trading and
networking group
is interested in
opening trade lines
and establishing
strong ties
between ATOs.

EQUAL
EXCHANGE
P.O. Box 2652
Cambridge, MA
02238
(617) 482-4945

Food-importing
cooperative that
works with
farmers in the
Third World.
American
distributor for
Stichting Ideele
Imports of
Holland.

MCC SELFHELP
CRAFTS
21 South 12th
Street
Akron, PA 17501
(717) 859-4971

Mostly volunteer
organization is run
by the Mennonite
Central Committee
with more than
sixty retail outlets.

ONE WORLD
TRADING
COMPANY
P.O. Box 310
Summertown, TN
39483
(615) 964-2334

Links Guatemalan
artisans with
American
consumers,
markets the crafts
of Guatemalan
refugees, and
supports the self-
sufficiency efforts
of indigenous
peoples.

SERRV SELF
HELP
HANDICRAFTS
500 Main Street,
Box 365
New Windsor, MD
21776
(301) 635-6464

Buys and markets
crafts from over
forty countries,
promoting
economically
disadvantaged
artisans, especially
those in workers'
co-ops.

THAI
INTERNATIONAL
DISPLAY
6030 90th Avenue
North
Pinellas Park, FL
33565
(813) 544-2429

Sells clothing and
crafts from Asian
producers working
in private
enterprise or small
home industries,
providing income
as well as training
for the artisans.

FRIENDS OF THE
THIRD WORLD,
INC.
611 West Wayne
Street
Fort Wayne, IN
46802
(219) 422-6821


Food and coffee
importers; also run
the Whole Worlds
Bookstore and the
Third World Shop.

OXFAM AMERICA
115 Broadway
Boston, MA 02116
(617) 482-1211

International
organization
supports
development at the
grass-roots level by
selling Third
World handcrafts.

For additional information on ATOs, see *Bridging the Global Gap*. Ordering information appears on page 217.

## The Future of Fair Trade with the Third World

The Fair Trade Foundation is quickly becoming the focal point for this important movement. With its goals of: educating the American public about the importance of linking their buying to their values, organizing the wholesale and retail marketplaces to feature and favor "fair-traded" Third World products, and providing technical and financial assistance to appropriate Third World producers, the Fair Trade Foundation is launching a major attempt to broaden awareness of fair trade. To support and obtain more information about the foundation, contact: Paul Freundlich, Fair Trade Foundation, 132 Highland Avenue, Middletown, CT 06457; (203) 347-5596.

# Part 5

# PEACE, NONVIOLENCE, AND HUMAN RIGHTS

*New opportunities through citizen diplomacy and legislative initiatives for reducing the military budget, peaceful purchasing, controlling television violence, and ending apartheid in South Africa*

## 23

# Who Is the Enemy?*

Four and a half billion years ago, the earth was formed. Perhaps a half billion years after that, life arose on the planet. For the next four billion years, life became steadily more complex, more varied, and more ingenious until, around a million years ago, it produced mankind—the most complex and ingenious species of them all. Only six or seven thousand years ago —a period that is to the history of the earth as less than a minute is to a year—civilization emerged, enabling us to build up a human world and to add to the marvels of evolution marvels of our own: marvels of art, of science, of social organization, or spiritual attainment.

But as we built higher and higher, the evolutionary foundation beneath our feet became more and more shaky, and now, in spite of all we have learned and achieved—or rather because of it—we hold this entire terrestrial creation hostage to nuclear destruction, threatening to hurl it back into the inanimate darkness from which it came. And this threat of self-destruction and planetary destruction is not something that we will pose one day in the future, if we fail to take certain precautions; it is here now, hanging over the heads of all of us at every moment.

The machinery of destruction is complete, poised on a hair trigger, waiting for the "button" to be "pushed" by some misguided or deranged human being, or for some faulty computer

* Excerpted from *The Fate of the Earth,* by Jonathan Schell, 1982. Reprinted by permission of Alfred A. Knopf, Inc., New York, N.Y. Originally appeared in *The New Yorker.*

chip to send out the instruction to fire. That so much should be balanced on so fine a point—that the fruit of four and a half billion years can be undone in a careless moment—is a fact against which belief rebels.

Since July 16, 1945, when the first atomic bomb was detonated at the Trinity test site near Alamogordo, New Mexico, mankind has lived with these weapons in its midst. Each year, the number of bombs has grown until now there are some fifty thousand warheads in the world, possessing the explosive yield of roughly twenty billion tons of TNT, or one million six hundred thousand times the yield of the bomb that was dropped by the United States on the city of Hiroshima, in Japan, less than a month after the Trinity explosion.

These bombs were built as "weapons" for "war," but their significance greatly transcends war and all its causes and outcomes. They grew out of history, yet they threaten to end history. They were made by men, yet they threaten to annihilate man. They are a pit into which the whole world can fall—a nemesis of all human intentions, actions, and hopes. Only life itself, which they threaten to swallow up, can give the measure of their significance. Yet in spite of the immeasurable importance of nuclear weapons, the world has declined, until very recently, to think about them much. We have thus far failed to fashion, or to discover within ourselves, an emotional or intellectual or political response to them.

Whatever the eventual shape of a world that has been reinvented for the sake of survival, the first, urgent, immediate step, which requires no deep thought or long reflection, is for each person to make known, visibly and unmistakably, his desire that the species survive. Extinction, being in its nature outside human experience, is invisible, but we, by rebelling against it, can indirectly make it visible. No one will ever witness extinction, so we must bear witness to it before the fact. And the place for the rebellion to start is in our daily lives. We can each perform a turnabout right where we are—let our daily business drop from our hands for a while, so that we can turn our attention to securing the foundation of all life, out of which our daily business grows and in which it finds its justification. This disruption of our lives will be a preventive disruption, for we will be hoping through the temporary suspension of our daily life to ward off the eternal suspension of it in extinction. And this turnabout in the first instance can be as simple as a phone call to a friend, a meeting in the community.

# 24

# Legislative and Legal Action

---

**Action 99**

*How to Defuse Nuclear Bombs on Your Coffee Break!*

# We Cut the Nuclear Issue Down to Size So You Can Do Something About it... in 20 Minutes a Month

*You already know the arms race is wasteful and dangerous. You wish there was something meaningful you could do about it. But you are busy.*

## We have a suggestion:

Subscribe to **20/20 Vision**. Every month our local committee does research to find the most useful 20 minute action you can take at home to stop the arms race.

## How it Works

Every month we call some of the nation's top arms-control policy analysts. They give us action recommendations tailored just for you and your neighbors - recommendations that take into account who your elected officials are and what national and local arms-related issues demand attention.

We review these analysts' suggestions and choose the one action you can take that will make the most difference. We send you our recommendation on a postcard – everything you need and nothing you don't need – so that you can spend 20 meaningful minutes a month working for our common security.

## 20 Minutes a Month... 20 Dollars a Year... Practical Peacemaking

Usually your monthly action will be to write a half-page letter or leave a brief phone message for a policy-maker facing an important national security decision.

Our research is so thorough, our actions so focused that you'll be getting the right message to the right person just when it counts. And your message will be heard. That's because you'll be writing and phoning along with hundreds of other **20/20 Vision** subscribers in our area.

## Focused on Results

**20/20 Vision Projects** across the country have a track record. Policy-makers pay attention. They change their minds and they change their votes on crucial arms race issues.

We won't guarantee you peace on earth by next Tuesday. But we do guarantee that you'll be satisfied with our service. That's because we do everything we can to turn the time you are willing to spend into time well spent.

### What You Get:

- A monthly postcard containing background information, our action recommendation and the address of the person to contact.
- Our short guide on how to write an effective letter in 20 minutes.
- A brief report every six months on the results of your actions.

### And we promise:

- No meetings.
- No mountains of mail.
- We won't ask you for more money.
- We won't give your name to other organizations.
- We won't call you during supper.

## 20/20 Vision—Something Practical We can do for Peace

### WHAT YOU CAN DO:

Currently there are 20/20 Vision projects active in thirty congressional districts with another six in development. To find out if there's a group in your district you can join, contact:

Lois Barber
20/20 Vision Eastern Office
69 South Pleasant Street, #203
Amherst, MA 01002
(413) 253-2939

Jeremy Sherman
20/20 Vision Western Office
1181 C Solano Avenue
Albany, CA 94706
(415) 528-8800

If there's no 20/20 Vision project in your area, the national offices can provide you with assistance to start your own project, including guidebooks and instructions, promotional materials, camera-ready artwork, on-site training, and ongoing support.

| Action | *A Rapid Response Network* |
|--------|----------------------------|
| 100    | *for Legislative Initiatives\** |

### Action 100    *A Rapid Response Network for Legislative Initiatives\**

A few moments of your time, on a consistent basis, can lead the peace movement to triumph.

In 1987 two of America's leading peace groups united under the single banner of Sane/Freeze. The two organizations—Sane, the Committee for a Sane Nuclear Policy, and the Nuclear Weapons Freeze Campaign—came together to pursue common goals:

—the creation of a just and peaceful world;

—the redirection of military spending into social programs;

—the prevention of developing the next generation of nuclear weapons;

—a comprehensive ban on nuclear testing;

—drastic cuts in nuclear arsenals;

—followed by the development of alternative means for solving international conflict; and finally

—complete disarmament.

Over 1,600 local groups, 24 state organizations, and 170,000 members are now part of the Sane/Freeze network. From Boston to Los Angeles, canvassers knock on six thousand doors every night to encourage fellow Americans to join the fight against nuclear weapons.

### WHAT YOU CAN DO:

Become a member of Sane/Freeze so you can join their Rapid Response Network (RRN). As an RRN participant, you will receive in addition to Sane/Freeze's quarterly magazine, a semiannual newsletter and more frequent postcards and/or phone calls targeted to congressional members in swing districts, alerting you to the upcoming vote on an important piece of legislation.

You'll be advised which of your local congressional repre-

\* Sane/Freeze brochure, 1988.

sentatives to contact, either by phone or mail, and what to say. Briefing papers will be available to provide you with complete background information on the issue, if you desire.

Your participation need not take more than a few minutes but may make a world of difference. Not unlike 20/20 Vision (see Action 99), the RRN is a way to cast your vote many times each year on the issues that concern you most.

To join Sane/Freeze and RRN send $25 ($10 for students, GIs, and those with low incomes) to 711 G Street, S.E., Washington, DC 20003; (202) 546-7100.

(NOTE: Along with your name and address mention your interest in joining the Rapid Response Network.)

---

## Action 101     *Nuclear Free Zones*

Nuclear Free Zones (NFZs) have been created by law, referendum, and resolution in cities, towns, and counties across the nation. All NFZs ban the manufacture and storage of nuclear weapons and the location of nuclear armament industries in the area. Some NFZs also prohibit investment of public funds in companies that manufacture nuclear weapons, the use of nuclear power, transportation of nuclear weapons, the storage or dumping of nuclear waste, and the irradiation of food (see Action 57).

Around the world there are more than 3,775 "Nuclear Free" cities, counties, and provinces in twenty-four countries:

    281 in Belgium (covering 45 percent of the population)
    169 in Canada (covering 64 percent of the population)
    184 in England
  1,135 in Japan
    105 in New Zealand
    305 in Spain
      1 in Tahiti
      1 in Vanuatu

In the United States there are currently 151 NFZs, representing more than 16 million people. If you don't already live in an NFZ, there are numerous activities you can participate in to help set one up.

## WHAT YOU CAN DO:

Contact Nuclear Free America (NFA) for information on how you can create an NFZ in your community, work with others who are already planning a campaign, find out what's happened in areas that have passed NFZ legislation, and learn about a variety of other information that NFA has available.

You can subscribe to the NFA newsletter, *The New Abolitionist,* six issues for $10. Write to Nuclear Free America, 325 East 25th Street, Baltimore, MD 21218; (301) 235-3575.

---

| Action 102 | *The Government Accountability Project (GAP)* |

The Government Accountability Project (GAP) has for over ten years protected and supported government employees in their struggle to speak out about a wide variety of dishonest, illegal, fraudulent and wasteful government activities.

The Government Accountability Project works to create a safety net for all the brave individuals who are willing to risk their jobs, and often lives, for their fellow workers, and at times the safety of their nation. While GAP's efforts cover whistle-blowers in all areas, they are mentioned here for their outstanding work in the military and nuclear industries. GAP has supported whistleblowers with legal protection, the drafting of new legislation, and Freedom of Information Act suits. GAP encourages individuals to take responsibility for alerting the public to safety violations in nuclear plants, faulty equipment, hammers that cost more than guns, payoffs to military consultants, and police brutality in Veterans Administration hospitals.

GAP has also worked to challenge the unlawful deregulation of the nuclear power industry, set safety standards in nuclear weapons facilities, cut massive governmental waste in space-related defense programs, and stop the government's attempt to deprive millions of federal employees with security clearances of their freedom-of-speech rights.

GAP has been successful in one landmark case after another. It has been responsible for the disclosure of:

—potential safety problems in forty-seven nuclear plants either in operation or under construction that the Nuclear Regulatory Commission tried to suppress

—the diversion of funds from defense appropriations to secret Central American military projects

—illegal and dangerous operational practices at uranium re-processing and nuclear weapons facilities owned by the Department of Energy in which hazardous wastes were leaking into water systems

—contract frauds by companies working for the Pentagon, the General Services Administration, and NASA

GAP has brought more than three hundred cases of dangerous government wrongdoing to the awareness of Americans through thousands of newspaper and magazine articles and television shows such as *60 Minutes* and *20/20*.

Whistleblowers take serious risks when they speak out. According to *The New York Times*, one out of five lose their jobs. Despite all this, these brave, conscientious men and women say they would speak out again—because they know that, thanks to GAP, *they* are making a difference.

What's more, they know that in *every* case where GAP gets substantive information about a problem, *they don't stop until a resolution is reached.*

## WHAT YOU CAN DO:

To support courageous whistleblowers around the nation and find out how you can help, contact GAP, 25 E Street, N.W., Suite 700, Washington, DC 20001; (202) 347-0460. Request a copy of their quarterly newsletter and consider making a financial contribution to their important work.

**Action**        *Telephone Hotlines*
   **103**

For Legislative Updates on Peace Issues

## WHAT YOU CAN DO:

The following taped legislative information is updated weekly and will help you play an active role in the Washington legislative process:

*Nuclear Arms Control Legislation* (202) 543-0006
   Sponsored by the Council for a Livable World

*Nuclear Testing Information* (702) 363-7780
   Sponsored by American Peace Test. [Contact the American Peace Test office (702) 731-9644, and request that you be notified every time a nuclear test is scheduled so you can assist in organizing your local community response.]

*Southern Africa Hotline* (202) 546-0408
   Sponsored by the Washington Office on Africa (see Action 119 for more information).

# 25

# Citizen Diplomacy

## The New Age of Diplomacy and Foreign Policy

Thousands of individuals, universities, unions, day-care centers, church groups, and cities have reached out across political, ideological, geographic, and governmental barriers to form relationships that will encourage peace, understanding, and partnership. These initiatives have given birth to a new age of diplomacy and foreign policy. They provide all of us with the opportunity to engage in meaningful foreign relations around the issues of our choice—almost anywhere in the world. Now we can set our own agenda, pursue the policies of our own choosing, and play a strategic role in our future relations with Russia, South Africa, and Central America with respect to development, military intervention, trade, hunger, economic policy, or education.

The following actions will explore your options as an individual citizen diplomat; as part of a sister cities program or partnership between your school, union, congregation or business and a similar group in a foreign country; and the new world of municipal foreign policy in which a city or municipality actively sets up and acts upon its own program of international diplomacy.

**Action
104**    *How to Become a Citizen
Diplomat\**

In a world of excessive military expenditures, nuclear ov-
erkill, endless Central American civil war, Middle East unrest,
apartheid in South Africa and international terrorism—diplomacy can clearly not be left to diplomats.

Global problems have simply become too complex to be solved
by just a few national leaders. If we ever hope to deal with these
problems effectively, we will need to harness the ideas, skills,
and goodwill of many of the world's five billion "unofficial"
leaders—people like ourselves. Thomas Jefferson once wrote that
"the good sense of the people will always be found to be the best
army." If more of us were involved in global problem solving, we
could begin to find more common ground on which to work together and more nonviolent ways to tolerate and reconcile our
differences.

Just as diplomats facilitate communication between governments, you, as a "citizen diplomat," can facilitate communication among the world's inhabitants. The more contact you have
with people in other countries through meetings, letters, visits,
lectures, and cultural exchanges, the more you can help everyone
recognize that they are all more than Americans, Chinese, Rus-
sians, or Indians—they are international citizens with a common
stake in survival.

Citizen diplomacy won't eliminate global conflict overnight;
nothing can do that. But it can begin transforming violent, na-
tion-versus-nation conflicts into nonviolent debates over specific
issues. As long as the world's controversies are framed terri-
torially—Israelis versus Syrians or Americans versus Soviets—
arms races and wars will remain and proliferate. But if international coalitions nourished through citizen diplomacy coalesce
among the world's developers, environmentalists, urbanites,
farmers, workers, and managers, controversies will increasingly
be defined in political, not geographic, terms. Once we find ourselves agreeing with people from other countries on some issues
and disagreeing on others, we can begin seeing them as more
deserving of persuasion than bullets. The more empathy we have

\*Excerpted with permission from *Having International Affairs Your Way,* by Michael
Shuman, published by the Center for Innovative Diplomacy, Irvine, Calif., 1986, pp. 4–5.

for foreigners, the less likely we will kill them—and the less likely they will want to destroy us. Only then will we begin finding lasting solutions to the world's problems.

## WHAT YOU CAN DO:

**1.** For a comprehensive introduction to citizen diplomacy— from personal preparation to setting an agenda, choosing your policy tools, developing a strategy, and successfully linking up with other groups—order a copy of *Having International Affairs Your Way: A Five-Step Briefing Manual for Citizen Diplomats,* $6 from the Center for Innovative Diplomacy (CID), 17931 Sky Park Circle, Suite F, Irvine, CA 92714; (714) 250-1296.

**2.** Also contact CID's Citizen Diplomacy Project, 424 Cole Street, Suite B, Irvine, CA 92714; (714) 250-1296.

**3.** For those interested specifically in U.S.-U.S.S.R. relations, the *Citizen Diplomat* is published bimonthly and is available for $10 a year from Citizen Diplomat, P.O. Box 9077, La Jolla, CA 92038; (619) 456-8049. The magazine covers a wealth of activities from tours, conferences, and projects to news, interviews, specific community-by-community interaction, coverage of new organizations, and reviews of relevant books.

**4.** Last, the following book will help put you in touch with thousands of peace groups with whom you can work:

*Peace Resource Book,* by the Institute for Defense and Disarmament Studies, 1988; $14.95. Describes five thousand peace groups across the country. Order from Ballinger, 2350 Virginia Avenue, Hagerstown, MD 21740; (800) 638-3030.

---

| Action | *Sister Cities, Unions,* |
|---|---|
| 105 | *Congregations, and* |
| | *Universities* |

In 1956 President Eisenhower formally established the sister cities concept, and twenty years later Sister Cities International picked up on his initiative. From 1976 to 1985, Sister Cities matched 786 American cities with 1,282 cities in eighty-six countries.*

*\*Bridging the Global Gap: A Handbook for Linking the First and Third Worlds,* by Medea Benjamin and Andrea Freedman, Seven Locks Press, Md./Washington, D.C., 1989.

Though this formal approach must be officially blessed by local city councils, with appointed city officials to oversee the program, less formal citizen-run and citizen-initiated partnerships have developed similar relationships through a variety of channels.

—Twelve Baltimore high-school students representing eleven public and private schools spent two weeks visiting Russian schoolchildren in Odessa. Three doctors from the Filatov Institute in Odessa met with U.S. doctors at the Johns Hopkins School of Medicine to discuss ophthalmological care.

—Vice-Mayor Alice Wolf of Cambridge, Massachusetts, led a sixteen-member delegation to Yerevan, U.S.S.R., to negotiate a three-year exchange program for educators, business executives, and environmentalists. Ten trade representatives from Yerevan attended Cambridge seminars hosted by the Chamber of Commerce and the Rotary Club to discuss joint business ventures.

—Brooklyn, New York, residents are raising money to help construct a new water system in San Juan del Rio Coco, Nicaragua.

—St. Paul, Minnesota, residents recently took out a half-page ad in a weekly South African newspaper to protest the forced eviction and relocation of Lawaai Kamp residents.

—Oregon State University has teamed up with the University of San Salvador in El Salvador to develop an exchange program.

These are only a few of the thousands of relationships that are building international understanding and laying the groundwork for more peaceful relations between countries.

## WHAT YOU CAN DO:

To find out how you can start or join groups already in place, contact the following:

### GENERAL SISTER CITIES INFORMATION

Center for Innovative Diplomacy
17931 Skypark Circle, Suite F
Irvine, CA 92714
(714) 250-1296

and

Sister Cities International
1625 Eye Street, N.W., #424-26
Washington, DC 20006
(202) 836-3535

## U.S.-NICARAGUAN SISTER CITIES

Wisconsin Coordinating Council on Nicaragua
P.O. Box 1534
Madison, WI 53701

and

Neighbor to Neighbor (see Action 121 for address)

## U.S.-CENTRAL AMERICAN SISTER CITIES

Faith Without Borders
c/o Network in Solidarity with the People of Guatemala
1314 14th Street, N.W., #16
Washington, DC 20005
(202) 483-0050

and

Partners of the Americas
1424 K Street, N.W., #700
Washington, DC 20005
(202) 628-3300

## U.S.-SOVIET SISTER CITIES

Institute for Soviet-American Relations
1608 New Hampshire Avenue, N.W.
Washington, DC 20009
(202) 387-3034

## U.S.-AFRICAN SISTER CITIES

American Committee on Africa
198 Broadway
New York, NY 10038
(212) 962-1210

*UNION TO UNION*

Labor Network on Central America
P.O. Box 28014, Department F
Oakland, CA 94604
(415) 272-9951

*DAYCARE TO DAYCARE CENTER*

MADRE
835 Broadway, #301
New York, NY 10003
(212) 777-6470

For more information see Chapter 2 of *Bridging the Global Gap,* by Medea Benjamin and Andrea Freedman, available from Global Exchange, 2940 16th Street, Suite 307, San Francisco, CA 94103. ($10.95.)

---

**Action    *Municipal Foreign Policy***
**106**

Today, cities from Minneapolis to Managua, Brooklyn to Bremen, and Oxford to Odessa are taking stands on the impact of the arms race on local economies, U.S. policy in Central America, the ozone crisis, international disarmament, homeporting, the conflict in Northern Ireland, and apartheid.

Eight hundred U.S. localities have passed nuclear freeze resolutions, forty-two municipalities have passed legislation prohibiting local governments from purchasing goods and services from nuclear weapons contractors or corporations that are active in South Africa, five hundred cities in Europe are providing direct development assistance to Third World communities involving millions of dollars and hundreds of thousands of residents, and twenty-two cities and two states offer sanctuary for refugees from El Salvador to Guatemala.

In the future, cities may send lobbyists to Washington, set their own international trade policy, and monitor human rights abuses. Municipal foreign policy has truly become an area in which citizens and local elected officials can affect international relations.

## WHAT YOU CAN DO:

To find out how you can play an active role contact Center for Innovative Diplomacy, 17931 Sky Park Circle, Suite F, Irvine, CA 92714; (714) 250-1296.

Consider ordering the following publications from the center:

*The Bulletin of Municipal Foreign Policy,* quarterly, $15 or free with a $35 membership to the institute. The bulletin is clearly the bible of the movement.

*and*

*Building Municipal Foreign Policies: An Action Handbook for Citizens and Local Elected Officials,* 53 pages, 1987. Costs $6.

---

| Action 107 | *Weaving Your Way to Soviet-American Understanding* **A Success Story** |
|---|---|

Peace Fleece is a business that was created out of one family's despair over the possibility of nuclear war.

Peter Hagerty and his wife, Marty Tracy, who live in rural Maine and raise lambs for wool, wondered daily "what was the point of raising all these lambs, growing all this feed, if all at once the sky could light up and everything we valued could disappear?"

Peter believed that we can all create a bridge of peace through personal relationships with Soviet citizens and thus begin to reduce the chances of war. His solution was to build his bridge with Soviet farmers by purchasing their wool and blending it with his own. Then he would market this Soviet-American wool to consumers along with knitting patterns and instructions and a booklet printed in Russian and English telling his story.

When Peter left on his first trip to Russia, with a group of American farmers to meet their Soviet counterparts, wool had never been exported to the United States. But Peter forged ahead to overcome the bureaucracy, an American embargo against certain Soviet products, and a punitive import tax on "Communist wool." In 1986 he received his first twelve hundred-pound shipment from Krasnodar, a beautiful farm district not far from the Black Sea. Since then, many more shipments have arrived, and the blended wool is now sold throughout the United States and Canada as well as overseas.

Peter has been to Russia three more times, to continue to promote understanding and friendship on a person-to-person basis. Recently, Peace Fleece even sponsored a trade conference for U.S. and Soviet business people under the heading of "Building Trust through Trade," and in January 1989, Peace Fleece signed an agreement with a Moscow cooperative to begin sale of their yarn in the U.S.S.R.

## WHAT YOU CAN DO:

To receive a Peace Fleece catalog with wool samples and designs for adults' and children's hats and mittens, vests, cardigans, and pullovers, contact Soviet American Woolens, RFD 1, Box 57, Kezar Falls, ME 04047; (207) 625-4906.

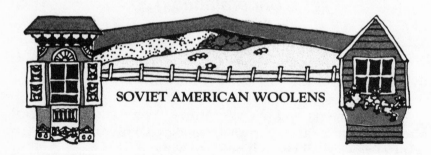

Peace Fleece also leads Soviet Sheep Tours. Write to the above address for more information.

# 26

# Reducing and Redirecting the Military Budget

**Action
108**

*1% For Peace*

There is no way in which a country can satisfy the craving for absolute security, but it can easily bankrupt itself morally and economically in attempting to reach that goal through arms alone.—DWIGHT D. EISENHOWER

Our government spends $300 billion on the military every year. 1% For Peace is a national grass-roots organization that tries to convince the government to spend just 1 percent of that $300 billion on exploring ways to eliminate the need for so many weapons.

1% For Peace is nonprofit and nonpartisan. It seeks to create a positive peace agenda. The goal is to pass a federal law based on the following resolutions:

—that 1 percent of the U.S. Department of Defense budget of the United States ($3 billion) be redirected to peace through understanding.

—that business, civic, religious, professional, trade, social, and educational institutions and municipal organizations *BE EN-COURAGED TO CONTRIBUTE 1 PERCENT OF THEIR RE-SOURCES* in the form of money, time, or in-kind contributions to *ACTIVITIES DIRECTED AT PEACE THROUGH UNDER-STANDING.*

—that *ACTIVE FORUMS BE CULTIVATED FOR THE AMER-ICAN PEOPLE TO SHARE AND PARTICIPATE IN THIS POS-ITIVE PEACE AGENDA.*

*The choice seems clear:*

| COST | COST |
|---|---|
| Here's what $3 billion buys in military hardware: | Here's what $3 billion could buy if spent on activities directed at peace through understanding: |
| 1 aircraft carrier (without airplanes) | A yearly exchange of 250,000 citizens between the U.S. and U.S.S.R. |
| **$3 BILLION** | **$750 MILLION** |
| | A multinational youth corps to start feeding the hungry, housing the homeless, and caring for the sick, here and throughout the world |
| | **$750 MILLION** |
| | 5 pilot projects to convert weapons factories to manufacturing alternate energy and mass transit equipment |
| | **$500 MILLION** |
| | Updating educational curricula to inform children of the multicultural and global realities of today |
| | **$500 MILLION** |
| | Multinational children's camps for 200,000 children a year @ $2,500 |
| | **$3 BILLION** |

**TOTAL:  $3 BILLION          TOTAL:  $3 BILLION**
**WHICH WOULD YOU RATHER HAVE YOUR MONEY BUY?**

1% For Peace has been organized mainly by Ben Cohen, Jerry Greenfield, and Jeff Furman of Ben & Jerry's Homemade Ice Cream.

## WHAT YOU CAN DO:

—Display a 1% For Peace bumper sticker on your car. Each sticker is a vote for 1% For Peace.

—Ask businesses that you patronize and organizations of which you are a member to support 1% For Peace.

—Distribute 1% For Peace bumper stickers and brochures.

—Organize and help out at 1% For Peace petition-signing efforts.

—Volunteer your time to 1% For Peace.

—Consider a financial contribution.

To order bumper stickers or buttons at $1 each, or to get more information, contact 1% For Peace, P.O. Box 94, Brooktondale, NY 14817.

Also

eat Ben & Jerry's Peace Pops; a portion of the profits go to support 1% For Peace.

---

**Action 109**    *Jobs with Peace\**
**"Build Homes Not Bombs"**

The National Jobs with Peace Campaign is run by an organization that does not focus on "peace" as the word is normally defined. It does not focus so much on avoiding nuclear annihilation as it does on organizing those who are most hurt by the current federal priority on military spending and the resulting loss of investment in human needs. These misplaced national priorities have allowed our federal government to spend fifty-five cents of every federal tax dollar on the military and only two cents on housing, nutrition, and other human needs.

*Excerpted with permission from *Building Economic Alternatives*, (Spring 1988). Subscription: $20 per year (4 issues plus Co-op America membership), Co-op America, 2100 M Street, N.W., Suite 310, Washington, DC 20063.

The political and economic vision of Jobs with Peace is clear: The United States cannot have a healthy economy or a free society while it squanders its resources on a military machine that absorbs over half of the federal budget.

## The Jobs with Peace Strategy

The Jobs with Peace strategy involves education, grass-roots organizing, and coalition building, including providing some of the hardest-hitting information about the military budget and its impact on our communities. It is organizing low-income people and people of color around a program that is both immediate and visionary. Coalitions are being built within the "triangle" of progressive forces represented by the peace movement, the labor movement, and the civil rights and women's movements.

Jobs with Peace campaigns fight for issues that immediately affect those constituencies. In Los Angeles, a campaign to provide 20,000 additional slots in the city's after-school child-care program is being organized. In Milwaukee, Jobs with Peace is organizing public-housing tenants over issues of rents and housing conditions.

## Neighbors Visiting Neighbors

Through personal visits and house meetings, the organization is steadily and consistently developing local leadership. In the personal visits, organizers ask an individual to become a "neighborhood leader," specifically to (1) pledge $20 per month, (2) hold a house meeting in his/her home, and (3) agree to contact fifty neighbors. The neighborhood leader is then responsible for asking those contacted to call or write elected representatives and remind them how to vote on issues that concern their constituents.

Jobs with Peace's basic belief is that all working people have a stake in peace but need to be approached from their own interests.

## Organizing Locally, Cooperating Nationally

The Jobs with Peace Campaign targets the federal government as the problem. It also sees the government as a necessary part of the solution. Local issues are emphasized, but local campaigns also cooperate nationally.

The national Jobs with Peace organization is now coordinating a "Build Homes Not Bombs" campaign that focuses on funding permanently affordable housing by cutting the military budget. It is coordinating a variety of local actions and federal legislation that will increase funding for housing.

## WHAT YOU CAN DO:

Jobs with Peace needs your help today! Contact them to discuss how you can get involved. Jobs with Peace, National Office, 76 Summer Street, Boston, MA 02110; (617) 338-5783.

---

**Action
110**     *Conscientious Objection
to Military and War Taxes\**

Henry David Thoreau is the most famous tax resister of all. Faced with the choice between supporting the U.S. war with Mexico and going to jail for refusing to pay taxes, he chose the latter. Thoreau said, "There is a higher law, and I have discerned it and placed myself in obedience to it."

When the Selective Service Act began allowing alternative service for conscientious objectors in 1940, U.S. citizens were given a legal way to refuse to participate in wars and remain true to their conscience and religious or moral principles.

Using this as a model, the founders of the National Campaign for a Peace Tax Fund (NCPTF) sought to create a similar mechanism for taxpayers to avoid paying military and war taxes. Legislation was written and introduced in 1972 in the U.S. Congress that would establish a Peace Tax Fund, financed by the military taxes of qualified conscientious objectors. The fund would promote disarmament, economic conversion of nuclear facilities, and educational programs on nonviolent resolution of conflicts. Like the Selective Service Act, this bill would resolve for some the moral dilemma of paying taxes for activities that violated their individual religious or ethical principles.

While lobbying and building support for the legislation became the priority for the NCPTF, the Conscience and Military

---

*Excerpted with permission from *Conscientious Objection to Military & War Taxes*, published by Conscience and Military Tax Campaign.

Tax Campaign (CMTC) was formed in 1979 to encourage people to refuse to pay military/war taxes immediately. Participants declared themselves "conscientious objectors" by signing the CMTC resolution and by informing their congressional representatives and/or IRS officials of their views and commitment. They began depositing their tax dollars in the CMTC Escrow Account or other alternative funds until pressure ensured passage of the bill. Thousands now refuse to pay portions of their income and telephone taxes. The escrow account contains nearly $300,000 from more than six hundred depositors nationwide. Upon passage of the legislation, the escrow funds would be turned over to the U.S. Treasury for nonmilitary purposes.

Because of this emphasis on a lawful mechanism to avoid direct complicity in warfare, conscientious objection can be distinguished from "war tax resistance," and is a way to work on restoring constitutionally guaranteed "rights of conscience" and freedom of religious expression.

However, despite references to pending or existing legislation and international law, any form of refusing taxes is currently a violation of the IRS code and federal law and could result in penalties, fines, property seizures, or even criminal prosecution (although the latter is extremely rare).

CMTC publishes a quarterly newsletter called *Conscience*, and a wide variety of other literature on the subject of tax resistance, including legal issues and the IRS's position on tax diversion.

### WHAT YOU CAN DO:

Write to CMTC for more information about tax resistance or subscribe to *Conscience*, $4 for four issues. CMTC, 4534½ University Way, N.E., Suite 204, Seattle, WA 98105 (206) 547-0952.

## 27

# Nonviolence—
# Toys, Television, Children,
# and Adults

| | |
|---|---|
| **Action 111** | ***The War Resisters League (WRL)**** |

*The War Resisters League . . . is indispensable for the preparation of a fundamental change in public opinion, a change that, under present-day circumstances, is absolutely necessary if humanity is to survive.*—ALBERT EINSTEIN

Across the political spectrum left, right, and center, everyone says they want peace. Usually they ALSO want a gun, an army, or an atomic bomb to make sure its the "right" kind of peace. In such a world, the War Resisters League (WRL) is unique. It believes, to quote A. J. Muste, "**There is no way to peace —peace is the way**," and rejects the use of violence for national defense or for revolutionary change. Deeply influenced by the teachings of the Indian leader, Mohandas Gandhi, as well as

*Excerpted with permission from the *War Resisters League* brochure.

Thoreau, Tolstoy, King, and others, WRL believes war is a crime against humanity. WRL believes in the use of peaceful means to help create a democratic society that is free of economic, racial, or sexual oppression. Their methods range from education to nonviolent direct action—trying at all times to see those they oppose not as enemies but as brothers and sisters.

Even where there seems to be "peace," the suffering of poverty is as real as war to those who are trapped at the bottom of our society. Thus the War Resisters League works for peace within a framework of social justice.

Feminist thinking has brought a better understanding of the connections between militarism and sexism. Our culture still equates masculinity with domination and concentrates economic and political power in the hands of men. The spirit and style of feminism offer a striking alternative to the military psychology of America, which stresses competition and aggressive (even violent) behavior. The league believes human survival depends on finding ways to negotiate and cooperate rather than continuing conflict through violence.

## Programs That Create Change

The War Resisters League centers its work on education and action. The educational work includes publishing pacifist literature, an annual *Peace Calendar*, organizers' mailings, and conferences. The emphasis is on ACTION, on war RESIST-ANCE, and on individual conscience—it is this emphasis that marks the difference between the league and the other peace groups. WRL organizes demonstrations, it forms coalitions with other peace and social justice groups, it opposes conscription, and supports young men who resist conscription at all levels. The staff helps train people in civil disobedience, in war tax resistance, and in other forms of putting conscience into action.

WRL is committed not only to eliminating war but the **causes** of war. The following list covers some of the specific areas of its work:

—Draft/counterrecruitment

—Central America

—Disarmament

—Local organizing

—Racism

—War tax resistance

—Stop War Toys Campaign (see Action 112)

—Feminism and nonviolence

Special literature includes the *Organizers' Manual*, the *Guide to War Tax Resistance*, and various packets of information, including those on High School Organizing, ROTC Dismantling, a Stop War Toys Campaign, Feminism and Nonviolence, and Racism and Militarism. Eight times a year, WRL sends its magazine, *The Nonviolent Activist*, to the entire membership.

## WHAT YOU CAN DO:

Join in one or more of the league's programs. Write for specific information on the activities listed above and also request a copy of their publications list, which contains a wealth of books and pamphlets on disarmament, draft resistance, feminism, nonviolent action, the teaching of peace, and a number of other subjects. The league has never charged membership dues. It depends entirely upon voluntary contributions from members and friends. Contact War Resisters League, 339 Lafayette Street, New York, NY 10012; (212) 228-0450.

---

## Children and Violence

We live in an increasingly violent world. Inner-city children often risk their lives just walking to school. Our nation spends half its budget on military-related activities. Wars can now be watched comfortably from living room couches. Domestic violence, terrorist activity, and human tragedy of every imaginable variety are part of our daily landscape. Children grow up with stories of babies being flushed down toilets and madmen with automatic weapons killing innocent people in a McDonald's that looks just like the one where they eat.

We support this violence when we give children war toys to play out the terror they've read about and seen on the screen, and when we take them to movies which let them see killing without pain and war without suffering. Even video games are

available that will let children pretend to cause a massive annihilation that the real world has yet to experience.

The following actions will help bring peace and eliminate
some of the unnecessary violence from the lives of our children.

---

## Action          *War Toys*
## 112

*Toy machine guns, death ray guns, tanks, war making robots and
space ships, stimulate hostile, brutal feelings even in very young
children, which gradually erode their capacities for tenderness and
sympathy.*—DR. BENJAMIN SPOCK

"Every time we purchase a toy, we communicate our adult
values to the children who receive these toys. Through play,
children imitate our values. Do we want children to assume that
war has a positive value to us by letting them play with war
toys? Do we want them to think that disputes and differences
are best settled by force, and that the world is divided up into
good guys and bad guys?

"We may not be able to shelter children from all forms of
violent play. They may still hold out a finger to imitate a gun.
But we need to explain to children, at their own level of understanding, the meaning and consequences of real war—that real
people don't get up when shot with a real gun.

"Mechanized war toys do not require or develop courage and
creative problem solving. They are substitutes for courage. They
lead children to think that everything can be settled by pushing
a button or pulling a trigger. Today, when war has become a
destroyer of whole populations, we must stop encouraging children to make a game of killing, especially with toys of destruction.

"Parents need to realize that the major objection to war toys
is that they condition children to accept something that is unacceptable. If, as adults, they try to use these weapons to settle
differences, they will fail, and the human race will be the
victim."*

---

*Excerpted with permission from *You and Your Children*, by Carol Jahnkow, Stop War
Toys Campaign, New England War Resisters League.

# WHAT YOU CAN DO:

### *"GI Joe: An American Hero"*

"GI Joe toys ranked in the top three selling toys for eleven months in 1986. It continued to be in the top ten in 1987 and is projected to remain there. GI Joe toys include: over 50 action figures of the Joe action force and enemy Cobra; battle gear accessories; weapons assortments; battlefield vehicles; strategic long-range artillery machines; tanks with artillery; underwater attack and aerial reconnaissance craft; roving vehicle fortress; helicopters with complete arsenals of bombs; supersonic jet with bombing equipment; the terror dome; aircraft carrier; a $200 space vehicle launch complex; plus more vehicles and weapons.

"GI Joe toys do not stand alone; every morning before school and each afternoon GI Joe cartoons are seen across the country. They average 84 acts of violence per hour. There are also GI Joe comic books, magazines, lunch boxes, sheets, kites, t-shirts, slippers and a GI Joe laser tag game. Over 30 companies are licensees for the GI Joe logo."*

The War Resisters League has initiated a campaign against war toys and cartoons that is presently focusing on GI Joe.

Write to:

Hasbro, Inc.
1027 Newport Avenue
Pawtucket, RI 02862

to protest the sale of GI Joe as well as the televised cartoon. Also protest "Transformers" and other war toys.

Other actions against war toys in general:

1. Write to the editor of your local paper.

2. Speak with family, friends, and especially other parents, encouraging them not to buy war toys.

3. Meet with the manager of your local toy store, share your thoughts, and urge the store to stop carrying war toys.

---

*Excerpted with permission from *GI Joe: An American Hero*, by Kate Donnelly, Stop War Toys Campaign, New England War Resisters League.

**4.** Order their Stop War Toys Campaign packet from:

> New England War Resisters League
> Box 1093
> Norwich, CT 06360
> (508) 774-3417 or (203) 889-5337

The packet includes a wealth of educational and factual information as well as organizing and action ideas, alternative play tips, and background and publicity material. For $6, it's a bargain and supports the outstanding work of the league.

**5.** Also available from the War Resisters League is a complete list of war toy manufacturers as well as a list of alternative toy, book, and music manufacturers whose products are available by direct mail.

**6.** Send your old war toys to:

> National Coalition
> on Television Violence
> P.O. Box 2157
> Champaign, IL 61820

which hopes to hammer, melt, and bend these toys of violence into a statue for peace.

---

**Action 113**        *Computer Games and Video Violence\**

Ever since the introduction of Space Invaders several years ago, toy and game manufacturers have exploited the profit potential of computers and video games which all too often bring additional violence into the lives of children. The latest wave of games out in the marketplace is far more sophisticated and realistic.

These descendants of Space Invaders are available for almost every type of home computer and video game system. Children and adults can spend time blowing away anything from ghosts and giant spiders to "alien monsters" to save humanity, the earth, or, occasionally, just themselves from certain death and destruction. Computer gamesters, with affectionate deri-

*Excerpted with permission from *Video Violence*, by Larry Erickson for New England War Resisters League.

sion, call these games "alien bashing," an idle pastime with no more meaning or significance—and with less connection to reality—than reading the Sunday funnies.

Of greater importance to war toy opponents—are "simulations," games that attempt in varying degrees to create the impression of a "true experience" that can be related to the player's knowledge of the real world.

In playing these games, one must think in terms of the most effective use of force and power to kill. No other route to success is permitted or even possible within the games' design. No other choice than "kill or die" exists. When combined with history-based "realism," which in some is fairly extensive, these games amount to training exercises for a militarized mind, one that thinks of the world solely in terms of "mission effectiveness" instead of morals and ethics.

Here are some of the more "realistic" titles: "F-15 Strike Eagle," by Microprose, with an add-on scenario disk to simulate bombing Tripoli; "Red Storm Rising," by Microprose, about a Soviet invasion of Western Europe; "Strike Fleet," by Electronic Arts/Lucasfilm Games, which offers scenarios of Soviet subs and the Falkland Islands; "PHM Pegasus," by Electronic Arts/Lucasfilm Games, where the player is pitted against arms smugglers to Nicaragua and ships from Libya; "B-1 Mission to Moscow," by Access, in which the "Evil Empire" has nuclear missiles that the player must destroy along with most of the Soviet Union; and "Contra," by Konami, where the enemy is the "Red Falcon" in the Amazon jungle.

Luckily the same sophistication that has made these games possible has also led to the release of a wide variety of creative, nonviolent alternative games. Unlike a few years ago, it's now possible to have a library of video games that don't require you to become an imitation Genghis Khan to play them. So when you shop for video games—exercise caution about what you buy.

## WHAT YOU CAN DO:

**1.** Write letters of protest to:

ATARI, INC.
P.O. Box 61657
Sunnyvale, CA 94086

NINTENDO OF AMERICA, INC.
P.O. Box 957
Redmon, WA 98052

as well as other manufacturers.

**2.** Protest to your local toy store.

**3.** Write the New England War Resisters League, P.O. Box 1093, Norwich, CT 06306, for more information.

---

**Action 114**  *Violence on Television**

*The evidence that televised violence contributes to aggressive and destructive behavior is overwhelming.*—U.S. SENATOR PAUL SIMON

In a recent episode of the TV cartoon "GI Joe," one of the heroes beats up a half-dozen terrorists.

"Has it ever occurred to you there might be an easier way to settle disputes?" one of the hero's sidekicks asks him.

"Yeah," the hero replies. "With a gun."

In the world of children's television, there is nothing remarkable about this episode. Violence is daily after-school fare.

On "Transformers," animated robots from outer space blast each other to bits in a never-ending war portrayed as centuries old. On "Captain Power and the Soldiers of the Future," actors fight to save Earth from enslavement by Lord Dread and his Bio Dread Monsters. On "Rambo," the animated hero kneels, ties on a headband, and wraps himself in bandoliers in a daily ritual that precedes the chatter of automatic weapons.

Children's television is more violent than ever.

The children's shows of twenty and thirty years ago—cartoons like "Tom and Jerry" and "Woody Woodpecker"—averaged twenty violent acts per half hour, says Dr. Thomas E. Radecki, a child psychiatrist at the University of Illinois. Today's war cartoons average forty-eight such acts, he says, with "GI Joe" leading the way with an average of eighty-four.

Children's shows are three times more violent than prime-time programs, according to recent congressional testimony by Dr. Lillian Beard of the American Academy of Pediatrics. She says the average child, exposed to both prime-time and children's programming, watches at least twelve thousand acts of televised violence a year.

The debate over whether TV violence produces antisocial

*Excerpted with permission from "TV More Violent Than Ever" by Bruce DeSilva, *The Hartford Courant*, 10/12/87, page A-14.

behavior in children is nearly as old as the television industry. The first congressional hearing on the subject was held in 1952.

Researchers have commonly approached the problem by sticking children in front of a television set to see how they behave afterward. Radecki says his review of the literature has uncovered thirty-three such studies. Thirty-one show that children behave more aggressively immediately after viewing televised violence, he says.

In a typical study, a group of four-year-olds was shown "Batman" and "Superman" cartoons every day for four weeks. A second group of children watched "Mr. Rogers' Neighborhood," a gentle, public television program. A third group watched educational films on such topics as visiting the post office. The study found that children who watched the cartoons were more likely to hit other children, call people names, and refuse to obey classroom rules.

The results are impressive, Radecki says, because the studies are based on only a few hours of television watching, a small fragment of the "massive number of such shows that children are exposed to."

## WHAT YOU CAN DO:

1. Write to Congress: Ask your congressperson and senators to support the National Coalition on Television Violence's proposed legislation on war toys and war cartoons. This would prohibit companies from using cartoon programming as a way of selling toys with violent themes. It would also require that the message of the Surgeon General on the harmfulness of violent entertainment be placed on children's TV. For every three ads promoting violent toys or violent TV programming for children, one advertising slot would be set aside to remind children that using violence as a way of entertaining themselves is a bad idea. Write to your congressperson at the U.S. House of Representatives, Washington, DC 20515, and to the U.S. Senate, Washington, DC 20510.

2. Write to local television stations that carry violent cartoons and ads for violent toys and protest this promotion of violence. Point out that this promotion is increasing attitudes of violence in children.

3. Write to the Federal Communications Commission (1919 M Street, N.W., Washington, DC 20554) and ask for an imme-

diate investigation of the use of children's programming to sell violent toys to children. Write to the Federal Trade Commission (633 Indiana Avenue, N.W., Washington, DC 20580) and ask for an immediate investigation into and ban on the use of advertising to sell violent toys to children, or for required counteradvertising time to get out the message of the Surgeon General.

4. Subscribe to *NCTV News*, published by the National Coalition on Television Violence. This publication will keep you informed about legislative efforts, actions you can take about everything from ads for war toys in *Parents' Magazine* to how to protest the latest new violent cartoon, and includes reviews of new research and publications that deal with violence and children.

   The newsletter also reviews new toys, monitors the number of violent acts on TV shows, movies, and cartoons, and covers conferences and events you may want to attend.

   Newsletter subscription is free with a $25 membership. Write to:

> NCTV
> P.O. Box 2157
> Champaign, IL 61820

5. Also contact:

> Action for Children's Television
> 46 Austin Street,
> Newtonville, MA 02160
> (617) 527-7870

for information about the organization and newsletter.

## 28

# Peaceful Purchasing and Consumer Boycotts

| | |
|---|---|
| **Action** | ***How to Keep Nuclear*** |
| **115** | ***Weapons Out of Your*** |
| | ***Daily Life*** |

Not unlike the Council for Economic Priorities' *Rating America's Corporate Conscience* (see Action 95), the *Socially Responsible Buyer's Guide*, published by Covenant for a World Free of Nuclear Weapons, will help you keep products manufactured by companies that make nuclear weapons out of your life.

The guide lists "acceptable" and "unacceptable" products in categories ranging from alarm clocks and answering machines to blenders and blow dryers, carpets and coffee makers, gasoline and garden equipment, glues and golf clubs, light bulbs and long-distance phone services to VCRs, washing machines, and watches.

Brand-name products made by companies or their subsidiaries that are also listed as the nation's top thirty nuclear weapons producers are categorized as "unacceptable," and companies that are among the top one hundred in overall military contracting are considered "questionable."

### WHAT YOU CAN DO:

Order a copy of the *Buyer's Guide* by sending $3 to Interfaith Council for Peace, 604 East Huron, Ann Arbor, MI 48104.

For $3, a similar and somewhat more expanded guide titled *Consumer Brand Names of the Top 50 Nuclear Weapons Contractors* is available from Nuclear Free America, 325 East 25th Street, Baltimore, MD 21218.

---

| Action 116 | Who Are the Nation's Top 100 Department of Defense Contractors? |
|---|---|

I thought you should know—and I am willing to bet that by just reading the list in the table below, actions will occur to you!

### FY '88 TOP 100 DEFENSE DEPARTMENT CONTRACTORS

| COMPANY | CONTRACT $ (thousands) | COMPANY | CONTRACT $ (thousands) |
|---|---|---|---|
| 1. McDonnell Douglas | $8,002,741 | 24. Singer | 784,616 |
| 2. General Dynamics | 6,522,124 | 25. ITT | 768,784 |
| | | 26. Allied Signal | 710,700 |
| 3. General Electric | 5,700,635 | 27. CRS Sirrine | 692,002 |
| 4. Tenneco | 5,057,922 | 28. Gencorp | 639,445 |
| 5. Raytheon | 4,055,346 | 29. Avondale | 579,797 |
| 6. Martin Marietta | 3,715,106 | 30. AT&T | 565,414 |
| 7. General Motors | 3,550,180 | 31. CFM | 532,707 |
| 8. Lockheed | 3,537,658 | 32. Northrop | 532,638 |
| 9. United Technologies | 3,508,055 | 33. Hercules | 498,937 |
| | | 34. Harsco | 495,916 |
| 10. Boeing | 3,017,839 | 35. Loral | 493,589 |
| 11. Grumman | 2,847,711 | 36. Teledyne | 469,497 |
| 12. Litton | 2,561,321 | 37. Bell Boeing | 426,674 |
| 13. Westinghouse | 2,184,957 | 38. GTE | 422,544 |
| 14. Rockwell | 2,183,875 | 39. Dyncorp | 421,440 |
| 15. Unisys | 1,379,517 | 40. MIT | 408,471 |
| 16. Honeywell | 1,365,830 | 41. Gibbons Green | 400,620 |
| 17. Textron | 1,275,992 | 42. Morton Thiokol | 391,500 |
| 18. TRW | 1,250,225 | 43. Royal Dutch Petrol. | 389,859 |
| 19. Texas Instruments | 1,232,422 | 44. Motorola | 381,280 |
| | | 45. Harris | 371,452 |
| 20. IBM | 1,064,658 | 46. Computer Sciences | 367,700 |
| 21. LTV | 941,595 | | |
| 22. FMC | 861,952 | 47. Aerospace | 367,000 |
| 23. Ford | 790,553 | 48. Mitre | 356,840 |

| COMPANY | CONTRACT $ (thousands) | COMPANY | CONTRACT $ (thousands) |
|---|---|---|---|
| 49. Pan Am | 356,681 | 76. Kodak | 186,154 |
| 50. Johns Hopkins Univ. | 354,830 | 77. Draper Labs | 186,011 |
| | | 78. Sundstrand | 184,847 |
| 51. Science Applications | $343,542 | 79. Kaman | 183,767 |
| | | 80. Emhart | 180,996 |
| 52. Olin | 330,789 | 81. Digital Equipment | 175,256 |
| 53. Penn Central | 328,570 | | |
| 54. Chevron | 327,769 | 82. Morrison Knudsen | 170,238 |
| 55. Control Data | 315,301 | | |
| 56. Atlantic Richfield | 303,207 | 83. Rolls-Royce | 168,779 |
| 57. Mobil | 302,333 | 84. Arvin Industries | 166,201 |
| 58. Philips | 291,302 | 85. United Industrial | 165,299 |
| 59. Exxon | 282,143 | 86. ITT & Varo | 164,698 |
| 60. E-Systems | 262,682 | 87. CSX | 160,928 |
| 61. Forstmann Little | 261,223 | 88. Daimler-Benz | 154,980 |
| 62. Oshkosh Truck | 259,932 | 89. Motor Oils Helas | 149,629 |
| 63. Emerson Electric | 253,105 | 90. Hewlitt-Packard | 148,739 |
| 64. Black River | 250,817 | 91. Honeywell Bull | 146,991 |
| 65. Zenith | 247,827 | 92. Tiger International | 145,192 |
| 66. Contel | 236,788 | | |
| 67. Sequa | 219,606 | 93. Day & Zimmerman | 144,765 |
| 68. Eaton | 217,926 | | |
| 69. Coastal | 213,368 | 94. Phelps | 141,036 |
| 70. Chrysler | 210,854 | 95. Royal Ordnance | 139,277 |
| 71. MIP | 198,016 | 96. Braintree Maritime | 133,527 |
| 72. Bahrain Nat'l Oil | 192,922 | | |
| 73. General Electric (UK) | 192,501 | 97. EG&G | 131,840 |
| | | 98. Texaco | 130,937 |
| 74. Westmark Systems | 191,959 | 99. Bundesamt | 129,607 |
| 75. Amoco | 187,826 | 100. Figgie International | 128,683 |

*Source:* DoD 100 Companies Receiving the Largest Dollar Volume of Prime Contract Awards, FY 1988

---

**Action 117**

## *Bringing GE to Light**

INFACT
THE GE
BOYCOTT

---

* Excerpted with permission from "INFACT: Bringing GE to Light," by Dion Nissenbaum, *SANE World/FREEZE Focus,* Summer 1988.

Join a boycott to get the nation's largest pro-military lobbier and
third largest military contractor out of the business of making
nuclear weapons.

General Electric, America's third largest military contractor, has run into a group of citizens who are taking the company's
slogan "We're not satisfied until you are" a little more seriously
than GE expected. INFACT, the Boston-based grass-roots organization that led a seven-year boycott against Nestle, is spear-
heading a now three-year-old boycott directed at General Electric
and its role in the nuclear arms race.

Following the success of the Nestle action, INFACT re-
searched other abuses by transnational corporations. Says IN-
FACT Executive Director Nancy Cole, "We had to target to be
effective. But we had to target in a way that would maximize
the impact on the whole industry." INFACT chose General Electric as a "strategic target" for two reasons: (1) It is involved in
more major weapons systems than any other corporation, and
(2) it grosses three times as much money from consumer products
as it does from nuclear products, making it susceptible to consumer pressure as well as sufficiently diverse economically to
respond to that pressure.

## Boycott Demands

When INFACT launched its boycott of GE in June 1986, it
made four basic demands of the company:

**1.** Cease production of nuclear weapons;

**2.** Stop interfering in the U.S. government's military decision-
making process;

**3.** Stop all direct marketing and promotion of nuclear weapons;
and

**4.** Implement conversion plans for the company.

In February 1988, INFACT released a 145-page report en-
titled "INFACT Brings GE to Light," extensively outlining GE's
role in every aspect of the arms race and governmental decision-
making process. Among the findings reported:

—11.8% of GE's overall sales are related to nuclear weapons
work;

—under President Reagan, who was the host of *GE Theatre* from 1958 to 1962, GE's share of government contracts increased more than 300 percent in six years; and

—GE is currently the sole producer of the neutron generator—the trigger for all U.S. hydrogen bombs—and develops components for the MX missile, Trident submarines, Trident missiles, the B-1 bomber, the Stealth bomber, and the Strategic Defense Initiative, to name a few.

The most important factor detailed in the report, and the issue that cuts to the center of the controversy, is General Electric's role in what President Eisenhower forty years ago spoke of as the "disastrous rise of misplaced power in the military-industrial complex."

Today GE maintains a Washington lobbying staff of 150 people, the largest of any weapons contractor. The company manufactures more nuclear weapons systems than any other. In 1986 GE received the third largest number of Pentagon research and development contracts, for work on the B-1 bomber, Trident I and Trident II missiles, and Star Wars.

Like other major U.S. corporations, GE routinely hires former government officials, perpetuating the incestuous relationship between the government and the defense industry. Among those presently on the GE board of directors are former Attorney General William French Smith and former Chair of the Joint Chiefs of Staff General David Jones.

In 1988 an independent poll conducted for INFACT determined that, after less than two years of the boycott, three million consumers, more than 1 percent of the U.S. population, were actively supporting the boycott. INFACT can also point to a number of specific victories. After learning of the boycott, a San Francisco architect canceled a $25,000 wholesale order for GE appliances. In another instance, a New England physician purchased half a million dollars' worth of Gamma cameras from GE's competitor. On an even larger scale, over 350 institutions now support the boycott, including UCLA, the City of Berkeley, California, and the ASC Health Systems Hospital in Illinois.

"You're dealing with a company whose principal reason to exist is to make money," explains Director Nancy Cole. "You have to create economic pressure on the company to change it. Right now it's so lucrative for GE to make weapons that there's no reason for them to consider anything else. What the campaign can do over a period of time is change that economic equation."

## WHAT YOU CAN DO:

Don't buy General Electric products, or products made by their subsidiaries Hotpoint and RCA (RCA Records is *not* part of the boycott). On your next trip to the supermarket or hardware store to get light bulbs, don't buy those made by GE (for a socially responsible alternative, see Action 1). For more information, to make a contribution, or to purchase a copy of their excellent book *INFACT Brings GE to Light* ($6.95 plus $1.50 postage), write to INFACT, 256 Hanover Street, Third Floor, Boston, MA 02113; (617) 742-4583.

## 29

# Human Rights, South Africa, and Central America

| Action 118 | ***Amnesty International***<br>**Your letter may help set someone free.** |
|---|---|

**AMNESTY**
**INTERNATIONAL**
**USA**

Here's what you can do to help set free men, women, and children throughout the world who are being illegally imprisoned and tortured. Their crimes range from practicing the wrong religion, to being born the wrong color, speaking out against oppression, even to speaking the wrong language. These people are not guilty of any crime. Peacefully they've followed their principles, stood by their moral beliefs, and spoken out against injustice.

In more than 135 countries, including the United States, fundamental human rights are violated by governments in power. One third of the world's governments torture their citizens. Fifty governments detain political prisoners without the benefit of charge or trial and more than 120 governments still permit the death penalty.

Hundreds of people have remained in prison for years without trial and, since 1961, tens of thousands have simply disappeared, never to be heard from again. Millions of friends and family members wait, losing hope day by day.

Amnesty International has set out to organize the world to take a stand against these injustices. Each year the group enlists more and more people to support the cause. Each year more letters are written to presidents, judges, military officials, prime ministers, jail wardens, and cabinet members.

In 1986 Amnesty International enlisted the support of rock musicians to bring the human rights message to American youth. The "Conspiracy of Hope" tour boosted national action to the international crisis.

In 1988, this time in fifteen countries throughout the world—from behind the Iron Curtain to Africa and Central America—Amnesty International carried its message of "Human Rights Now" to one million or more potential letter-writing activists.

At present, more than 700,000 individuals in 150 countries are working for the release of over 3,500 people identified by the movement as prisoners of conscience. Other goals are to ensure prompt and fair trials for political prisoners and an end to torture and executions. As of 1989, Amnesty International has taken on more than 30,000 individual cases, and of the 3,534 it took on in 1987 alone, 1,689 political prisoners had been released.

The "Conspiracy of Hope" concert tour publicized six of these prisoner-of-conscience cases. Throughout the United States, audiences signed postcards, wrote letters, and circulated petitions to government officials calling for the prisoners' release. As a result, today Thozamile Ggweta, a South African trade union dissident; Lee Kwang-ung, a South Korean high school teacher who had distributed poetry written by a North Korean writer; and Tatyana Semyonova Osipova, a Soviet computer specialist who joined a human rights group—*are free*.

Over the years, letter-writing campaigns have been effective in stopping human rights abuses. Together with Amnesty International's publicity, the program has helped set free thousands of prisoners of conscience and continues to try to end torture, "disappearances" and executions worldwide.

Everyone can help. Your letter may help set someone free.

## *WHAT YOU CAN DO:*

Join Amnesty International today and receive their bimonthly publication, *Amnesty Action*. This magazine offers special opportunities to participate directly in working for the release of prisoners and helping to stop torture and executions. Each issue contains requests for letters to government officials appealing for the release of individual prisoners of conscience. Postcards and action alerts are often included.

You will also have the opportunity to join a variety of local and national volunteer groups, including:

FREEDOM WRITERS: A network of individuals who write letters on behalf of prisoners. Amnesty International USA sends names of three prisoners of conscience, along with sample letters to be addressed to appropriate officials, to network participants each month.

URGENT ACTION NETWORK: Participants of the Urgent Action Network are called upon periodically to send airmail letters and telegrams to assist individuals who are in immediate danger of being tortured or executed. Within the network are included academics, journalists, lawyers, business people, union members, and religious congregations, who work on behalf of colleagues and peers imprisoned abroad.

HEALTH PROFESSIONALS: Health professionals work together to help imprisoned colleagues and prisoners with serious health problems. They also work to aid health professionals who are threatened with torture and execution, and present educational programs on medical ethics and human rights.

LEGAL PROFESSIONALS: Lawyers and other legal professionals work for imprisoned colleagues, assist in research, offer advice to amnesty groups on relevant legal issues, and present educational programs on human rights.

To become a member send whatever you can. The suggested membership fee is $25, or $15 for students and seniors. Write to National Office, Amnesty International USA, 322 Eighth Avenue, New York, NY 10001; (212) 807-8400.

---

**Action 119**  **Ending Apartheid in South Africa**

It's 4:00 a.m., there's a knock at the door. Four men push aside the mother in the doorway and walk into the house. At the bedroom they pause, and then pull 13-year-old Cleopatra Molefe out of bed and take her away. Two months later, Cleopatra's parents had still not seen their daughter. . . .

*EVERY TWELVE MINUTES* another person is detained in apartheid South Africa. Men and women, church, trade union and community leaders, journalists, students and their teachers have all been swept up. Forty percent of those detained are 18 years old or younger, some only five years old. The detainees are denied access to lawyers or family. In one recent study, doctors reported that more than 80 percent of the detainees they examined showed signs of torture. Many prisoners have died in police custody. The Detainees Parents' Support Committee estimates that more than 30,000 people have been detained without charge or trial since the State of Emergency began in June 1986. Countless others have disappeared without a trace.*

History will inevitably look upon apartheid as one of humanity's great steps backward into dark and evil times. Yet, as harshly as history judges white South Africa for its widespread murders, acts of torture, and repression of human rights, the rest of the world will be judged even more harshly. For we have just stood by and watched. Our failure to respond to this tragedy will echo through generations of history texts, and surely rank with humankind's other disgraces, from Nazi Germany to Pol Pot's destruction of Cambodia.

Apartheid is legalized racism. Apartheid is the denial of political, economic, social, and human rights. Apartheid does not recognize black South Africans as humans; it does not allow them to vote, own land in 87 percent of the country, decide where they want to live, marry anyone of another race, receive a decent education, be employed for a fair wage, live in decent housing, or even receive the health and medical care that's often necessary just to stay alive.

The white South African government controls every black person through a sophisticated computer network requiring all blacks over the age of sixteen to carry a "passbook" at all times. The passbook contains fingerprints, a photograph, and employment records. If it is not produced upon demand, blacks are jailed and fined. More than thirty-one million Africans have been convicted of pass-law offenses since the National Party came to power in 1948—almost one thousand every day!

White South Africans have stolen the land that once be-

*From *Unlock Apartheid's Jails,* The American Committee on Africa.

longed to the black majority. Black workers are paid one third of what whites are paid for the same job. Sixty percent of urban blacks earn less than what the white government defines as necessary to survive. The black population is denied any rights to protest its plight, improve its life, or reach out for help.

Recently the United States has begun to awaken from an indifferent sleep. One by one, individuals have begun to speak out. Corporate America has started to halt the financing, technical support, and moral approval of the racist South African regime. Our government has taken small, slow, and nervous steps against its military and economic ally.

We must force this movement into high gear, refuse to accept what is so clearly unacceptable, come to terms with our own conscience, and take as many of the following actions as we are able—to end apartheid.

## WHAT YOU CAN DO*:

**1. EDUCATE YOURSELF:** The American Committee on Africa, 198 Broadway, New York, NY 10038; (212) 962-1210, distributes a wide variety of written material describing apartheid and U.S. involvement in South Africa. The ANC News Briefing—weekly clippings from the South African press—is available from the African National Congress (ANC) of South Africa, Suite 405, 801 Second Avenue, New York, NY 10017 (212) 490-3487. Food First distributes a book, by issues analyst Kevin Danaher, called *In Whose Interest?: A Guide to U.S.-South African Relations*. Contact Food First, 145 Ninth Street, San Francisco, CA 94103; cost is $11.95. For a wide range of films and other audiovisual materials, contact the Southern Africa Media Center, 630 Natoma Street, San Francisco, CA 94103; (415) 621-6196.

**2. DIVESTMENT:** The divestment movement has grown in this country as more and more people decide that they do not want to profit from apartheid. As a result, churches, universities, and trade unions throughout the United States have taken funds out of companies and banks doing business in South Africa. Even local and state governments are divesting from South Africa because taxpayers are demanding that their hard-earned dollars

* Excerpted in part by permission from *Organizing Against Apartheid*, Washington Office on Africa.

stop supporting a system opposed to democratic ideals. So far, five states, Massachusetts, Connecticut, Michigan, Nebraska, and Maryland, and many cities, including Boston, Philadelphia, and Washington, D.C., have responded by passing divestment laws. More than twenty-one other states, cities, and counties are considering such bills.

**a. STATE/MUNICIPAL LEGISLATION:** Support laws to stop public funds from being invested in banks and corporations that invest in South Africa. Such funds should be used to rebuild local communities and create new jobs. See Action 106 on municipal foreign policy to find out what specific actions you can take.

**b. RELIGIOUS GROUPS AND UNIVERSITIES:** Pressure your school, college, or religious institution to divest itself of any financial interests it currently holds in companies doing business in South Africa.

**c. PERSONAL INVESTMENTS:** Sell the stock you may own in any company operating in South Africa. Invest in South African free money funds, municipal funds, banking institutions, and corporate stocks. For a list of these see Actions 69 through 80 on socially responsible banking and investment.

**3. SHAREHOLDER RESOLUTIONS:** If you do own stock in a company that is operating in South Africa, you may want to support or sponsor a shareholder resolution that forces that company out of South Africa before you sell your stock. See Action 82 for more information.

**4. NATIONAL LEGISLATION:** Voting is only the first step in exercising your democratic rights. You must also make sure your elected officials really represent your views and positions. Calls, letters, and telegrams can influence congressional votes and encourage your representatives to speak out on key issues affecting southern Africa. The Washington Office on Africa maintains a legislative information service, the Anti-Apartheid Action Hotline (202) 546-0408, to keep you up to date on the actions that you and your congressperson can take.

**5. PROTEST:** The Free South Africa Movement has spearheaded anti-apartheid protests in Washington and many other cities. For a local affiliate, contact the Free South Africa Movement, c/o TransAfrica, 545 8th Street, S.E., Washington, D.C. 20003; (202) 547-2550.

**6. PROVIDE MATERIAL AID:** One concrete way to support liberation in South Africa and Namibia is to collect clothing, school supplies, and medicine for shipment to refugee camps in southern Africa. This campaign can involve large numbers of people in your community, make the issues more visible locally, and facilitate joint work. The ANC and SWAPO offices, Suite 405, 801 Second Avenue, New York, NY 10017; (212) 490-3487, can provide further information.

**7. ISOLATE SOUTH AFRICA:** Local groups are ideal for protesting white South African attempts to build cultural, sporting, business, entertainment, and political ties with the United States. Monitor the local media for news of visits to this country by South African athletes, academics, officials, and performers. Protest these visits and publicize the issue of apartheid. Make your community an "APARTHEID FREE ZONE":

—Boycott performances, concerts, and records by artists who visit South Africa.
—Demonstrate against South African consulates to local officials and to the State Department, and picket these buildings. Los Angeles, New Orleans, and Pittsburgh activists forced the consulates in those cities to close down.
—Protest visits by South African scholars and scientists to local universities.

**8. BOYCOTT SOUTH AFRICAN PRODUCE AND WINES:** Check labels in the supermarket or liquor store to make sure you don't purchase South African products. If any store sells these products, speak to the manager and voice your objection.

**9. KRUGERRANDS:** If your bank or coin dealer sells these or other South African gold coins, protest to encourage the stopping of this practice. The United States is the largest market for these coins.

**10. BOYCOTT U.S. COMPANIES DOING BUSINESS IN SOUTH AFRICA:** Boycott the following fifty U.S. companies, who are the largest employers operating in South Africa:

| RANK | COMPANY | | EMPLOYEES |
|------|---------|------|-----------|
| 1 | Mobil Corp. | | 2,927 |
| 2 | Goodyear Tire & Rubber Co. | | 2,443 |
| 3 | USG Corp. | GT | 2,300 |
| 4 | RJR Nabisco Inc. | GT | 2,205 |
| 5 | USX Corp.* | GT | 1,809 |
| 6 | Colgate-Palmolive Co. | | 1,391 |
| 7 | Johnson & Johnson Co. | | 1,369 |
| 8 | American Cyanamid Co. | | 1,343 |
| 9 | Owens-Illinois Inc.* | | 1,239 |
| 10 | Minnesota Mining & Manufacturing | | 1,106 |
| 11 | Chevron Corp.* (Caltex) | GT | 1,070 |
| 11 | Texaco Inc.* (Caltex) | GT | 1,070 |
| 13 | United Technologies Corp. (Otis) | | 1,060 |
| 14 | Joy Technologies Inc. | | 1,041 |
| 15 | Phelps Dodge Corp.* | | 865 |
| 16 | Tenneco Inc. | | 855 |
| 17 | Baker Hughes Inc. | GT | 822 |
| 18 | British Petroleum Co.* (Kennecott) | | 758 |
| 19 | Crown Cork & Seal Co. | | 739 |
| 20 | Unisys Corp. | | 707 |
| 21 | Dresser Industries Inc. | | 682 |
| 22 | Kimberly-Clark Corp.* | | 639 |
| 23 | St. Paul Cos. | GT | 614 |
| 24 | H. H. Robertson Co. | | 585 |
| 25 | Arvin Industries Inc. | GT | 584 |
| 26 | Warner-Lambert Co. | | 558 |
| 27 | Lastarmco Inc. | | 555 |
| 28 | American Home Products Corp. | | 554 |
| 29 | NCR Corp. | | 510 |
| 30 | Banner Industries Inc. | | 490 |
| 31 | Strategic Minerals Corp. | | 489 |
| 32 | Unilever (Chesebrough-Pond's) | | 484 |
| 33 | Ingersoll-Rand Co. | | 450 |
| 34 | Foote, Cone & Belding Communications Inc. | | 430 |
| 35 | Deere & Co. | | 399 |
| 36 | Interpublic Group of Cos. Inc. | GT | 386 |
| 37 | Reader's Digest Association Inc. | | 380 |
| 38 | AM International Inc. | | 370 |
| 39 | Gillette Co. | | 360 |
| 40 | Fruehauf Holdings Inc.* | | 350 |
| 41 | March & McLennan* | | 347 |

| RANK | COMPANY | | EMPLOYEES |
|------|---------|---|-----------|
| 42 | Union Carbide Corp. | | 337 |
| 43 | Young & Rubicam Inc. | GT | 330 |
| 44 | Heinemann Electric Co.* | | 330 |
| 45 | Saatchi & Saatchi Co. Plc | | 325 |
| 46 | Echlin Inc. | | 320 |
| 47 | Kellogg Co. | | 320 |
| 48 | MacAndrews & Forbes Holdings (Revlon) | | 300 |
| 49 | Precision Valve Corp. | | 280 |
| 50 | Borden Inc. | | 276 |

GT = greater than
*Company employee figure is prorated.

*Note:* This table only shows those companies for which employee figures are available. Data are prorated for companies that own 50% or less of their South African/Namibian subsidiaries. Rankings are only approximate, as data for different companies are not always directly comparable. Companies are listed by their ultimate parent organization, even if the parent is not a U.S. company. The table does not include non-U.S. companies unless they have a U.S. subsidiary which in turn has a subsidiary in South Africa or Namibia. Plus it only includes companies with ownership in South Africa, so those that have franchising, licensing, or distribution agreements in South Africa and Namibia are not indicated. Also excluded are companies that are in South Africa/Namibia for news-gathering purposes only.

This list of companies is excerpted from the *Unified List of United States Companies Doing Business in South Africa & Namibia,* which is published by The African Fund, 198 Broadway, New York, NY 10038, and is available for $10. The book provides detailed profiles of more than 150 companies with regard to ownership, employment revenues, and business activities in South Africa. It's an invaluable resource for making personal decisions as a consumer and for developing local actions specifically targeted to these corporations.

The *Unified List* also covers U.S. bank loans to South Africa, indicating the total amount lent and the value of third-party loans or underwriting of the vast majority of the outstanding loans, $2.1 billion, is owed by South Africa to Bankers Trust, Chase Manhattan, Chemical, Citibank, Continental Illinois, Manufacturers Hanover, and J. P. Morgan.

**11. UNION SOLIDARITY:** Black South African trade unions need your support. If you belong to a union, ask your union officers what concrete steps they are taking to oppose apartheid and support black unions in South Africa. Call for the withdrawal of union pension funds and other investments from South Africa. Urge the passage of a resolution on South Africa.

**12. NATIONAL CELEBRATIONS:** Organize events to commemorate dates of southern African resistance movements, such as Sharpeville Day (March 21), Soweto Day (June 16), and Namibia Day (August 26). Coordinate with national groups to ensure national action. Many universities have annual activities starting March 21 (Sharpeville Day) and continuing through April 4 (commemorating the assassination of Martin Luther King, Jr.).

**13. SUPPORT ORGANIZATIONS WORKING TO END APARTHEID:** All of the organizations listed in this action can use direct financial support. Consider making a contribution to any or all.

---

Action
120

## *How You Can Save the Lives of Activists in El Salvador* \*
## CISPES—Rapid Response Network

On Thursday, March 10, 1988, the Salvadoran air force dragged Humberto Centeno, a leader in the National Unity of Salvadoran Workers (UNTS), away from a demonstration protesting the capture of fifty-three workers. Centeno was thrown into the back of a treasury police truck, beaten, and hospitalized. CISPES, the Committee for Solidarity with the People of El Salvador, responded immediately.

On Thursday night, March 10, 1988, the national CISPES office in San Francisco received an urgent call from San Salvador. "Centeno's been captured and beaten by the treasury police. We're afraid they'll kill him!" The phones were buzzing— five regional CISPES offices were alerted as well as dozens of other labor, religious, human rights and solidarity organizations, supportive congresspeople, and the national media.

SF CISPES, one of eighty Rapid Response Networks in the United States, went into action: fifty telexes to El Salvador; five phone calls to the U.S. embassy and Salvadoran military; fifty

---

\* Excerpted with permission from "You Can Save Lives of Activists in El Salvador," by Sharon Martinas, *S.F. CISPES Update,* Vol. 3:4, May-June 1988.

people mobilized within hours to demonstrate at the Salvadoran consulates; dozens of calls to local congresspeople and the media. Nationally the network activated five protests outside Salvadoran consulates, one hundred phone calls to El Salvador, one hundred telexes, and sixty-five calls to congressional offices—all within twenty-four hours!

Meanwhile, on Friday morning in San Salvador, thousands of workers demonstrated, defying police tear gas and bullets to demand Centeno's freedom. By Saturday afternoon the phones were abuzz with the news: Centeno was free!

Although the repression in El Salvador is escalating, CISPES's work makes a difference. From January through March 1988, the national CISPES office received information about 101 incidents of human rights violations, almost all involving more than one person. The Rapid Response Networks were activated sixteen times. Of the seventy-five people whose captures they protested, forty-eight were released, five imprisoned, three disappeared, and the whereabouts of nineteen are unknown.

Can the Rapid Response Networks stop the death squads? Realistically, no. But who knows how many assassinations have been prevented by unremitting protest?

## WHAT YOU CAN DO:

To find out how you can support CISPES's work and join a Rapid Response Network contact CISPES, P.O. Box 12056, Washington, DC 20005; (202) 265-0890. You can also subscribe to their newsletter *Alert! Focus on Central America* ($15 for 10 issues), which contains additional actions you can take.

---

Action
121
### *More Opportunities for Peace and Human Rights in Central America**

## WHAT YOU CAN DO:

**1. PEACE BRIGADES INTERNATIONAL:** Peace Brigades International (PBI) advocates and trains people for nonviolent conflict resolution throughout the world. One of PBI's

* Excerpted from *Bridging the Global Gap: A Handbook for Linking the First and Third Worlds;* by Medea Benjamin and Andrea Freedman, Seven Locks Press, Md./Washington, D.C., 1989.

tactics in the fight against human rights abuses is the "escort." For three to twelve months each year, international volunteers (primarily European, but also Canadian and American) form teams of unarmed escorts and accompany members of local human rights commissions in El Salvador and Guatemala.

One of PBI's first assignments was working for the Guatemalan Mutual Support Group (GAM), as a shield against attacks by government security forces. According to Chip Coffman, a member of one of PBI's escort teams, the GAM was organized in 1984, and suffered the murder, torture, and disappearance of its leaders. Since the PBI escort service began in 1986, the threats to the GAM continue on a daily basis but no one has been killed.

In addition to the Guatemalan and Salvadoran escorts, PBI volunteers monitor border clashes between Nicaragua and Honduras, and consult with groups in Sri Lanka, Thailand, and Big Mountain, U.S.A. about nonviolent confrontation tactics. PBI recently received requests for help from South African groups, and is considering working in the Middle East.

> Peace Brigades International
> 722 Baltimore Avenue
> Philadelphia, PA 19143
> (215) 727-0989 or
> (215) 727-1464

**2. MARIN INTERFAITH TASK FORCE ON CENTRAL AMERICA:** The Marin Interfaith Task Force on Central America (MITF) is another United States-based group that chooses to act directly in another country to protect indigenous human rights efforts.

In the summer of 1986, all the members of the Independent Human Rights Commission of El Salvador (CDHES) who could be found were arrested and tortured in San Salvador's Mariona Prison.

MITF responded by offering to send North American volunteers to San Salvador to protect and assist the remaining commissioners. CDHES accepted the offer, and MITF has supplied volunteers ever since. Bill Hutchinson, one of those who volunteered, describes MITF's work: "We took testimony from people about the killings and disappearances of their relatives. Some of the disappeared were campesinos; most were urban-based people who were part of some organizing work. Those who disappeared included members of other human rights groups, labor unions, farm cooperatives, teachers, truck drivers. Some were even members of cooperatives set up by the Duarte government itself. We kept food on the stove for the hungry who came to testify. We also accompanied commissioners on their work, in order to thwart any further attacks against them."

> Marin Interfaith Task Force
> 1024 Sir Francis Drake Boulevard
> San Anselmo, CA 94960
> (415) 454-0818

MITF publishes a bimonthly newsletter, *Central American Report,* for all members who contribute a minimum of $12.

**3. NEIGHBOR TO NEIGHBOR:** Neighbor to Neighbor (N2N) was started in 1985 to stop U.S. government support of the contras in Nicaragua. District by district, N2N organizers set up lobbying networks to turn around U.S. congressional votes. "We reach people through local campaigns, which includes standing on street corners to get petitions signed, phone banks, and TV ads," explains Robyn Macswain, an N2N organizer.

Kit Miller, also of N2N, adds, "The contra aid votes have been so close—each time within a handful of congresspeople—that even turning around a few votes counts a lot. But this kind of lobbying takes persistence. We know that we generated one hundred thousand letters in one campaign, for example, but we didn't see the representatives respond to the pressure for six months."

> Neighbor to Neighbor
> 2601 Mission Street
> San Francisco, CA 94110
> (415) 824-3355

N2N also publishes an *Action Alert* for all members who contribute a minimum of $25.

# 30

# Resources and Tools for Peace

## *A Global Computer Network Working for Peace*

PeaceNet will let you talk, plan, learn from and work with individuals and peace groups throughout the United States and seventy countries around the world!

With a personal computer and modem you'll be able to attend special conferences; gain access to vast data bases on arms control initiatives, local military contracting, and comprehensive lists of the nation's peace groups; review a current calendar of events to which you may add your own; enjoy the use of electronic mail, which is quicker and cheaper than Federal Express; and be alerted to *opportunities for action* on legislative issues, letter-writing campaigns, and local protests and public meetings.

Sharing PeaceNet with you is a host of the leading peace groups (many of which have been discussed in other actions), including: Amnesty International, Beyond War, Center for Innovative Diplomacy, Citizen Diplomacy, Mobilization for Survival, National Peace Institute, Nuclear Times, and Sane/Freeze.

With a touch of your finger you'll be able to:

—Call up the Council for a Livable World's nuclear arms control hotline.

—Send an overnight message to the U.S. Congress and the White House.

—Read the American Friends Service Committee's legislative updates.

—Contact others in your area who share your concerns.

—Obtain up-to-date information about nuclear weapons tests.

—Review a list of Star Wars contractors.

—And much, much more!

## WHAT YOU CAN DO:

To join or obtain more information, contact PeaceNet, 3228 Sacramento Street, San Francisco, CA 94115-2007; (415) 923-0900. If you join the service, you'll be charged a one-time $10 sign-up fee and a monthly basic subscription charge of $10, which entitles you to one hour of free off-peak usage.

---

**Action 123**     ## *Resources for Peace\** ## A Survey of Activist and Educational Organizations

*ACCESS*
1755 Massachusetts Avenue, N.W.
Washington, DC 20036
(202) 328-2323

Access is a nonprofit clearinghouse of information on international security and peace issues.

*AMERICAN FRIENDS SERVICE COMMITTEE*
Peace Education Division
1501 Cherry Street
Philadelphia, PA 19102

---

*Excerpted with permission from *Building Economic Alternatives*, Spring 1988. Subscription: $20.00 a year (4 issues plus Co-op America membership), Co-Op America, 2100 M Street, N.W., Suite 310, Washington, DC 20036.

An activist group that works for peace, justice, and equality. Worldwide programs are based on the conviction that nonviolent solutions can be found to problem situations.

### BAY STATE CENTER FOR ECONOMIC CONVERSION
2161 Massachusetts Avenue
Cambridge, MA 02140
(617) 354-8325

Educates the public about disarmament and the effects of military spending and promotes economic conversion projects.

### BROOKINGS INSTITUTION
1775 Massachusetts Avenue, N.W.
Washington, DC 20036
(202) 797-6000

Conducts research on public policy issues in the social sciences, particularly in economics, government, and foreign affairs.

### CENTER FOR ECONOMIC CONVERSION
222C View Street
Mountain View, CA 94041
(415) 968-8798

Promotes positive economic alternatives to excessive military spending and serves as a national resource center on military economics and conversion planning.

### CHILDREN'S DEFENSE FUND
122 C Street, N.W.
Washington, DC 20001
(202) 628-8787

Publishes an annual Children's Defense Budget, which advocates increased federal spending for human services and decreased spending for the military.

### CITIZENS NETWORK
Anabel Taylor Hall
Cornell University
Ithaca, NY 14853
(607) 256-6486

A nonpartisan network committed to educating Americans about the true nature of U.S. nuclear policy

*CLERGY AND LAITY CONCERNED*
198 Broadway, Room 302
New York, NY 10038
(212) 964-6730

Interfaith peace and justice organization advocating citizen action on militarism, economic justice, human rights, and racial justice

*COMMITTEE FOR NATIONAL SECURITY*
1601 Connecticut Avenue, N.W.
Suite 301
Washington, DC 20009
(202) 745-2450

Informs Americans about national security and arms control issues and encourages citizen participation in the debate on U.S. military and foreign policy.

*DEFENSE BUDGET PROJECT*
Center on Budget and Military Priorities
236 Massachusetts Avenue, N.E., Suite 305
Washington, DC 20002
(202) 546-9737

Research and publications concerning the impact of defense spending on the federal budget, the American economy, and national security. Examines the politics and bureaucracy of defense and spending.

*GRASSROOTS PEACE DIRECTORY*
P.O. Box 203
Pomfret, CT 06258
(203) 928-2616

Computer-based directory of information on religious and secular groups working in the areas of peace, disarmament, and international security

*GRAY PANTHERS*
311 South Juniper Street
Philadelphia, PA 19107
(215) 545-6555

Advocates of a shift from military spending to social programs

## INTERNATIONAL ASSOCIATION OF MACHINISTS AND AEROSPACE WORKERS
1300 Connecticut Avenue, N.W.
Washington, DC 20036
(202) 857-5200

Represents members in collective bargaining and lobbies on legislation affecting working people. Promotes conversion from military to civilian industry.

## NATIONAL COMMISSION FOR ECONOMIC CONVERSION AND DISARMAMENT
Box 15025
Washington, DC 20003
(202) 544-5059

Promotes greater awareness about the ties between disarmament, economic planning, and the military economy, through citizen forums, and publications, and by planning with industries, universities, and other nongovernmental groups.

## NUKEWATCH
315 West Gorham
Madison, WI 53703
(608) 256-4146

Educates the public about nuclear weapons and power. Advocates the establishment of nuclear free zones and socially responsible investing.

## PEACE DEVELOPMENT FUND
44 North Prospect Street
P.O. Box 270
Amherst, MA 01004
(413) 256-8306

Awards grants to community-based peace projects that educate the public on the arms race and the economic issues related to military spending.

*UNION OF CONCERNED SCIENTISTS*
26 Church Street
Cambridge, MA 02238
(617) 547-5552

Studies the hazards of U.S. nuclear policy. Promotes public education through conferences and publications.

*U.S. NUCLEAR FREE PACIFIC NETWORK*
842 Market Street, Room 711
San Francisco, CA 94102
(415) 434-2988

Liaison center between the international Nuclear Free Pacific movement and peace, environmental, and human rights groups in the United States.

*WOMEN'S ENCAMPMENT FOR A FUTURE OF*
*PEACE AND JUSTICE*
Box 5440, Route 96
Romulus, NY 14541
(607) 869-5825

Ongoing women's peace presence and center for nonviolent action. Networking materials available.

*WOMEN STRIKE FOR PEACE*
5440 South 13th Street
Philadelphia, PA 19107
(215) 563-2269

Women of all races, creeds, and political beliefs determined to end the arms race

*WOMEN'S ACTION FOR NUCLEAR DISARMAMENT*
New Town Branch
P.O. Box 153
Boston, MA 02258
(617) 643-6740

Disseminates information and encourages local affiliates to lobby and work in congressional campaigns in support of a bilateral nuclear weapons freeze.

*WORLD POLICY INSTITUTE*
77 United Nations Plaza, 5th Floor
New York, NY 10017
(212) 490-0010

Conducts research and provides information on global issues, including disarmament, peacekeeping, new international
economic order, human rights, and social justice. Promotes college teaching on these topics.

---

Action          *Publications About Peace*
124                *and Disarmament\**

Since the late seventies, antinuclear groups and magazines
have been proliferating almost as fast as warheads have. The
mainstream media's studied reluctance to cover the movement
without dismissing or red-baiting it has made it all the more
necessary to develop a network of alternative publications. Some
are simple grapevine facilitators, guaranteed to put nonactivists
to sleep; others are full-scale magazines with their own angle
on militarism and disarmament. They cover the political gamut
of the movement, from the arms controllers of the Federation of
American Scientists to the peace-with-justice activists of Clergy
and Laity Concerned (CALC).

*Nuclear Times* ($2 an issue, $15 a year, monthly, 298 Fifth
Avenue, Room 512, New York, NY 10001) aims to be *the* magazine of the antinuclear weapons movement. It gives a thorough,
intelligent overview of organizing efforts from direct action to
lobbying. Professionally produced, crisply illustrated, and reli-
able, this is the magazine to read for an overview of the movement.

*Bulletin of the Atomic Scientists* ($22.50 a year, monthly,
from the Educational Foundation for Nuclear Science, 5801 South
Kenwood, Chicago, IL 60637). As old as the atomic bomb itself,
this bulletin is the origin of the famous doomsday clock, recently
moved forward to three minutes to midnight. Scholarly, liberal
essays on foreign policy, arms control, and disarmament, with

---

*\*Reprinted with permission from *The Utne Reader Field Guide to the Alternative Press*,
No. 3, April 1984. See pages 299–301 for subscription information.*

a regular "weapons tutorial." A major forum and excellent resource for activists and others.

*Sojourners* ($15 a year, $27 for two years, monthly, from P.O. Box 29272, Washington, DC 20017). The well-designed, glossy-cover magazine of the radical Christian community is undogmatic, consistently interesting reading even for atheists, especially for its inspiring accounts of pacifist civil disobedience actions.

*Peace Work* ($10 a year, monthly, from the American Friends Service Committee, 2161 Massachusetts Avenue, Cambridge, MA 02140). New England "peace and social justice" newsletter— sixteen pages of organizing news and intelligent, radical discussion of international and movement issues. Particularly good on the Middle East, thanks to the contributions of the AFSC's Joseph Gerson.

---

## Publications from Peace Groups

*The Mobilizer* (voluntary subscription of $5 or more, quarterly, from Mobilization for Survival, 853 Broadway, Room 2109, New York, NY 10003). Mobe, one of the oldest post-Vietnam peace groups, describes itself as "the cutting edge of the possible." Covering nuclear weapons, nuclear power, military intervention, and social justice issues, the newsprint magazine combines radical analysis with realistic organizing strategies.

*CALC Report and Third World Caucus Bulletin* (8 times a year with Clergy and Laity Concerned membership, $20, or $7 for limited income, from 198 Broadway, New York, NY 10038). Nonactivists should read this for its excellent investigations into the effects of the arms race on the Third World, the economics of southern poverty, and the plight of black farmers. The emphasis is on making the links between militarism, poverty, and exploitation; CALC, founded during the Vietnam War, is the only peace group to give prime place to black and Third World concerns.

*Fellowship* ($1.25 each, $10 a year, 8 times a year, from the Fellowship of Reconciliation, P.O. Box 271, Nyack, NY 10960). FOR's members are traditional pacifists, believing in "the power of love and truth" to resolve human conflict. They are also efficient organizers with close links to the movement in Europe, and their activities are covered here better than in any other American peace magazine. First-class national and international news roundups, networking notes and book reviews.

*F.A.S. Public Interest Report* ($25 a year, 10 times a year, from the Federation of American Scientists, 307 Massachusetts Avenue, N.E., Washington, DC 20002). Scrupulous and well-documented reports on arms control and disarmament proposals, military hardware, the effects of defense spending on the economy. Facts and figures with impeccable credentials.

*The Defense Monitor* ($25 a year, 10 times a year, from the Center for Defense Information, 303 Capitol Gallery West, 600 Maryland Avenue, Washington, DC 20024). Contains the same kinds of material as the *F.A.S. Public Interest Report.* C.D.I. is a liberal research center; its publication provides cool-headed, fact-packed arguments against military build-up as well as close critiques of Pentagon planning.

*Arms Control Today* ($25 a year, 11 times a year, from the Arms Control Association, 11 Dupont Circle, N.E., Washington, DC 20036). Includes a thorough bibliography of recent books, pamphlets, and articles on military matters.

# Part 6

# TWELVE ESSENTIAL RESOURCES

*How to stay informed, inspired, and ready for action as you continue to make the world a better place*

## A Concise Guide to Some of
## the Most Essential Resources

For my own ongoing education, helping to research this book,
nourishing my inspiration, and the simple joy of their excellence,
I owe the resources and publications described in this section a
great debt. To me, they are essential to forging ahead into the
future, discovering new actions that need to be taken, recharting
courses that need to be corrected, making connections with other
kindred souls, and simply for their own marvelous contribution
toward making the world a better place.

While inevitably the list is far too short and fails to recognize
many whose good work deserves recognition, please accept it as
a very personal statement of those forces that have found their
way into my life.

### 1. COMMUNITY JOBS

For more than ten years, this monthly publication has provided the only nationwide listing of socially responsible jobs and
internships. Organized geographically, it lists hundreds of opportunities to work for social change, complete with job descriptions, background requirements, salary levels, and where and
how to apply.

As the magazine describes itself, "In a job market full of

square holes, we find the round pegs." The unique listings give
you a chance to work for much more than a paycheck.
    Available at selected newsstands or from:

> Community Jobs
> 1516 P Street, N.W.
> Washington, DC 20005
> (202) 667-0661

Single issues cost $2.50; six monthly issues, $12; or twelve issues,
$15.

### 2. DOLLARS & SENSE

No publication—*Forbes, Fortune, Business Week, The Economist,* or *The New York Times*—explains economics as clearly
and concisely as *Dollars & Sense*. Its socialist perspective never
seems to be biased or interfere with careful and meticulous explanations of the gross national product, what causes interest
rates to go up or down, why we perpetually have unemployment,
who benefits from the new tax laws, how much corporate executives really make and who pays for it, and what choices exist
for eliminating the budget deficit.
    Ten issues are just $14.95.

> Dollars & Sense
> One Summer Street
> Somerville, MA 02143
> (617) 628-8411

### 3. THE GIRAFFE PROJECT*

—Claude and Louise Montgomery of Portland, Maine, entered
their seventies with some money saved "for an emergency." But
when they saw a homeless man climb into a dumpster to keep
warm, they decided *that* was their emergency. Today they live
in Friendship House, where they invite twelve homeless "guests"
to stay every night.

---

*Excerpted with permission from *The Christian Science Monitor,* "They Didn't Say 'I
Gave At the Office,' " by Kirsten A. Conover, August 21, 1987.

*Stick Your Neck Out*

—John DeMarco of Philadelphia stood up to racism in his community. The thirteen-year-old testified in court against an adult neighbor he saw paint a racial insult on a house that a black family wanted to buy.

—New York City police officers George Hankins and George Pearson pooled their savings and borrowed from their pensions to start a youth center in the violent Fort Apache section of the Bronx.

These people aren't just do-gooders; they've taken personal risks on behalf of others.

All of them are "Giraffes." They're named after an animal that sticks its neck out, can see for miles, has a heart that weighs up to twenty-five pounds, and leads a peaceful life with grace and dignity.

The Giraffe Project is a national organization inspiring people to stick their necks out for the common good. Its mission is to generate a new level of grass-roots participation in public life by helping people believe in their own good instincts and in their own ability to help create a better world.

The program is "a celebration of attractive and powerful qualities of human beings," says Roger Pritchard, president of Financial Alternatives in Berkeley, California, a consultant to socially conscious small businesses and a member of The Giraffe Project.

Giraffes are nominated by members and reviewed by a committee of staff and volunteers. The criteria for commendation include typical Giraffe qualities as risk taking, compassion, humor, courage, action beyond the call of duty, and service for the common good, as well as credibility and role-model appeal.

Stories about giraffes reach people around the country in the form of public-service announcements on radio (read by actors like Candice Bergen and Eli Wallach or by station DJs) and in magazines and newspapers. They're also featured in the *Gi-raffe Gazette,* a quarterly newsletter for members of the project and the press.

Find out about the best humanity has to offer and support this work, which has inspired so many to "stick their necks out." Become a member of The Giraffe Project. Your $25 membership fee entitles you to receive the quarterly *Giraffe Gazette.*

> The Giraffe Project
> P.O. Box 759
> Langley, WA 98260
> (800) 344-TALL

### 4. *THE LEARNING ALLIANCE*

Since I only lasted eighteen months in college, in many ways my education continued at the Learning Alliance. Reflecting the nature of this book, the Learning Alliance seeks to combine education with action, and has done so with astounding success.

Working with more than one hundred community organizations, the Learning Alliance provides the most current information on a wide range of community and social concerns, including peace, the ecology, homelessness, Native American issues, personal and community health, economics, and practical living skills.

The Learning Alliance attempts to integrate these issues and provide a thorough and holistic perspective that examines critically the roots and future implications of problems. It is the alliance's goal to help each participant develop his/her own critical analysis, which it is hoped will lead to action in some form.

Workshop participants have been encouraged to create, work with, and maintain ongoing activist groups, including:

—adolescent-service providers who have been meeting to focus on the problems of school dropouts in Brooklyn, New York. The group first came together for a Learning Alliance-sponsored conference that officially involved more than forty social-service agencies.

—the recently formed New York Food and Agriculture Network, whose commitment to promote and support sustainable agriculture in Hudson Valley arose from a forum on New York farming and food production.

—the Health Network, a group of holistic health and community health practitioners dedicated to finding the means to assist each other professionally and personally, and to provide quality alternatives to community health needs. This group became organized in the fall of 1987, and is working on a pilot program for shelters and community centers in low-income neighborhoods.

—A program concerned with ecological/green politics has been instrumental in forming study groups on alternative economics and green politics. These groups grew out of forums held on those issues.

The Learning Alliance has also been instrumental in coordinating or providing assistance to many major gatherings and conferences, such as the Conference on Tri-State Economics; the Homelessness and Housing Justice Popular Assembly; the Conference on International Rain Forests; the Save Our Schools Teach-in and Speak-out; and an International Gathering on Poor People.

In addition, many practical projects have been actualized using the resources and contacts provided by Learning Alliance workshops:

—Individuals and organizations have started recycling programs for office waste paper and newspapers.

—Ecological and socially responsible design projects have been implemented at urban and suburban dwellings.

—People have used their newly acquired skills to help nonprofit groups in organizational development, mediation, and leadership training, and communication skills.

—People have joined, volunteered, and even gained employment at numerous community and neighborhood organizations working on a wide range of social issues.

David Levine founded and has directed the Learning Alliance for over five years.

Twice a year the Learning Alliance publishes a free catalog of events. For a copy of the catalog or to make a tax-deductible contribution contact:

Learning Alliance
494 Broadway
New York, NY 10012
(212) 226-7171

Unfortunately, most activities take place in the New York vicinity, but the Learning Alliance has a national network of contacts and is interested in helping set up new programs across the country. Any community would benefit from the open, activist spirit that the Learning Alliance seeks to create. It is a model for helping to create positive change, and it is committed to finding answers to the questions others are often afraid to ask.

### 5. *MULTINATIONAL MONITOR*

A hard-hitting magazine that is bound to make big business nervous. The *Monitor* arrives none too soon, fills a void in the reporting of corporate activity and is a valuable resource for the union activist and concerned citizen.—William Winpisinger, president, International Association of Machinists and Aerospace Workers

The only magazine that keeps track of multinational corporations, the *Multinational Monitor* is filled with: *Hard-Hitting Exposés:* the role of the U.S. government in arms trading with South Africa; how the Reagan administration helped U.S. businesses relocate to Mexico. *Provocative interviews:* Labor strategist Ray Rogers on organized labor's newest corporate campaigns; Bishop Desmond Tutu on multinationals and apartheid. *In-depth analysis:* high-tech industries and Third World development; multinational banks, debt, and the quality of life in the Third World; women fighting against repression in Guatemala.

An intelligent, well-written, and forceful publication. Highly recommended! Monthly, $22 per year.

Multinational Monitor
P.O. Box 19405
Washington, DC 20036
(202) 387-8030

### 6. *NEW OPTIONS*
Edited by Mark Satin, *New Options* consistently reviews, discusses, questions, and evaluates the issues that are on the

forefront (and often frontier) of progressive thought and action. At times irreverent and unpredictable, it is the only publication (other than the *Utne Reader*) that I've saved every issue of. It helps me think through the most difficult issues that confront our society, introduces me to individuals and organizations that are involved in truly remarkable pursuits, and reviews almost every (nonfiction) book I'd consider buying. All that in only eight pages, eleven times a year.

*New Options* has had articles about "How to Shrink Our Big Corporations," "Alternative Solutions for South Africa," "Why the Democratic Party Keeps Letting Us Down," and even "What We Can Learn From Pat Robertson."

*New Options* provides you with practical idealism and intelligent hope. It gives you a vision of the future that's worth working on and working for. Costs $25 per year.

> New Options
> 2005 Massachusetts Avenue, N.W.
> Washington, DC 20036
> (202) 822-0929

### 7. PUBLIC CITIZEN

Founded by Ralph Nader, Public Citizen is both an activist organization and a monthly magazine of consumer protection and corporate accountability. Public Citizen's research, lobbying, and precedent-setting lawsuits have resulted in major victories for millions of Americans. From unsafe drugs and food additives, to stronger environmental programs, safe energy, and tax reform, to battles with the auto industry and fighting for union rights—Public Citizen isn't afraid to stand up to corporate America.

The $20 membership fee includes a subscription to the magazine:

> Public Citizen
> 2000 P Street, N.W.
> Washington, DC 20036

Public Citizen is also involved in the following projects: Buyers Up, Congress Watch, Critical Mass Energy Project, Health Research Group, Litigation Group, and Tax Reform Research Group. Write for more information about these projects and request a copy of the publications list.

## 8. THE REGENERATION PROJECT*

There is a new pioneering spirit afoot in America—the Regeneration Spirit. Thousands of people are cultivating this spirit of hope and possibility and discovering ways in which they can make use of it to improve their lives and their communities.

The message of regeneration is that we all have a vast untapped capacity to improve our lives and our environment by making better use of our abilities and resources. We can simultaneously improve our personal lives and the lives of those around us.

Every time you pick up a newspaper you read about problems and crises, but you seldom have the pleasure of learning about successes and opportunities. The Regeneration Project provides an outlet for the good news, with a voice that is realistic but hopeful. Even during difficult times there are thousands of people who are doing good work. The project tells some of these people's stories and about their new, their regenerative visions.

Just what does "regenerative vision" mean? Regenerative vision is a way of looking at our lives and our communities. It enables us to discover opportunities where others would find only crises. It looks beyond scarcity to discover the abundance that is in our midst. It identifies and builds on our capacities rather than just trying to meet our immediate needs.

The *Regeneration Newsletter,* published bimonthly, provides readers with both success stories and specific, practical, do-it-yourself tips on "Regenerating the Environment" or "Regenerating Local Schools." Art, agricultural, outdoors, senior-citizen, hunger, health care, home-improvement, and family projects are also described.

The Regeneration Institute, founded by Bob Rodale of Rodale Press, is dedicated to making the world a better place, one step at a time, starting right in your backyard.

Membership is $15 annually and includes the newsletter.

> Regeneration
> 33 East Minor Street
> Emmaus, PA 18098
> (215) 967-5171

*Excerpted from *New Visions*, Regeneration Project, Rodale Press, 1987.

### 9. *TRANET*

Each issue of *Tranet* is filled with hundreds of little notices about meetings, events, publications, and conferences throughout the world on subjects ranging from alternative technology to municipal foreign policy. The publication of new books, papers, and reports is noted, news items, ranging from debt-for-equity swaps to green/political gatherings, are summarized, and each issue covers international developments in the areas of transportation, direct aid, water and sanitation, the environment, peace work, the family, and food.

*Tranet,* published by Bill and Margaret Ellis, is committed to informing us all about the resources we need to create a sustainable and locally self-reliant future. *Tranet* is a truly transnational publication that helps build grass-roots people-to-people networks. Published bimonthly, it costs $30 per year.

Tranet
P.O. Box 567
Rangeley, ME 04970
(207) 864-2252

### 10. *UTNE READER*

The *Utne Reader* (*utne* means "far out" in Norwegian), named after its publisher and editor, Eric Utne, hit upon a brilliant idea a few years ago. The United States publishes thousands of alternative publications covering everything imaginable, from *Maledicta: The International Journal of Verbal Aggression* to

*Spare Rib,* a British women's magazine, and *World War III Illustrated,* to say nothing of less unusual publications such as *Aviation Week and Space Technology, Employee Ownership,* and *Sinsemilla Tips,* or even semimainstream publications like *Tikkun, Harrowsmith, New Age Journal,* or *The Progressive*—many of which we wouldn't know where to find, let alone have time to read. *Utne Reader* sifts through these and over a thousand other publications each month and presents you with the best (and only the very best) examples of the alternative press.

The magazine does more than just reprint articles; it finds a common thread and related themes as a focus for each bimonthly issue. That focus is often embellished by the magazine's own commissioned pieces and by the conscious selection of material that presents different and often conflicting points of view.

You'll read pieces by some most interesting and compelling writers, including:

Barbara Ehrenreich on today's crazed pursuit of "excellence" . . . Ken Kesey on coming to terms with the death of his twenty-year-old son . . . Alice Walker on saying good-bye to a dying friend . . . Gary Snyder on life in general . . . the meaning of marathoning according to Hunter Thompson . . . the jogger's prayer according to Tom Wolfe . . . Chris Mullin on Vietnam today . . . Allen Ginsberg on Nicaragua . . . Deena Metzger on careers in prostitution . . . Jonathan Rowe on Ralph Nader . . . Noam Chomsky on disarmament, and Garrison Keillor on porches.

Past articles have focused on child abuse—how parents can scar their kids worse than any molester. Dieting—why are health authorities now telling you to forget it? Central America—how is the U.S. administration censoring the news? Nazis—if you think that they're ancient history, why must you think again? AIDS—what's more dangerous than the disease? Family farms—how does saving them start at your supermarket? World peace—what might you be doing to help? Stress—how can you lessen it by taking on more responsibility?

Each issue includes excellent magazine and book reviews that have a common subject, a quick series of "In Brief" articles that deal with important and current news items from an alternative point of view, and some of the most interesting advertising to be found anywhere. This magazine is filled with the information and inspiration you need to help make the world a better place. It runs a solid 128 pages; and is an unbelievable bargain for only $18 per year.

Utne Reader
Subscription Services
P.O. Box 1974
Marion, OH 43306-2074
(612) 338-5040

## 11. *THE WORKBOOK*

*The Workbook* is the closest we have to an encyclopedia that addresses social, environmental, and consumer problems. Its goal is to be a critical link in connecting you with the necessary information to assert control over your life. *The Workbook* is a quarterly catalog, running over 125 pages, and is filled with sources of information about agriculture, business, education, energy, food and nutrition, government and the military, minorities and the Third World, natural resources, health and safety, pollution and the environment, women's issues, and much, much more.

All this information focuses on providing you with the tools to help create a world that is economically just, pollution free, and environmentally sound; that provides meaningful work at a fair wage, health care for all, child care for those who desire it and decent housing for everyone; that helps small towns and communities create self-sustaining economies; and that uses the best scientific and technical resources to design programs and technology to benefit all people equally.

*The Workbook* has been my guide to much of the information contained in this book.

I recommend it highly. Subscriptions are $8.50 for students and senior citizens, $12 for individuals, and $25 for institutions.

The Workbook
P.O. Box 4524
Albuquerque, NM 87106

## 12. *THE WORLDWATCH INSTITUTE*

The Worldwatch Institute, founded and directed by Lester Brown, provides thorough, complete, and relevant information about the physical health of our planet. Through a bimonthly magazine, *World Watch*, an annual book, *The State of the World,* and periodic reports highlighting specific topics, the Worldwatch Institute has been a primary source of facts, statistics, and research about the environment.

## WORLD WATCH MAGAZINE

This bimonthly magazine's goal is to help reverse the environmental trends that are undermining the human prospect and to raise public awareness of these threats to the point where an effective political response will be formulated and supported. *World Watch* is concerned with the social consequences of the earth's physical degeneration. Soil erosion leads not only to the degradation of the land but eventually to the degradation of life itself. Ozone depletion, with the resulting increase in ultraviolet radiation, will disrupt the oceanic food chain, reduce crop production, increase skin cancer and eye damage, and suppress the human immune system.

A decline in the human condition is no longer entirely hypothetical. Africa and Latin America will end this decade with lower living standards than they started with. For both continents, a combination of rapid population growth, environmental decline, and rising external debt is undermining progress.

Feature articles have included "Harvesting the Wind," "The Vulnerability of Oil-Based Farming," "Building a Market for Recyclables," "Energy Efficient Housing," "Bicycling Into the Future," "Brazil's Landless Lose Again," and "The Growing Grain Gap." Subscriptions are $20 per year.

## THE STATE OF THE WORLD

Published annually, *The State of the World,* by Lester Brown and Worldwatch Associates, is the definitive overall statement on the health, healing, and continued destruction of the planet. The book covers in great detail major issues from population to the future of nuclear power, rain-forest destruction and reforestation, energy efficiency, new approaches to recycling solid wastes, the economics of cleaning up the environment, and the mass extinction of species.

Hardcover, $18.95; paperback, $9.95. Available in your local bookstore or directly from the Worldwatch Institute.

## THE WORLDWATCH PAPER SERIES

These special, in-depth reports cover a broader range of issues and often go into greater detail than the magazine or book. Topics include "Defusing the Toxics Threat: Controlling Pesticides and Industrial Waste," "Beyond the Green Revolution: New Approaches for Third World Agriculture," and "Investing in Children." More than eighty-two different reports have been published and are available for $4 each.

To subscribe to *World Watch* magazine, order *The State of the World,* or receive a complete listing of individual papers, write:

Worldwatch Institute
1776 Massachusetts Avenue, N.W.
Washington, DC 20036